Writing: The Bridge Between Us

A Step-by-Step Guide to Writing Well

TEACHER'S MANUAL

Marcy McDonald

Popular Weasel Press.

Writing: The Bridge Between Us
A Step-by-Step Guide to Writing Well
Teacher's Manual

Printed in the United States of America

Book Cover Design: Greta Matus Design
Book Design and Typesetting: McDonald Communications

ISBN: 0-9715781-1-7

Contents

PART I: Teaching the Course

PART II: Chapter-by-Chapter Assistance

Section 1   What Is a Bridge?

Section 2   How To Build a Bridge

Section 3   Why Build a Bridge?

Section 4   Cleaning up the Construction Site

Section 5   Bridge-Building in Action

PART I: Teaching the Course

"To teach is to learn twice."
Joseph Joubert

INTRODUCTION

Writing: The Bridge Between Us is designed to teach writing by virtue of its own style and organization as well as through its content and exercises. The book has an ongoing, central theme, and its chapters are meant to be read as units, then re-examined and discussed. The exercises at the end of each chapter work together and build on one another in conjunction with the whole. Doing them is essential if this course is to have the desired impact.

Comprehension, discussion, and analytical skills are three fundamental yet oft-neglected elements of effective writing which the text emphasizes. They are considered, demonstrated, and practiced throughout, as are organization, wording, and editing skills.

In general, the book is aimed at students in eleventh and twelfth grades or to college freshmen who have had insufficient preparation in composition. Occasionally an exercise will be more suitable for a high schooler than a college student, but alternative exercises are provided as necessary, and teachers can tweak the assignments to suit the needs of particular students.

Many homeschool students of high school age study mostly independently, and this is feasible for many courses—but not this one. This is an interactive course; writers need guidance and feedback to improve. You will have to *teach* this class.

Homeschoolers typically know their children well enough to assess at what point they would be ready for this book. It is a demanding course and not for those wishing a touchy-feely, everything-you-write-is-wonderful kind of experience. Everything a student writes is *not* wonderful, just as everything I, a professional writer, put on paper is not wonderful (at least not at first). Hard work, painstaking analysis, perseverance, and revision are what stand between strong writers and feeble ones. Those qualities, plus solid, inspired instruction (partly your job, partly mine), are what I hold out to your students, with the guarantee that their writing will improve if they do every assignment and you provide supportive but critical feedback—or your money back.

Using the Textbook

The text is suitable for a full-year language arts course or for one semester if the class works intensely or, for those with less time, if some of the exercises are skipped. Some homeschooling families might run the course over two years' time if they wanted to do less writing each week or more rewriting overall.

"Process," Part I of the book, incudes fifteen chapters, each a building stone in the writing bridge. It lays the foundation for Part II, "Application." While you may choose to use the book out of sequence, I think that students will benefit more from proceeding in the given order. Successfully completing the assignments in Part II, for instance, depends on fully understanding the material in Part I. In addition, the exercises in each chapter are linked to those in preceding chapters; taken out of sequence the exercises would lose some of their logic and applicability.

A chalkboard or erasable board will come in handy for writing vocabulary words and quotations, for revising sentences together, and so forth.

To simplify the language, I shall refer to students and teacher as a "class" regardless of the number of students or the setting.

If possible, read at least a few chapters ahead of the class, and try to make yourself familiar with the whole book by at least scanning it before you have your first class. You need to be prepared to interact during discussion and critiques.

Schedule Options

I urge homeschoolers to hook up with one or more other families to work this program together. Peer editing and group discussions will immeasurably accelerate the student's growth as both a writer and a thinker. If joining with others is out of the question, then I suggest that you, the parent, try at least the early writing exercises. (This is good practice even for the traditional teacher.) For those with several children in high school, another option would be to teach the class to the different age levels. Be sure that the siblings are encouraging to one another, and tailor your expectations to the grade level. No matter how brilliant the child, lack of experience and exposure usually (but not always) keeps the younger child from analysing or writing as well as the older. Nor should he or she be expected to.

Another idea worth considering is to set up a weekly or bi-weekly supervised e-mail or chat room for exchanging writing assignments. You can arrange that the participants post assignments on a certain day, for instance. Since I live and work in a rural setting, I depend on e-mail to exchange manuscripts and to do exercises with fellow writers. It works well. If you can connect with some other families also using the same textbook, "peer editing" will be within your reach.

How you structure the course will depend on the amount of time available for the class weekly, whether you choose to teach over a semester or a year, and on how many and which exercises you choose to do. Most of the exercises in Chapters 16-18, such as writing a research paper, a letter of application, and a résumé, consume more time than do the assignments for earlier chapters. Yet every assignment has its place in the overall tapestry the student is weaving; no thread is of lesser importance. Clearly, the more exercises you can fit in, the better prepared each student will be for the larger undertakings of the later chapters and their future writing needs. Of course, your instincts and the responsiveness of the class will play a big role in determining your best schedule.

Be sure to leave ample time for class discussions, writing, and editing. Discussion and interaction among writers are key components in the writing process, and the exercises reflect that position. Nurture the confidence of your students and encourage their ability to discuss anything of relevance to the class, from the assigned topics to a particular paper's improvements to articles in that day's newspaper.

For a one-semester course, you may wish to work with one chapter a week, for a total of seventeen weeks, and then take the eighteenth week and the final exam period (if you have one) for a larger project or several projects from the last three chapters. Alternatively, you could cover Chapter 12 and 13 in one week, and 14 and 15 in another, so as to leave more time for the longer projects in Part II. These four chapters, however, could easily take a week each because the lessons and exercises are essential for developing editing skills.

If you give yourself a year to tackle the course, you will have ample time for outside reading, discussions, and thorough editing. In this case, I would expect that while some chapters might take only one week, many will take two; some you could work on for many weeks. The chapter on purpose, for example, could easily take six weeks. Don't rush if you don't have to. Take what time your student needs to master each lesson before you go forward. The beauty of homeschooling, after all, is that you can move at the student's pace.

Philosophy and Structure of the Textbook

Without a doubt, careful reading skills are a necessary prerequisite to effective writing. Many of the exercises in the book are therefore geared toward improving the students' ability to read and process what has been read. Overall, the exercises direct students to analyse the material's content, organization, and style, and then to apply what they learn.

Discussion, within one's own mind and then with others, is the first stage of analysing what has been read. Students work through this stage on their own when they answer the questions in SUM UP and REACT, which ask them to summarize, dissect, and respond to each chapter and related ideas. They then bring these responses to class for open discussion. These discussions, especially if lively, should help the students clarify, firm or discard, and add to their own ideas. Afterward, the students are asked to revise their initial response to the exercises. Communicating thoughts, feelings, and reactions by writing them, voicing them in group discussion, and rewriting will challenge and expand students' understanding of the material.

Those families who cannot meet with others can still engage in meaningful teacher-student discussions. Whether homeschooler or traditional teacher, remember that the idea is not to tell the students what to think but to help them think for themselves.

Discussion leads the way to application, as students practice the material and test their understanding via the exercises in ACT. The total operation—reading/responding, writing/responding, discussing/rewriting—blends analysis with intuition. Analysis alone is too dry; intuition alone is ungrounded. Together, they sizzle. To put it another way, dynamic writing requires creativity, but effective writing requires structure. The exercises work to give the class a sure footing with both. By the end of the course, they should be responsible readers and reliable writers.

Supplementing the Textbook

Vocabulary
A deep chest of language will offer the class the most dazzling riches: greater clarity and more precision when writing and speaking. Many homeschoolers have an advantage over traditional students in this arena, partly because they have more time to read, and partly because of the many wonderful vocabulary programs available to them. Nevertheless, students

should look up even well-known words to refresh their memories about exact definitions as well as subtle nuances.

This manual provides vocabulary lists for each chapter. The first section uses words from within the chapter (if any) that call for definition, emphasis, or practice. The second lists enrichment vocabulary (to learn new words and to learn how to use customary words more precisely). I suggest you assign the vocabulary words for the chapter ahead of time—whether all at once or a certain number daily is up to you. Require the class to provide definitions and original sample sentences before beginning a day's lesson. A "good" sentence demonstrates true comprehension of the word, is inventive, and is well crafted.

Reading the sentences aloud will help students hear the flow of the language (or its awkwardness). Teachers should from time to time ask for definitions of words from past chapters. In a larger class, you might randomly call on the students for a sentence as part of the "warm-up" vocabulary time. This invites class participation and encourages innovative sentence-writing. A homeschooling parent might call on the student during dinner time for a family reading session.

If you'd like to build your students' vocabulary even more (which I advocate), I recommend the following books:

> •*Vocabulary from Classical Roots* by Norma Fifer and Nancy Flowers
> •*Vocabulary Energizers/Stories of Word Origins* by David Popkin (Hada Publications). My son and my sister's kids love this two-part series; the etymological stories and exercises are fascinating. I wish the series were longer. A word of warning, however: fundamentalist Christian families may not like the examples. Nevertheless, the books are worth a peek to see if you could use them.

Outside Reading

Supplementary reading requirements will enlarge your students' base of knowledge. Use outside reading to demonstrate specific points within the chapter, to provide models, and to show writing's broad spectrum of styles. Throughout the chapters here and in the textbook are suggestions for outside reading. At the end of the manual, I make a few additional suggestions. In general, draw upon your own experience, ideas, and the students themselves when you select additional reading material. Homeschoolers have the opportunity to choose reading that reflects or expands upon other subjects currently under study.

Aim to expose students to excellent writing in as many genres and styles as possible. Seek to develop in them critical reading skills and to open their minds to ways to apply their outside reading to class discussions and their writing. In other words, I can suggest that they read more, and I can suggest what they might read, but only you can show them why they should read and how to capitalize on what they have read.

Homeschoolers, requiring daily reading (an hour minimum) is one of the best things you can do for your children's education.

The Journal

Most of the students' written exploration and practice will take place in a formal journal. The journal format has several advantages over full-dress assignments. For one thing, the writing is not "up for show" in the same way it would be if the assignments were "turned in," and this fact gives the students time and latitude to develop confidence. The personal nature of the journal enables students to feel comfortable using it as a forum for their internal discussions. In addition, the format emphasizes the concept of writing for individual growth and development. Lastly, it puts the onus of the work on the student, where it should be.

A caveat, especially for those teaching large classes, is in order. Do not let students get away with delaying making journal entries. Every student's journal must be kept up to date. A student racing to finish the assignments at the end of a grading period will not get enough out of them.

While a loosely structured, free-flowing style has a place in developing generic writing skills, well-defined guidelines are essential to form discipline in the thinking and writing of the students. Because the ultimate goal in keeping the journal is to refine thinking and writing capabilities, the students should *always* write entries in full sentences unless an exercise dictates otherwise. The students should date and identify *all* entries, additions, and comments (for example, "January 4, 2005; Chapter 5; REACT, Question 2"). Date your comments, too. An outside reader should be able to tell what a student is working on at any given time. In addition, any reader must be able to find a particular entry when needed, for some of the later exercises refer back to earlier entries. Since students will be adding comments to SUM UP and REACT after class discussion, they should leave space after their initial entries for doing so.

Any book, notebook, or binder is appropriate for a journal so long as it is expandable or fat enough to accommodate a great deal of material. The journal should be divided into four sections (six if making sections for vocabulary and outside reading). The student will label these in order: SUM UP, REACT, ACT, and Quotations. With the exception of some of the later exercises from ACT, students will write their responses to each activity in the appropriate section.

If you make a section for outside reading, require students to write one-sentence summaries for all the books they read. They should include the title and author and may want to rate the book on a scale of one to ten. They might also use the section to record everything they read for the course (but only summing up books); it will be a hefty list and may one day be a useful reference.

Teachers who grade their students will probably make the journal count for a large percentage of a student's grade (more about this in the "Grading" section). Graded or not, review journals after each assignment. Frequently ask students to read from them aloud. If working in a group or traditional class, incorporate responses into class discussions and provide (or help students discover) ways to improve their answers.

Fostering Discussions

Because learning to discuss ideas is basic to sharpening writing skills, a quick study of ways to listen and respond effectively might profit your class. Listening skills parallel reading skills in that feedback is a necessary test of comprehension. In verbal communication, however, the response is immediate, and acknowledgment of the speaker is vital to a confident exchange of ideas. When students feel heard, discussions go more smoothly, and students are more likely to participate. "Hearing" the person speaking requires attentive listening and responses that are respectful, assertive (but not aggressive), and to the point.

Suggest that students study the physical manifestations of attentiveness (or inattentiveness) during a class period. Direct eye contact, leaning forward, arms and legs in open posture, and close proximity to the speaker are signs that someone is actively listening. Homeschoolers, clear the work area and sit close to the student so attention is centered on the writing and discussion. Classroom teachers, try placing seats in a semi-circle to encourage physical involvement.

Invite students to talk by asking open-ended questions, one at a time, and by responding with non-judgmental commentary. Set ground rules. Teach students to avoid responses which squelch discussion, such as directly negative comments ("that stinks"; "an ape could write better than that"), stereotyping ("what a typically male-chauvinist-pig's point of view"), preaching, and knowing all the answers or "solutions." Advise students of these basics, and practice them yourself:

1. Don't fake understanding. If you don't get it, say so, neutrally and specifically. "I'm unclear about your thesis," or, "The second sentence confused me."
2. Don't merely say that you understand; demonstrate that you do: "When you said, 'the principle was untested,' your whole argument crystallized," rather than, "I get your point," or "Nice job."
3. Keep comments and suggestions concrete, relevant, and open-ended. Be affirming yet genuine: "In the third paragraph the mixed sentence structures picked up the pacing of the piece, but I'm wondering about using fragments when your audience is formal. Talk to me about your reasons for using them."
4. When analysing work, define problems in terms of needs, not solutions: "Think about the need for descriptive writing to appeal to the senses. How can you meet that need better?"

Discussions carry with them one curse: the tendency to stray from the subject. I sometimes think that students take a special course in getting teachers off the subject; they are more expert at it than any other skill. Yet you must persevere in keeping to the point, not only to prevent wasting time but to teach your students how to concentrate. Interrupt digressions with non-critical statements such as, "These points are interesting but irrelevant. What was the last relevant point? [response] Good, let's start from there." Follow your track back to the topic with an open-ended question.

The more involved students are in the class, the more they will stay involved. In *People Skills* Robert Bolton warns that when listening "for a long time without doing any talking or responding, our listening efficiency begins to drop drastically and finally our minds drift off...." Lecturing minimally and urging maximum participation will counteract this problem and, in the process, make the class a challenge and a delight for you and your students.

Evaluations

A survey in *English Journal* (February 1987) queried high school and college students concerning evaluations of their writing. Specifically, the survey asked what marks or comments helped them the most in improving their writing. The most helpful techniques included writing an explanation about how to fix a mistake, giving an example or making suggestions of how to improve the paper or aspects of the paper, individual conferences, suggesting a better word, showing how to add new ideas, and marking or circling a mistake. The least helpful techniques included just grading a paper without comments or marks, grading on neatness, and grading every single mistake. The lesson in this is that students learn best when they have specific feedback. In other words, when teachers work the hardest, students gain the most. But this is not news, and certainly not good news, to the typically overworked parent/teacher. How, then, to accommodate the needs of the students in the most efficient manner?

For those in a traditional class or who have formed a cooperative venture with other homeschoolers, one option, again, is to establish peer writing and editing systems early in the course; students can share the work of critiques and evaluations, and their participation provides additional opportunities for growth. The listening/responding skills developed for class discussions are virtually the same as those needed for useful evaluations in writing partnerships and groups. All such partnerships work best if you interact with them regularly and regroup them if necessary (as well as for variety). On the other hand, while peer writing groups are helpful, the most telling evaluations will come from the teacher.

Besides using any available sibling, parents, friends, and "class" mates for critiques, it may also help to use newspapers, magazines, and essay collections as subject matter for reviewing together with the criteria established in the text. Much published work could stand revision, and an isolated student (or even one in a large class) can practice on professionals.

Some teachers use—and ask students to use—evaluation forms to save time during peer review. These can be valuable in teaching assessment skills to students. In the long run, however, standard forms are limiting. The time they save may not counteract minimized teacher impact. I suggest using forms just to get a handle on how better to analyse work if you think this will help you and the students, and otherwise, eschew them. True, it takes longer to write comments, make editing suggestions, and engage in student conferences, but such efforts reap dividends. That said, a comprehensive evaluation/critique guide is offered in the textbook and again at the back of this book; feel free to revise it to suit your needs.

Grading

Many homeschoolers forego grades. I did, but I still had to make some up to satisfy the local school board. I found that thinking about grading helped me see my son's strengths and weaknesses objectively. It is worth considering how you would grade if you did, to ascertain how well the student is or isn't progressing, whether you need to push a little harder or if you're both doing fine.

When evaluating student writers, the exercises and revisions in the journal should reveal both effort and improvement, which count a great deal in this course. Until Chapters 12-15, when students study editing and presentation, put your focus on improving organization and style rather than on implementing grammar. Emphasizing the latter in the early stages deters students from finding their own voices and from gaining a love of writing for its own sake.

On the other hand, these elements cannot stay in the background forever. I suggest making notes on students' papers and in their journals that corrections are needed, but not making the corrections themselves unless needed for clarity (and then by all means, point them out). They will have to fix them for the exercises in Section 4 anyway. Homeschoolers could use these mistakes as examples if teaching grammar as a separate class. Of course, don't discourage a student who spontaneously corrects errors, since you want proofing to become an automatic skill eventually. Sometimes, however, a student will be distracted from finishing an assignment because of excessive rewriting and correcting in early drafts; put a stop to this and insist that the student finish the work and follow the criteria for revising it as described in the two chapters on rewriting.

If grading, don't "mark down" for grammatical errors until after Chapter 12. Assign the exercises in each chapter in lieu of quizzes and exams. Writing is the best test of writing.

Here are some possible proportions to use in grading:

Journal	35%
Journal revisions	25%
Major essays	25%
Class participation	15%

The First Day

On the first day give students a reading schedule for the chapters (and any additional reading) and assign the book's first chapter. Homeschoolers, let the students, at least for the first reading, read the chapters on their own, and don't race ahead in a predetermined reading schedule lest you inadvertently limit those golden "learning moments."

Explain the set-up for the journal, and assign the exercises from SUM UP and REACT. From then on, students (and teachers) should read each new chapter or a portion thereof (as it suits you and the class), and do the exercises for SUM UP and REACT before the class discusses the chapter. If you find it works better to read sections and discuss them as you go, that is fine as well; the point is to let the students answer the questions in SUM UP and REACT without first going over them with anyone else, since they are meant to write about them on their own, *then* discuss them, and *then* rewrite them. Students must learn to develop the self-discipline this format requires.

Whether you assign vocabulary in conjunction with the reading or as homework for the next lesson is up to you. If you don't like to assign homework (obviously this only applies to homeschoolers), use class time for the reading and exercises. A high school or college student can certainly learn to manage time outside of "school" well enough to do reading independently, however, so as to maximize the use of the teacher's involvement.

Back to the first day—once you have taken care of business, initiate a warm-up writing exercise instead of a lecture. Aim for participation right away to set the tone for the entire course. One warm-up I have used successfully is to introduce myself and in turn ask the members of the class to introduce themselves, following the guidelines below. Even families can do this successfully and have fun in the process.

First, discuss the idea that all writing, even fiction, comes from real life in some way. (Nonfiction, of course, comes directly from life, but even facts are subject to interpretation.) In a sense, everyone is a "character taken from real life." What makes up each character is a bundle of details, put together a particular way. Some of those details can reveal a great deal about the whole person, in the same way that a few choice words can reveal a character's nature in a story or the gist of an article.

Next, introduce yourself (yes, the teacher/parent must go first). Act as though you are a character in a book (fiction or non-fiction); limit yourself to just a few sentences in which you try to reveal something *visual* as well as *personal* about yourself. If you are a parent, try to pick details your child is unfamiliar with. Before you do so, warn your students that they will have to do the same for themselves so that they have some time to think about the idea. You may even write a few questions on the board at the beginning of the class and ask them to be thinking about how to answer them. Some sample questions might be, "Name something unusual about yourself that I don't know. Compare one of your physical characteristics to those of an animal, a vegetable, or a car. What is your secret getaway? What makes you laugh now that you didn't find funny when you were younger? What are three adjectives that describe your attitude toward life? What is your most burning desire?"

It is fundamental to the success of the exercise that you participate and have some fun doing so. Think about your response ahead of time, but don't write it down. If you teach more than one class, change your description each time. Then ask the students to introduce themselves in the same manner, in some way that will give not only their names but reveal something of their inner character.

How long the exercise takes will depend on the size of the class and the length of the responses. If you have time, mention a few ways that the descriptions could have been more vivid, and ask students to recall any details that impressed them. Analyse why they were memorable. Have students write their descriptions down to save as the first entry in their journal. They should feel free to improve upon their verbal effort.

The more involved students are with the class, the more successful the class will be. Your vocabulary sentences offer one invitation for class participation. In addition, regularly use warm-up exercises to loosen up the students. Every time a student speaks aloud, the student is forced to practice thinking, and thinking inherently improves writing. I've listed warm-up exercises in many of the chapters in this manual, and a few worthy writing books are listed in the back if you want more ideas.

I promote not only student but teacher involvement, for those in both traditional and non-traditional environments. Immerse yourself in the class and the class's experience. Answer the exercise questions and do as many of the activities as your schedule permits. If possible, keep a journal yourself. Your class will respect you for your efforts, and the process will help you identify potential problems, give you a reference for future classes, and improve your own writing. As your writing increases in excellence, so will that of your students.

PART II: Chapter-by-Chapter Assistance

"A teacher affects eternity; he can never tell where his influence stops."

Henry Brook Adams, *The Education of Henry Adams*

one

Writing: The Bridge Between Us

Objectives for This Chapter:

After studying this chapter, students should:

- •Be able to list many reasons to write
- •Understand and be able to explain the benefits of writing
- •Know why there is power in writing
- •Be able to explain how writing improves thinking
- •Be able to give examples for all of the above.

Vocabulary

Write the list of vocabulary words on the board at the beginning of each chapter. The class should write a sentence for each one that demonstrates clear understanding of the word. They can make a separate section in their journals for vocabulary, as I have already recommended, or use a separate notebook (useful if also teaching vocabulary from another book). Words listed in combination with another provide opportunities to study subtle differences in meaning and to practice precise wording. Make sure students are reading the section on synonyms, listed beneath a word in the better dictionaries, to learn the sometimes fractional yet critical differences among words.

Chapter Vocabulary

plight	diligence
denunciation	compassion
unrefined	testament
anecdote	stint
potency	

Enrichment Vocabulary

decry	arraign
paraphrase/sum up	harbinger
echelon	cogency
anemic	infallible
preliminary/introductory	nascent

Suggested Outside Reading

Have the class read some examples of writing that has endured through the ages, such as are mentioned in the text:

•Charles Dickens—"against the harsh poverty of the working classes"—try *Bleak House*, Chapter 15, "Bell Yard," the description of Charley and her family
•William Lloyd Garrison against slavery—try a biography of him or look for a collection containing reprints of *The Liberator*, January 1, 1831
•John Steinbeck speaking on the plight of migrants—almost any section from *The Grapes of Wrath* is stirring, but the rest of the passage cited in the text is a suitable choice; in the 1940 Viking Press edition, page 477.
•Try comparing Mark Antony's "Friends, Romans, countrymen" speech from Shakespeare's *Julius Caesar*, the Lord's Prayer, the entire Preamble to the Constitution, the opening of the Declaration of Independence, and the Gettysburg Address. Discuss what makes these passages so impressive.

Caveats

At first you may have to work hard to get students to speak up in class (especially in a traditional setting). Try doing some of the early journal exercises and reading your own responses aloud. If working with a group, call on everyone in turns so that no one can avoid participation. Have students read their responses to SUM UP and REACT and open the floor to discussion if your class is larger than one; you and the student discuss the responses otherwise. Try to avoid saying a direct "yes" or "no" to the ideas put forth. At the end of the discussion, the class should reiterate the main points while you write them on the board. Remind the class to make additions and revisions in the journal apropos the discussion.

SUM UP

1. State in one to five sentences the main points of the chapter.
2. Highlight or star the point you consider most important.
3. After class discussion, add any new points, and circle (or add, if you missed it) the point that the class agreed was most central to the chapter.

This task is vital because it will help you ascertain whether the class can find and differentiate major and minor points. "<u>Because writing reaches into all aspects of your life, it is important to do it well</u>" is the central theme. It doesn't matter how the students write this idea, as long as the meaning is the same. The other major points are that:

- There are many reasons to write—personal, political, social, etc.
- There is power in writing.
- Writing improves thinking.
- Before you can write you must pin down content to one idea and then organize the support for your content.

REACT

1. Do you agree with the author that "you can express some things in writing that you cannot express as well in speech"? Give the reasons for your response and at least two examples for each reason.

The student must comprehend and accept this concept, as it is motivation for improving writing. If the discussion is moving slowly, come up with a list of your own reasons and phrase them as open-ended questions to stimulate discussion.

2. Give examples of occasions in history when the pen has been "mightier than the sword." State in a few sentences your thoughts about this statement.

The class should not view the quotation too narrowly; the idea is to consider instances when writing has influenced the way mankind thought. A few of the many possibilities:

- Thomas Paine: *Common Sense*
- Henry David Thoreau: *Civil Disobedience*
- Harriet Beecher Stowe: *Uncle Tom's Cabin*
- Martin Luther: *Ninety-five Theses*
- Sir Thomas Aquinas: *Summa Theologica*
- Sir Isaac Newton: *Principia Mathematica*
- Charles Darwin: *Origin of Species*
- Karl Marx: *Das Kapital*
- Rachel Carson: *Silent Spring*
- Sigmund Freud: *The Interpretation of Dreams*

3. Why is it necessary to be able to write clearly? Write a few sentences about a time when the ability or inability to write made a difference to someone you know. (If you can't think of an instance, make up an example of when it might make a difference.)

This question (and indeed, the whole chapter) aims to help students find personal motivation for writing. The focus of the paragraph should turn around the phrase "made a difference"; try to think of your own examples in case prompting is needed.

4. The central metaphor for the chapter and the book is that writing is a bridge between minds. What are some other metaphors for the process or aims of writing?

Before assigning this exercise, discuss metaphors and the ways they help make abstract concepts more tangible. Give examples of metaphors for concepts related to religion, science, math, or politics.

5. After class discussion, add any new points to your reactions.

Every so often check the students' journals to see whether they are adding to their notes after class discussion. One way to do this would be to ask students to read from their revised notes the day after a discussion to clarify certain points.

ACT

1. Write a list of five or more words or phrases from the chapter or another source that "sound" good to you. Use each word or phrase in a vivid sentence of your own.

Students can choose single words or phrases based on verbal appeal. The exercise is meant to awaken students' sense of the music in writing. Some possibilities from the chapter:

- •eloquent
- •scrutinize
- •"a crime...that goes beyond denunciation"
- •thoughts forged of steel
- •"a sorrow...that weeping cannot symbolize"
- •ideas crafted of gold
- •"a failure...that topples all our success."

2. Record sentences from the chapter that describe something physical about the writer. Now write sentences that describe something physical about yourself. Do not merely state the color of your hair, eyes, or skin. Do not mention height in inches or weight in pounds; use non-numerical descriptions, and tell the kind of person you are.

Discuss some possibilities for description ahead of time. You can refer to some of the ideas generated in the first day's introductory exercise, or you could describe your physical characteristics to the class. Another option is to read several brief descriptions from writers who convey vital characteristics in a few swift strokes. Donald Westlake's writing is humorous and to the point; in *Drowned Hopes*, the 1990 Mysterious Press edition, try pages 34, 47, or 79. Ray Chandler's *Farewell My Lovely* offers incisive character descriptions every time he introduces someone, and almost every story by Eudora Welty or Flanner O'Connor will provide a great model as well.

The slew of memoirs to come out in the last decade offer a myriad of examples of nonfiction description of the key players. To name just two: Lucy Grealy's memoir, *Autobiography of a Face*, is a powerhouse of writing; two telling descriptions come within the first three pages. The prologue of Rick Bragg's *Ava's Man* is packed with vivid description (as is the rest of the book and his previous one, *All Over but the Shoutin'*).

Students should have fun with this assignment. You might suggest that the assignment be considered the opening passage of a memoir; they should try to write honestly, creatively, and compellingly enough so that a reader would buy the book.

3. Record one anecdote about the author's life. An anecdote is a true story, usually told to illustrate a point. Write one sentence stating the point of the anecdote. Next, write an anecdote (no shorter than three sentences and no longer than ten) about yourself. In one sentence state the point of the anecdote.

Students must learn that what they say and write has to have a point. The anecdote is a perfect practice ground, because anecdotes are accessible and personal but not inherently interesting to a reader. To succeed as writers, students will have to apply the principle behind this exercise to what they say and write. Be prepared to relate and state the point of your own anecdote as a model for the class.

4. Pick two writers, fiction or non-fiction, whom you admire. Write one sentence about each stating the author's name and why you respect that person. Then record one quotation (and the source) from each person that demonstrates your point.

Students need heroes, heroines, and models. The desire to emulate someone can be a tremendous motivation. Answer this question yourself.

two

Syntax: Building Blocks

Objectives for This Chapter

After studying this chapter, students should understand:

- What syntax is
- "Logic of order"
- "Logic of thought"
- The ways in which syntax forms a base for all writing
- What a thesis is
- Why writing is and must be based on a single, dominating idea.

Vocabulary

Chapter Vocabulary

gobbledygook   inherent

Enrichment Vocabulary

congruence   propitious
anathema   serendipity
eschew   secular
obfuscation   aggregate (v.t.)
mitigate   fetter
succor   hackneyed/trite/banal

Caveats

Beginning writers (and many practiced ones) typically have difficulties comprehending the notion that writing can and must boil down to a single dominant idea. Even more difficult than recognizing a single-sentence thesis is writing one. For the first several weeks you may have to check students' journals (either by looking at them or having students read from them) to help them reduce verbiage. If, when students read aloud, they find themselves wanting to cross out words and/or add others, allow them to do so. Reading aloud is one of the best tests of writing. Have them compare the first version to the second.

Warm-Up

Without explaining the exercise, ask the class to write a list of all the verbs they can think of related to a particular profession (or do this as a group activity, writing on the board). For instance, for "auto mechanic," a student might write: tune up, grease, rewire, or unscrew. For "gardener," the verbs might be dig, shovel, plant, haul, weed, hoe, and the like. The students should try to list at least eight verbs—the more the better.

Next ask students to turn over the page (or start a new column on the board) and write a greatly varied list of seven nouns, having nothing to do with the profession or taken from another profession. Then ask the class to write a sentence for each noun using a verb from the "occupation" list. The combinations should be unique, but the sentences must still be logical. "The bullet edits the burglar" and "Night types my sleep" are two examples stemming from the occupation "writer." Ask students to read aloud their two best sentences. Make a collection of the strongest ones and use them to jumpstart creative essays, short stories, or poems.

SUM UP
1. In three to five sentences write the main ideas in Chapter Two.
2. After class discussion, add to your understanding of these ideas by revising the sentences you wrote or writing additional ones.

Be sure students stick to the sentence restriction. Their responses should mirror these ideas (the dominant theme is underlined): Syntax is duplicated and magnified in every piece of writing via the nature and logic of its structure. <u>All writing is based on a single, dominant idea, which can be completely expressed in a sentence.</u> A sentence, the model of syntax, is the building unit of writing.

REACT

1 Do you understand the idea that all writing is based upon a single sentence? Write a few sentences saying in your own words what this means. If you are confused about the idea, mention specific points from the chapter that are unclear.

The class must understand this concept before proceeding. If necessary, spend extra time answering questions and playing with additional examples. Reread the chapter together and discuss it point by point if the class is still not getting it.

2. What is meant by "logic of order"? Give two examples from the text that demonstrate this concept. In one or two sentences, say why logical order is important.

"Logic of order" is the sequencing of ideas to parallel the way English speakers think; most commonly the idea comes first and the action second. The examples in the text use language for one model and placement of the word *only* for the other. For more examples, look outside of language to activities which require specific sequencing, such as model-building, or loading a program onto a computer.

3. What is meant by "logic of thought"? What examples are given in the text that show illogical thought?

Combining words and ideas so that they make sense according to our language and experience is "logic of thought." The examples use word order according to other language patterns, as well as the notion that "Birds type."

4. In a few sentences, explain what a thesis is.

The predominant, focused idea which is the driving force of a written work is the thesis. It is also called the theme; main, central, or governing idea; or the universal (also, the closing universal).

5 After class discussion add to your responses.

Ask the class to read aloud their amended reactions.

ACT

1. Rewrite your summary of the chapter into a single thesis statement. Compare it to the previous summary.

Discuss ways to determine the dominant idea in a body of writing, as well as how to reduce the idea to one sentence. As a class try rewriting a few of the students' statements before assigning this exercise; if a class of one, simply work together on this.

Essentially the main point is that all writing is based on one idea. Students can state this several ways.

2. Give an example of an illogical subject-and-verb combination. Write the subject and verb into an illogical sentence. Now rewrite the sentence, using the same subject and verb to create a logical idea.

Students need to be able to figure out what is logical or illogical and why so they can recognize faulty structure and logic in their own writing. If they get stuck on this assignment, they could use the "occupation" nouns and verbs from the warm-up.

3. Write at least three sentences that tell full (and different) stories; each should have a subject, action, and a plot. We'll cover plot more fully later, but for now you might view plot as something that complicates the action.

This is another exercise which should be fun. No matter how outlandish the "plot" of the sentences, however, they must have logic, a sense of story, and the three structural parts (introduction, body, and conclusion). The lesson emphasizes the complete nature of a sentence and shows the might of its structure.

4. In the same section, write the thesis of three of your favorite novels in one sentence each; also, write the thesis of a favorite movie in one sentence.

Students must exercise the ability to recognize and express a thesis. Identifying the thesis in more than one medium broadens their abilities. Framing the single-sentence thesis for a current movie or recent TV show is a valuable class activity. It may take the class a while to distill the essence, but doing so is within their grasp. You may want to do this exercise frequently.

5. Rewrite the following sentences so that they contain only one main idea that is clearly and logically expressed. (HINT: Sometimes you will be able to write two sentences with a different idea in each; with other sentences, you will have to drop some ideas altogether. Be sure to eliminate repetitive thoughts.)

> 1) Love cannot fill a vacuum of identity, and physical activity helps one face stress, because both things are important to mental and physical well being.
> 2) Knowledge that is applied is powerful, and although power is an elusive idea, it is attainable, but only if you use it well.
> 3) In order to be successful, a perfect situation, a great mind, and exceptional abilities are not necessary, but determination and confidence are, so long as you do not work so little that what you must do is overwhelming.
> 4) Setting limits gives people, from toddlers to law-abiding citizens to teenagers and even the elderly, something to define themselves against, measure up to, obey, and rules to abide by or rebel against.
> 5) Focusing attention on the speaker, when you want to listen effectively, you need to still your own inner dialogue, and observe the speaker's body language, too.

As a preliminary to this assignment, practice rewriting some sample sentences in class. "Letters to the Editor" may be a source for sentences that could be more clearly rendered.

Students may pen vastly different revisions; as long as the new version contains only one idea (per sentence) that was at least implied in the original, any logical revision is acceptable. Work with revisions that still contain more than one idea. In discussion you might point out how marvelous it is that there can be different versions, as this variety demonstrates the impact of individual minds on the same ideas.

Here are some possible revisions:

> 1. Love cannot fill a vacuum of identity. Physical activity helps reduce stress.
> 2. Knowledge has power only when it is applied.
> 3. To be successful, one only needs to be determined and confident.

OR: Work steadily lest what you must do overwhelms you.

4. Limits are needed for self-definition.

OR: Limits define the boundaries of one's place in society.

5. Effective listening requires focusing attention on the speaker rather than on your own inner dialogue.

three

Content: The Bridge Itself

Objectives for This Chapter

After studying this chapter, students should:

•Understand what focus is and why content needs focus
•Be able to identify and give examples of event, chronological, and thematic focus
•Be able to differentiate between a thesis statement which is substantial and developable—and one which is not
•Understand why content needs support
•Be able to identify and use different types of support: examples, anecdotes, and quotations
•Be able to explain why examples must be concrete, give an example of concrete vs. vague support, and begin to recognize vague or insufficient support in a given piece of writing
•Understand the concept that support must in some way add to the central idea, and should begin to recognize support which does not
•Understand that a single idea can be developed different ways
•Be able to define content and explain its place in writing.

Vocabulary

Chapter Vocabulary

emaciation	sparsely
credibility	frail
orator	debilitate

Enrichment Vocabulary

involute	pandemic
insurgent	puerile
fulminate	assay
invoke	kith
bailiwick	expurgate

Discussion Points

In class discuss the proposed thesis statements in the section, "Without Focus, the Picture's Blurry." Bearing in mind that the students will work with this list for REACT #3, ask the suggested questions and list sub-ideas for some of the topics. Students must learn to differentiate between insubstantial and solid ideas if they are to write workable thesis statements.

Caveats

Beginning writers need practice distinguishing between developable and untenable themes, obtuse and clear ideas, and mushy versus solid examples. The class should have a good grasp of these elements before you advance to the next chapter.

Warm-Up

Use warm-up exercises not only to help with a specific topic, but also to bring a sense of play to the work. Play word games such as "Fictionary," in which one player chooses an unknown word from the dictionary, writes the definition, and the other players write what they think it might mean. The responses need not always be serious, nor should competitiveness rule the sport. Some of the most inventive and amusing writing by our kids is put forth during Fictionary.

Play word games such as Scrabble, Upwords, Boggle, and Pass the Bomb; play visual games such as Club Cranium, Pictionary, and charades. All will loosen and improve the writer's mind.

SUM UP

1. What is the subject of this chapter?

Content is the subject.

2. What is the focus of this chapter?

The chapter pivots around the idea that content is the transformation of a subject.

3. In one sentence using your own words, state the thesis of this chapter.

<u>Content is a subject with a focused thesis, developed with support to convert that subject into a body of thought with a purpose.</u>

Of course, that's only how *I* would say it. What matters is how the class says it.

4. State the major supporting points for the thesis, writing one sentence for each point.

    1. Before it becomes content, a subject must be narrowed to a single, developable idea—the thesis.
    2. Focus is a narrowing-in process.
    3. Thematic focus overrides other types of focus.
    4. A thesis must have enough substance to be developed and supported.
    5. Content is supported through general and explanatory statements backed by examples, anecdotes, quotations, and analysis.
    6. Support must be concrete and relevant, and it must add to the reader's understanding of the subject.
    7. Content is a body of thought that has purpose.

5. After class discussion add any new points, and if necessary, rewrite the thesis in a sentence that concurs with the view of the teacher or class.

Have the class read and comment on their revisions for the first few chapters and sporadically thereafter (more often if it's providing additional insights).

REACT

1. Briefly note what in this chapter is significant to you, and why. Give an example that demonstrates your main point.

As a means of involving themselves and increasing motivation, students need to look for and find personal significance in what they read as well as what they write.

2. In your own words say why focus is important to content.

Students will probably express this thought a number of different ways—the greater the variety, the better. When something can be stated in one's "own words," the lesson is being absorbed. The class should give examples as support.

3. Look back at the list of thesis statements. Write down the statements that you think are substantial enough to develop.

> •Everything around us operates according to basic principles of physics.
> (This is too broad for a short paper but acceptable for a longer work.)
> •Wrestling is a sport that requires discipline on and off the mat.
> •Performing in plays has given me confidence because I have faced and survived situations that used to terrify me.
> •College entrance exams should be banned.
> (This needs a bit of elaboration to indicate the direction of the argument.)
> •Nailbiting may seem like a solution to relieve stress, but it causes its own problems.
> (I've rewritten this to give it a developable slant.)
> •For years I've kept a papier maché shoe that I made in kindergarten, for the shoe reminds me of a calmer, simpler time in life.
> •The more kinds of music the ear can appreciate, the more kinds of thoughts the mind can think, and the more kinds of emotion the soul can experience.

The others were too loose; you might try rewriting them as a class to show how you develop more focus.

4. Why is support important to content? Give an example.

Support helps the reader process the thesis by showing a new way of looking at it as ideas and facts are tied together.

5. How are focus, purpose, and audience linked? Think of examples besides those in the chapter.

Why you write (purpose) and for whom you write (audience) help determine what you write (content), and by limiting the material to be included (focus), you give shape to what you write.

The correlation of these three is developed in depth in Chapters 8, 9, and 10, but the class needs time and exposure to many examples to grasp the connection. You might wish to skim those chapters now if you yourself are unclear about the relationships.

For examples, look to television news and radio broadcasts (reminding the class that these are written beforehand), in addition to printed materials.

ACT

1. Develop the following general ideas into focused thesis statements, finding for each a slant suitable for development.

I have given one suggestion for each; the possibilities are boundless. The only requirements for the students' themes are that they must in some way reflect the original idea, be focused and developable, and be stated in a single sentence. Otherwise, the themes can and should run the gamut. Read my suggestions to the class before they do this assignment.

If you are in a class of one, both teacher and student should do this exercise to demonstrate the diversity possible. You may even wish to come up with two or three clearly expressed themes per idea.

•Cruelty to animals is unfair.
Sales in the fur industry have plummeted in the last decade because of charges that killing animals for pelts is cruel.

•Communication is important to everyone.
Neighborhood crime watch organizations fail when communication systems break down.

•Euthanasia is the practice of deliberately putting to death those suffering from terminal illnesses.
The legality of euthanasia has remained unsettled throughout recent, contradictory court decisions.

•Immigrants do not always know how to read or speak English when they first arrive in America.
Illiteracy in English can prevent immigrants from gaining citizenship.

•Relationships can be stressful.
The greatest times of stress in parent-child relationships are likely to be when the child is a toddler or a teenager.

2. Write two or more supportive ideas (not examples, but points that could be further developed) for each of your focused thesis statements. For example:

•Thesis statement: An effective conclusion satisfies the reader that all has been said that needs to be said.
•Supportive points: 1) One way to conclude is to refer to the introductory remarks without repeating them verbatim.
2) A summary that recapitulates the chief points but frames them in different language lends broader understanding to the thesis.

Sometimes the intended support conflicts with the thesis or competes with it for dominance. The work in this and the previous exercise provides students with much-needed practice in developing themes and suitable support. A great additional exercise is to ask the class to write supportive points for every thesis statement in ACT #1. You could also do this verbally.

3. Rewrite the following vague sentences, making them more specific and visual. If necessary, use more than one sentence.

You might try rewriting some sample sentences in class before assigning this exercise. Later, try as a group exercise to make some of the revisions even more specific and visual; discuss successful techniques. Discover together which words and phrases are vague and why, as well as what makes certain revisions successful.

I took a lot of liberty in my sample rewrites; the students may, too, as long as the resulting sentences contain at least a germ of the original and are sharply defined. When the student begins the process of finding a theme to develop into an actual essay, the results may veer far from the original, perhaps not even including a "germ" of the original. Unless you have a specific need for a certain subject and scope (for instance, to merge the assignment with a history topic), this should be allowed. Notice that some of my rewrites are considerably longer; this may or may not be the case with the students' responses.

•Nature is a marvelous, special, bounteous world that offers new vision to careful viewers.
One dawn I saw a dewdrop on a spider's back, and reflected in that dewdrop I saw my face. Nature offers many such marvels to the careful viewer.

•Sports are meaningful because they are both cool and hard.
Many sports participants find personal reward in the discipline required to endure rigorous training, long hours of practice, and grueling competitions.

•I have kept a certain item, which is beautiful, for years because of its importance.
Buried at the bottom of my dresser drawer is the split spiral of a conch shell that a friend brought me from the shores of Greece. Whenever I come across it, I can picture the young man tying it to a rough string and looping it around my neck. I was nineteen at the time, and seeing that necklace again sends me whirling through a window to a time, place, and an awakening sense of self that comes once in a lifetime.

•Littering has a definite impact on the planet.
Litter is a visual blight and a permanent one when not biodegradable, as is the case with such common trash as broken bottles, Styrofoam food containers, and disposable diapers.

4. Give examples for each of the following statements.

•Through several acts I let go of my childhood and accepted the responsibilities of my adulthood.
•Many readers are easily distracted.
•Temptation confronts everyone, but morality must prevail.
•There are many ways to say, "No."

These statements are so general that the class should be able to think of a wide range of supportive examples. They may use examples or anecdotes from their own lives, but they should also try to come up with some third-person examples for all but the first.

5. Develop the following statement into a focused, supported paragraph. Use two different types of examples (anecdote, textual reference, etc.). Write a second paragraph developing the same statement in a different way with new examples.

> Opponents of censorship point to the First Amendment for support: "Congress shall make no law...abridging the freedom of speech, or of the press."

This exercise is designed to strengthen skills in developing support, to help students understand that one thought can be developed in different ways, and to teach students that they have the ability to control the outcome of their writing.

If no ideas are forthcoming on the quotation, students might look up editorials on the First Amendment (especially from the time period) in history books, *The Reader's Guide to Periodical Literature*, or on the Internet.

four

Organization: The Blueprint

Objectives for This Chapter

After studying this chapter, students should:

•Understand what organization is and why it is essential to writing
•Understand the processes of analysis and synthesis and why they are fundamental to organization
•Understand the organizational principle of proceeding from the general to the specific to the general
•Be able to recognize this pattern
•Begin to be able to create this pattern in their own writing
•Be able to identify structural parts (introduction, body, and conclusion)
•Be able to write a paragraph in the hourglass pattern with a definite introduction, body, and conclusion
•Understand the concept of organizational coherence
•Begin to be able to recognize problems with coherence, both in their own and others' writing
•Be able to develop a paragraph according to spatial order, chronological order, order of importance, or a zigzag order (comparison or contrast), and to identify these patterns in other people's writing
•Be able to write a formal outline (including full-sentence introductory and concluding thesis statements)
•Be able to revise an outline so that it is better organized.

Vocabulary

Chapter Vocabulary

hierarchy
analysis
coherence

palatable
synthesis

Enrichment Vocabulary

perspicuous/manifest
extrinsic/intrinsic
inveigle
recondite
moil

enmity
delineate
spume
phlegmatic
conjecture/surmise

Discussion Points

Discuss the way the wrestling outline developed. Ask students to figure out what has been deleted from one outline to the next and to explain the rationale behind the changes. Could the writer of the outline have developed the content in other ways? What are some other directions for the material?

Caveats

A recurring problem in student writing is mindlessly repeating (or barely changing) the thesis rather than restating it in the conclusion in a way that reflects the information presented in the body. For this reason, in the chapter and again here I emphasize the need to write full-sentence introductory and concluding statements, and I urge you to require students to follow this practice. Writing both statements in sentences insures that the ideas are complete and well considered. Writing the sentences back-to-back makes it easier for students to keep the idea the same in each but to phrase them differently because they can compare the two.

Warm-Up

To practice outlining, in class create one from an essay no more than two pages long. Include full-sentence introductory and concluding statements. Essay collections abound. Or use editorials.

You can do this verbally, writing on the board as you go. If you are teaching more than a few students, divide the class into two or more groups and ask each to outline the same essay. Compare the results.

SUM UP

1. Write a paragraph summary of this chapter's thesis and its major supporting points. Use the hourglass principle to structure the paragraph.
2. Using those points, write a broad outline of the chapter to see its structure and development.

For the outline students should write the introductory and concluding statements as full sentences, but they may write the points in abbreviated form (one to several words). Remind students that both the paragraph and outline should form an hourglass pattern.

The summary and outline must both contain the following points, phrased in the students' own words. (Although the students may include more points than I list, they may not include less.) The thesis statement is underlined in both the introduction and conclusion. The "narrowest" point of the hourglass is the list of types of order.

Organization is the process of separating an idea into supportive points and determining a hierarchy among them (analysis), in conjunction with the process of shaping those points into a logical, unified order (synthesis).

A. Analysis
  1. Paragraph: basic unit of organization, with a central point and supportive points
  2. Paragraph (and all organization) has an introduction, body, and conclusion
  3. Paragraph (and all organization) follows hourglass pattern (moves from general to particular to general)

      B. Analysis and Synthesis
         1. Paragraph (and all organization) must have coherence
         2. Types of order
            a. Spatial
            b. Chronological
            c. Zig-Zag
            d. Order of importance
      C. Synthesis
         1. Creating a formal outline
         2. Creating an informal outline
      D. Analysis and synthesis again
         1. Evaluating and revising an outline a mix of both
         2. Steps for creating organizational structure

<u>Active evaluation—taking ideas apart and putting them together to make something new—is an essential preliminary to writing a well-structured first draft.</u>

REACT

1. Define analysis and synthesis. Describe the process by which a writer analyses and synthesizes.

    Analysis is the process of separating material into its essential features and related parts. Synthesis is the opposite: the process of combining the constituent elements of separate material into a unified entity. A writer analyses an idea by considering (and jotting down) ideas about a topic, deciding on a focus and a theme, and writing ideas about that theme. Then the writer examines the list of ideas to determine a hierarchy—how important points are and how they fit with other points of lesser importance. Once the hierarchy is determined, the writer can group ideas and place the points in an outline format, which will provide the lay-out for the first draft.

    The writer cannot give order to points if the points are not known (yet many students attempt to do so). Only analysis reveals the points and hierarchy of points. Putting the points together in a logical way—synthesis—enables the writer to transform the points from a random listing into a unified whole.

    Of course, the class isn't going to write their responses the way I just did; what matters is that the salient points are evident and coherent.

2. Why are both processes necessary for sound organization?

Working through the steps of analysis and synthesis gives the writer control over the direction and shape of the material. The processes together enable the writer to include relevant and delete irrelevant ideas, to cluster points for coherence, and to provide sufficient support.

3. Why is the paragraph the basic unit of organization? How does its structure duplicate the structure of a longer piece?

A paragraph is a complete body of thought in miniature. In the same way that you could not create a paragraph without sentences, you could not create a longer work without paragraphs. It structure, with a beginning, middle, and an end, along with its hourglass pattern of development, are the same as for a longer piece.

4. Why is it important to follow the "hourglass pattern"?

Although writers have some leeway as to the exact shape of the pattern, structuring thoughts according to the hourglass pattern insures that the development will be logical and accessible. Just as a sentence has an inherent rationale of order and thought, so does a paragraph. Dickering with that logic confuses readers, who generally expect writers to develop information in a certain way.

5. Think about conversations you have had during the past few days. Which were "coherent" and which not? Could you repeat those that were *not* coherent to a third party, or would you need to reorganize them to do so? You don't need to write your answers (unless your teacher asks you to), but be prepared to discuss these questions.

Observing your own conversation can reveal clearheadedness or disconnectedness in your thinking. It takes practice to think coherently, and working on speech habits is an excellent arena for such practice. In class ask students to speak in full sentences during discussion. Suggest that they continue their surveillance of themselves and others during conversations. Urge them, too, to get into the habit of amending their speech on the spot to give it greater coherence and impact.

6. What is an outline? How does making an outline help you organize? Do you have good organizational skills? Be honest in self-evaluation. How would greater self-discipline and organization benefit you? How could you introduce more order into your life and your thinking?

An outline is an ordered list of main ideas and, optionally, the supportive ideas regarding a topic and theme. An outline helps a writer ascertain whether a thesis is tenable, what support is needed for adequate development, whether the ideas are substantial and relevant, and how short or long the material need be to develop the thesis fully. A writer saves time by writing an outline and sorting ideas before attempting a draft, which is then far more likely to be to the point.

It may be obvious to you how organizational skills in one area translate to another, but it is usually not apparent to students until they investigate the idea. As with the exercise dealing with conversation, this assignment ties writing to real-life concerns, and it broadens the ability to think in a disciplined manner.

ACT

1. Write a series of sentences (at least six) that shift from the biggest idea to the smallest detail and back again. Start with the general idea, "Body language often speaks louder than words."

This assignment affords students latitude in content. Have the class read the finished exercises aloud to demonstrate the diversity possible when more than one mind considers an idea. If a class of one, then both teacher and student should do the exercise and read aloud in turn. The assignment offers the opportunity to show how a single idea may be supported and directed many different ways. This assignment can work well with an on-line writing group, although of course you'll forego the chance to read aloud with a larger audience.

Students must grasp the "hourglass" principle before you go on to the next chapter, so be prepared to spend time exploring and reinforcing this basic tenet as much as needed. Involve the class in assessing the organization of others' work and in revising sentence order when necessary; the process will improve their comprehension of the material.

2. Rewrite the following paragraph so that it has a sound structure (a beginning, middle, and end) and a logical organizational pattern (from general to specific to general).

Instead of my slender, strong fingers, I imagine my grandfather's gnarled, arthritic fingers tracing the cover pattern of geese in flight. By that point, I have settled down, and I can carry myself as I should, with my grandfather's composure. I pull out the watch whenever I feel tempted to yell at someone, to be hasty, or to ignore my responsibilities. The watch's three-inch diameter is too big to fit comfortably in my jean pockets, but it nestles in my hand, the worn gold smooth against my palm. My only heirloom, my grandfather's watch, reminds me to be courteous, as he was. I rarely notice the time but just think while the second hand methodically clicks. I close the cover gently and slowly wedge the watch into my pocket. The contrast slows me down: my impatience compared to his patience, my restlessness next to his sturdy will. I see him fumble with both hands for the catch as I flick it open with my thumb.

My only heirloom, my grandfather's watch, reminds me to be courteous, as he was. I pull out the watch whenever I am tempted to yell at someone, to be hasty, or to ignore my responsibilities. The watch's three-inch diameter is too big to fit comfortably in my jean pockets, but it nestles in my hand, the worn gold smooth against my palm. Instead of my slender, strong fingers, I imagine my grandfather's gnarled, arthritic fingers tracing the cover pattern of geese in flight. I see him fumble with both hands for the catch as I flick it open with my thumb. The contrast slows me down: my impatience compared to his patience, my restlessness next to his sturdy will. I rarely notice the time but just think while the second hand methodically clicks. I close the cover gently and slowly wedge the watch into my pocket. By that point, I have settled down, and I can carry myself as I should, with my grandfather's composure.

3. Using spatial order, in one paragraph describe a room that your best friend would hate.

Because the elements involved are tangible, organizing according to spatial order appears easy to students. Their efforts tend to be somewhat boring as a result, and the point of the assignment is lost in a superficial attempt. Making the assignment fictional increases students' interest in it and forces them to work harder.

Students can test their success at conveying spatial order by having another student briefly restate the description, or to draw the room as they picture it.

4. Write a paragraph on one of the following topics. Before you begin, think about your focus, and write a thesis statement. Develop the paragraph in either chronological order, order of importance, or a zigzag order.

Family secrets
Life without television
Life without books
A personal memento
Something that irritates you
Why your dog needs disciplining
A sports event
Something you feel guilty about
Your worst habit
An embarrassing incident

Discuss possible slants for the topics. You may wish to have students choose a topic, come up with a slant, and write a thesis statement during class time so that together you can check the feasibility of the themes.

5. Rewrite the paragraph using a different developmental order.

The ability to manipulate organization is a tremendous asset to a writer. Review the students' work for ACT #4 before assigning #5; students should rewrite that one if not properly organized before moving on to #5.

6. Practice outlining by making one for a hypothetical paper. Write a thesis statement for a topic of your choice. Jot down your major supporting and minor supporting points. Sift through the ideas and eliminate irrelevant points. Cluster related points. Number the ideas so that they fit into the overall organizational pattern (the hourglass). Fit the ideas into outline form with opening and closing thesis statements. Refer to "Packaging Paragraphs" and "Patterning Paragraphs" for guidance.

Have students use a different topic than the one used in ACT #4 so that they will have to work harder and from "scratch"; this will give them additional practice. If possible, revise the outlines in class as needed, and have students rewrite their outlines until they are soundly organized. Stay with the lesson until students can create a solid outline. The students must master structure to succeed with the more complicated tasks ahead.

five

Other Approaches to Organization

Objectives for This Chapter

After studying this chapter, students should:

- Understand and be able to explain the role of prewriting exercises in preparing them to write
- Understand and be able to explain why reading is a helpful prewriting exercise
- Understand and be able to explain why brainstorming is a helpful prewriting exercise
- Understand and be able to explain why timed writing is a helpful prewriting exercise
- Be able to use several prewriting exercises
- Be able to build a "model" for a draft, clustering and reclustering ideas for greater effectiveness
- Be able to write a full-sentence ("working") outline
- Be able to write a draft based on a full-sentence or formal outline.

Vocabulary

Chapter Vocabulary

slew (n.)

Enrichment Vocabulary

nadir	surmise
insipid, jejune	truncate
winnow	obtuse
inequity	froward
tractable	fractious

Discussion Points

In class examine the chapter's model. Discuss reasons for abandoning or including certain points. Ask students to conjecture about other directions the writer could have taken. Try writing an alternative outline.

Caveats

Students have difficulty recognizing irrelevant ideas and unworkable themes, and they are inclined to hold onto what they have written even if it does not make sense. Encourage students to view their efforts less dearly.

Warm-Up

If you have not yet set up writing partnerships or groups, now is a good time to do so if possible. Students will require a great deal of feedback for all the activities henceforth.

Try some of the prewriting exercises in class. "Brainstorming" and the circle activity are especially suitable for a group; one student or the teacher can write ideas on the board as they arise. Work through the whole process to test and enlarge students' comprehension and give them additional practice in a controlled, supportive environment. Finish by writing a working outline together (first rewriting the thesis if necessary).

For another exercise that will serve to loosen things up, release tension, and heighten awareness of language, try the following. Make a list of twenty words on the board. Choose provocative (but not fancy) words. You can select the words or do it as a class (but don't tell them ahead of time what you will be doing with them). Ask the class to write a poem using ten of the words. They may change the form (e.g., the tense of a verb) if they want. You have tens of thousands of words from which to choose, but here is one list of twenty. I chose words that are somewhat common but have some grit to them.

belly	plunk
grimy	shiver
bald	hum
grieve	gleaming
stagger	chapped
mud	crackle
nick	panting
round	joyful
splendor	abundance
ice	cringe

SUM UP

Write a short summary paragraph of this chapter. Include a brief explanation of the various prewriting exercises.

The paragraph should include the following points:
1. <u>Alternatives to the formal outlining procedure may work better for some.</u>
2. Reading is a way to stimulate ideas, get focused, and learn about style.
3. Brainstorming is a process of writing down everything imaginable about a topic and sifting through the thoughts for ideas.
4. "Automatic" or "timed" writing is a non-stop writing practice meant to "warm up" writers and help them find interesting ideas and phrases.
5. Forming a circle pattern is a process of writing thoughts in a circle to find ideas about a topic.
6. A full-sentence (or "working") outline clusters and reclusters ideas to determine significance, relevance, and coherence.
7. A full-sentence outline contains main ideas which can be developed into paragraphs and a first draft.
8. <u>Trying a variety of approaches to sort out major and minor points, as well as to discover the thesis, will expand the writer's tools for pre-draft work.</u>

REACT

1. In the past what have you found most difficult about writing?

This question should stimulate discussion about the students' problems, likes, and dislikes regarding writing and give you a forum for addressing their concerns. What you learn from and about the class may give you cause to reshape your curriculum.

2. What advantages are there in having more than one option for getting started writing?

Options provide flexibility. The more choices available, the more likely it is that the writer will be able to come up with good ideas.

3. Which prewriting exercise appeals to you the most and which the least? Why? Can you think of other exercises that might be effective? Make up one and describe it so that someone else could try it. If you can't think of one, look one up in another writing book (*Getting the Words Right* or *The Courage to Write*, for example) and explain it briefly.

What works for one person may not work for another. Determining which exercises work best personally and why will help the writer gain a sense of autonomy and control over writing. Look through *Writing the Natural Way* and *Writing Down the Bones* for more exercises.

4. After class discussion add any ideas generated in class for other prewriting exercises.

From time to time check to insure that students add to their comments. Whether they do is really up to them, as the process is for their benefit. Nevertheless, it won't hurt to nudge them toward that benefit with an occasional surprise review.

ACT

1. Start a quotation section in this part of your journal. Go to the last page of the section (so it will be easy to find in the future), and working backwards, title several pages with the heading "Notable Quotations." For entries in this section (unless otherwise noted), the quotations can be as short as a phrase or as long as a paragraph. Find and record some strong or stirring quotations (and their sources) to begin the section. Include one

about writing (not from this book), one that is funny, and one that is personally meaningful.

The quotation exercise extends throughout the rest of the book; managing it successfully requires that students read carefully and purposefully. At the same time it exposes them to quality writing. By the end of the course, the students will have a collection of quotations for future reference. Unless a source is specified, students may take quotations from any source originally written, including radio, television, movies, and speeches, as long as they cite the author and title (or the title alone, if the author is unknown).

Be prepared to give the students examples before they work on the assignment. Following are some samples, one for each category.

> Writing: "Talent is helpful in writing, but guts are an absolute necessity." Jessamyn West, as quoted in *Writing the Script* by Wells Root

> Humor: "The best contraceptive is a glass of cold water: not before or after, but instead." Pakistani delegate at International Planned Parenthood Federation Conference

> Personally meaningful: "In the midst of winter, I finally learned that there was in me an invincible summer." Albert Camus, *Actuelles*, January 6, 1960

2. Using the guidelines in the section, "Try a Brainstorm," pick one of the following topics and brainstorm about it alone or with a partner. Remember as you write and while you review your brainstorming list that you are looking for two things—a focus for your topic and support for your focus. Your aim is toward a general essay written for an audience of your peers.

> Creativity
> State lotteries
> Censorship
> "Workfare" vs. "Welfare"
> Girl or Boy Scouts
> Cameras in courtrooms
> Teenage curfews
> Sports

Provocative topics help stimulate students' interest in the writing process. It is to your advantage, therefore, to find topics which appeal to many types and levels of interest. You may wish to brainstorm as a group for topics. Feel free to replace topics on the suggested list with ones more fitting to your class.

3. Do a ten-minute timed writing, using one of your quotations as a catalyst. Do not lift your pencil or pen from the page, and do not worry about grammar. Just write everything you think; begin with thoughts that relate to one of the quotations you have selected, and let your mind rove freely from there. This exercise is less focused than the brainstorming one. You are trying to summon forth ideas pulsing deep in your subconscious mind. When you're done, put the writing aside for a while. Later read what you've written, and mark any expressions or thoughts that appeal to you.

Students may have a hard time letting go and relaxing enough to do this exercise. It is, in addition, just plain difficult to write nonstop. The benefits may not be immediately visible, particularly if no writing "gems" appear. Yet the exercise does loosen up both writer and writing, wherein lies its value.

4. Reread "Going in Circles Yet?" Beginning with the topic of your choice, form a circle pattern from your ideas. Read what you've written, and highlight the main points. If these lead to a different idea, form a second spiral of thoughts with the new idea at the center. Again, select and list the main points.

This exercise works mostly because its somewhat silly nature automatically relaxes students and may help them to dig deeper for ideas as a result.

5. Follow the steps in the sections, "A Model of Your Ideas" and "Remodeling the Model," and build a working outline, using a sentence for each major supporting point, from one of your prewriting exercises (#2, 3, or 4).

Make sure the class is clear about the process of creating a working outline before assigning this exercise. Insist that students write full sentences for the entire outline. I cannot emphasize enough my conviction that writing full sentences forces students to clarify ideas before beginning a draft. The work at this stage is more than paid back by the ease in writing the draft later.

6. Write a first draft from your working outline.

The aims of these assignments are to experience and practice the writing process studied thus far. You may wish to take some time to assess the students' achievements since beginning the course, stressing their strengths and pointing out their weaknesses (rather than emphasizing grades).

Plan enough time in class to work on students' outlines and drafts. Allow students to rework both. The essays should not be long—between 350 and 550 words. Do not assign a specific word count, for students pay more attention to quantity than quality when a minimum is specified.

Do not worry about rewriting at this point; the student is writing a *draft*—something to learn from. What must be attended to is the success of the organization; some revising may be necessary for the student to grasp the lessons of this chapter, but otherwise, wait for the lessons of the next one.

"Revise! Revise! Revise!"

Wallace Stegner

"Endlessly, endlessly, endlessly."

Frank O'Connor

both as quoted in *Revision: A Creative Approach to Writing and Rewriting Fiction*, by David Michael Kaplan

six

Rewriting: Analysis

Objectives for This Chapter

After studying this chapter, students should:

- Understand why rewriting is essential to effective writing
- Be able to scan a written work to detect obvious problems
- Be able to assess and revise a written work using the first set of content and organization questions in the chapter
- Be able to assess and revise further using the second set of questions (that is, to edit sentence by sentence)
- Be able to conduct a word-by-word examination of a written work and revise it for greater conciseness, vividness, and precision
- Be able to improve a first draft's content, organization, and wording enough to write a significantly better version.

Vocabulary

Chapter Vocabulary

serendipity

Enrichment Vocabulary

baneful   rescind
recant   eclectic
ebullient   poltroon
make/construct/manufacture
thwart/frustrate/baffle

Suggested Outside Reading

See REACT #2.

Discussion Points

Discuss the chapter's examples and the logic behind all changes. Try to get students to say in their own words why particular points had to be deleted and others revised. Ask them to explain how the content and organization questions directed the analysis and reshaped the essay.

Caveats

Most students (and many professional writers) are loathe to toss out their first draft, which seems to them to have been penned on stone with their own blood. Moreover, they resent doing what they see as "extra" work. Thus, they tend to treat rewriting as recopying or retyping. Working on these assignments in the journal focuses the efforts on revision as opposed to neatness. Even so, you will have to labor hard to motivate them to work. And work they must, for writing is nothing without rewriting.

If you have time, search your local library or bookstore for biographies of famous writers that include early drafts of great works. It will encourage your class to compare the disorganized scrawls of master's first draft to the final brilliance.

Warm-Up

The home-schooling company, Critical Thinking Books and Software, publishes workbooks with activities to improve writing skills. They're worth looking into. Try the following exercise, modeled after some of theirs.

Write a description that another person will then read before trying to draw the object. Machine parts, such as those found in drafting books, make suitable subjects. If a class of one, then the teacher and the student should privately select a picture to write about; exchange descriptions and try to draw the object.

SUM UP

1. In a brief paragraph sum up the chapter's main points, and briefly describe the rewriting process.

The paragraph should include the following in its lists of main points:
1. Rewriting, a process of analysing and revising, is a chance for writers to see what they really said or did not say and to try again to say what they mean.
2. Broad, instinctive evaluation is the first step of rewriting because it catches many problems intuitively.
3. Determining content and organization problems and fixing them are the next steps, before focusing on lesser details which are shaped by the broader ideas.
4. Sentence-by-sentence analysis, the next step, is a chance to look at and refine the details making up content and organization.
5. Word-by-word analysis follows; every word must count.
6. Writing is not sacred, and what does not work should be thrown out.

2. After class discussion, review your summary to see whether you stated clearly enough the importance of rewriting.

This is self-explanatory.

REACT

1. What role does analysis play in rewriting?

Like a broken radio, writing must be "taken apart" if the writer is to determine what is wrong and how to fix it. Subjecting the elements to increasingly focused review enables the writer to find and correct problems.

2. How do you feel about rewriting a paper? Why is rewriting so important a phase? What does the maxim "Hard writing makes easy reading" mean?

Students must come to terms with the need to rewrite. It does no good to parrot the ideas in the chapter about the value of rewriting; they must seize upon its value themselves.

That "hard writing makes easy reading" is unbelievable until you see it in another's work or make it happen yourself. As an outside reading assignment, the ending (the last page) of Hemingway's *Farewell to Arms* provides a perfect model of the maxim. Ask students to read it and discuss it in class. Is it well oiled? Could it flow any better, say any more, be organized more effectively or efficiently? Is it "easy" reading? Lead your class through these questions, and then ask them to guess how many times Hemingway rewrote the ending alone. Thirty-nine times. (In an interview for *Paris Review*, Hemingway was asked what the problem was. He answered, "Getting the words right.")

3. In what ways can revisions make a difference in the quality of your writing and thinking? (Address both points.)

Again, students must come to a personal understanding of the value of rewriting. As a class exercise you might revise sentences which the students volunteer from their journals as needing help. Seeing their own and each other's writing improve—and taking a role in that improvement—can be gratifying and motivating. If you are a class of one, try asking for sentences from Internet buddies or look at writing from the previous year (in addition to selections from the journal).

Any time students use analytical skills, they develop them further. They think more clearly and deeply as a result.

4. What do you find the easiest to improve when rewriting? The hardest?

Writers need to learn their weaknesses so they can counteract them. At the same time, they need to push themselves to develop beyond their current levels of ability. Weaknesses are not static; what a writer needs to improve today will be replaced by something different tomorrow.

5. After class discussion add any suggestions which might help you revise more effectively.

Remind students that learning to write is an ongoing, open-ended proposition. Every day I learn to write and revise more effectively—as should the class. I find this rewarding rather than daunting. Rewriting, if viewed positively, offers the joy and excitement of a challenge that grows along with the writer.

ACT

1. Add three strong quotations to the "Notable Quotations" section. One quotation should refer to an issue of national concern, one to an issue of international concern, and one to a personal issue. Credit the sources. Here is one by James Joyce that I like: "Errors are the portals of discovery." Discuss its meaning and see how it relates to your life.

> •National: "I have a dream that one day on the red hills of Georgia the sons of former slaves and the sons of former slaveowners will be able to sit down together at the table of brotherhood."
> Martin Luther King, Jr., Speech at Civil Rights March on Washington, D.C.

> •International: "We shall defend every village, every town and every city. The vast mass of London itself, fought street by street, could easily devour an entire hostile army; and we would rather see London laid in ruins and ashes than that it should be tamely and abjectly enslaved."
> Sir Winston Spencer Churchill, Radio broadcast

> •Personal: "Do not have your concert first and tune your instruments afterward. Begin the day with God."
> J. Hudson Taylor
> [NOTE: This last may not hold any meaning for you; it is not meant to. It is personally relevant, and so should the students' be.]

2. You should have a first draft from the exercises in Chapter 5. Apply the first set of "Content and Organization Questions" (page 79 of the text) to it. Write down your responses. If the answers show problems in these areas, revise the essay's content and/or structure before going on to Exercise 3. Date your revisions. (It may help to work with a writing partner or group.)
3. After you have examined content and organization and rewritten to satisfaction, examine the essay in more detail. Ask and answer the second set of "Content and Organization Questions." (See page 83 of the text for the list of questions.) Rewrite again to correct any problems you find. (It may help to work with a writing partner or group.)

You can approach questions ACT #2, 3, and 4 (below) one of two ways. Have the class do revisions independently and then work with a partner or group to answer the questions; if necessary, make further revisions. You would check and assess the final versions of each essay. Or, have the students work with a writing partner (in a class of one, that may be you) or group after each phase. Then you can check the final versions, if you haven't already, or they can work in class with new partners for one "final" revision. However you work it, when it is your turn to review the revisions, look at not only the "final" results, but at effort, achievement, and signs of improved comprehension. At this stage, the journey counts as much as the destination.

4. Count and record the number of words in your essay, and review each word for clarity, preciseness, and vividness. Then rewrite, cutting at least twenty-five percent of the words from the essay. That means you'll cut one of every four words. At least.

At this point students may have enough cross-outs, marks, and comments to warrant making a fresh copy (still in the journal and dated) of the shortened version.

Some students may argue that they have already reduced word count twenty-five percent. Your counter: "Fantastic. Now reduce it twenty-five percent more. If you did it once, you can do it again." An important note: Compare the recut version with the previous one. It may be better, but it may not be. Conciseness sometimes shortchanges content. In this case, compare, discuss, and have the student put back in only what is essential.

5. In one sentence answer the question, "What is the one most important thing I am trying to convey?"

This step brings the students back to the general review after such detailed revisions. Regaining an overview at this juncture is essential. It enables the writer to check the revisions against the thesis, and it puts the work back in perspective. Sometimes details can take on lives of their own. This step helps resist that tendency.

6. Show the essay to a writing partner who has not previously read your essay. Without revealing your answer to #5, have your partner read your essay and answer the question. Do the answers match? Discuss ways to improve the essay.

A small class may need to enlist other family members or friends for this exercise. If no one is available, skip the exercise.

7. Photocopy an article from an encyclopedia (usually tightly written and well organized), and try to rewrite it, reducing the number the number of words by one quarter, without omitting any facts. (The "Booker T. Washington" sketch in *The Dictionary of American Biography* is a good one to try.)

Depending on how much time you have for each chapter, this exercise may prove to be too much for the class. Do it if possible, for the practice is excellent. In a large class pressed for time, do the exercise verbally, as a group exercise.

"A writer should concern himself with whatever absorbs his fancy, stirs his heart, and unlimbers his typewriter."

E. B. White

seven

Rewriting: Style

Objectives for This Chapter

After studying this chapter, students should:

- •Be able to define style
- •Be able to name, describe, and give examples of the elements of style (coherence, conciseness, smoothness, and sound—page 90 of the text)
- •Be able to use the transitional devices described in the chapter (transitional words and phrases, repetition of key words or phrases, phrase variations, and pronoun reference)
- •Be able to recognize problems with coherence and revise accordingly
- •Begin to be able to select words according to subtle differences in definition and implication
- •Begin to eliminate qualifiers from their writing
- •Be able to condense wordy writing
- •Begin to use the active voice more than the passive
- •Begin to recognize inconsistencies in voice and tense and revise accordingly
- •Be able to recognize stiff, awkward phrasing and revise it
- •Be able to explain and give examples for the role of punctuation in style
- •Be able to explain the role of sound in style and be able to experiment with rhythm and pacing
- •Demonstrate noticeable improvement in their own style.

Vocabulary

Chapter Vocabulary

jargon

Enrichment Vocabulary

ingratiate/cavil	recondite
vacuous/vacant/blank	denunciate
precise/concise	roil
resilient	feasible
honor/honesty/integrity/sincerity	

Suggested Outside Reading

Students should read Chapter 5, "An Approach to Style (With a List of Reminders)" in *The Elements of Style*. Although many of the points in the textbook's Chapter 7 are reiterated there, Strunk's language is far more eloquent.

Discussion Points

Ask a student to read the incorrect punctuation example aloud; have another student (or you) read the corrected version. If necessary, work with the class until they understand and *hear* the differences. (A warning, however: neither student may read punctuation well enough to make the example effective. In this case, stop and direct the students, read it yourself, or ask another student to continue so that the class can get the full impact of the passage.) No punctuation = no breath.

Caveats

Developing an awareness of style, discovering voice without copying others, and refining style are knotty problems for all writers, let alone beginning ones. Engage the student in analysing the samples they read in class and for class (see Warm-Up). Be enthusiastic about any breakthroughs the students experience in recognizing or achieving style.

Warm-Up

Reading aloud alerts students to stylistic elements better than reading silently. Warm up for style by asking the class to read aloud short samples of a wide range of styles. Selections need not be longer than a paragraph and might include writing by Charles Dickens, Graham Greene, Gabriel Marquez, Toni Morrison, Thomas Wolfe (one sentence of his is long enough to demonstrate his style), Ralph Ellison, Joyce Carol Oates, Barbara Cartland, Thornton Wilder, Amy Tan, Ray Chandler, or Japanese haiku writers. Ideally, every student would have a chance to read, and every selection would show a different style. If you have time, spend an entire class period exploring and comparing styles.

Here's another warm-up you can do in class. Line up five to seven books by different authors and read aloud the opening paragraph of each. Discuss the differences in approach and tone. Then have the students pick one to rewrite in their own voices.

Here is another option: Have the class try writing three compelling, opening sentences for a story; the catch is that all the words must have only one syllable. Have them rewrite the opening, keeping the same essential content, but changing all the words to two-syllable ones. Then revise with all (or mostly) three-syllable words; see how high up you and the class can go. This will likely be a team effort, but it could just as easily be a competition.

SUM UP

1. Write a two-paragraph summary of the chapter. In the first paragraph state the chapter's thesis and major supporting points, and show their relationship. In the second paragraph give a brief explanation of and example for each stylistic element.
2. After class discussion review your examples and add any others which seem more to the point.

The paragraphs should include the following:
1. <u>Style distinguishes writing.</u>
2. Style relies on sight and sound.
3. Stylistic coherence links material through transitional devices.
4. Conciseness invigorates writing with precise wording.
5. Through consistency and well-considered phrasing, smoothness gives fluidity to writing.

6. The "sound" in writing is the measure of words, created through punctuation and sentence variety.
7. <u>Style is the writer's individual voice.</u>

REACT

1. What is your own definition of style?

Because students are striving to find their own voices, they need a personal definition of style. That definition can and should incorporate their own stylistic goals.

2. How is it possible to write in your own voice and still improve and change your style?

Awareness of stylistic elements and problems directs writers in their revisions. The guidance shapes and supplements but does not eradicate their own natural way of assembling words and ideas. The warm-up exercise above should help demonstrate the uniqueness of voice.

3. Your style is uniquely you; what characteristics do you think your style shows? What aspects of your personality do you want to shine through?

Associating personal characteristics with writing style is a new idea to most students, but doing so will help them grasp the relationship between their lives and their writing. In class discussion ask students to give an example of their style.

4. What is meant by the "rhythm and pace" of a sentence or paragraph? Give examples. Read aloud to yourself samples of your writing. Are you pleased with the rhythm and pace? On a scale of one to ten, how would you rate your beat?

Discuss with the class their feelings about reading aloud. Do they feel differently when asked to read their own work as opposed to someone else's? Talk about developing confidence within the class; what makes an audience trustworthy?
Homeschoolers who aren't working with anyone else might try reading to family members; at your church, synagogue, or mosque; or at any public forum.

ACT

1. Add at least three quotations to your "Notable Quotations" (crediting the sources) that demonstrate distinctly different styles. Read them aloud and try to figure out which most appeal to you, and why.

Listen to and discuss students' choices and their reasons for making their selections. Discuss how effective style makes for compelling reading, even if you're not personally interested in a subject. In recent years, for example, I have found myself reading more and more nonfiction simply because the writing is so engrossing, and despite a previous lack of interest in a subject. Some examples are *Flu* by Gina Kolata, about the 1918 influenza pandemic; *A World Lit Only by Fire* (William Manchester) about Europe during the Dark Ages; *The Railway Man* (Eric Lomax) about the building of the Burma-Siam railroad by Japanese prisoners-of-war; and *How the Irish Saved Civilization* (Thomas Cahill).

2. Rephrase one of the quotations in your own words, as though you were telling a friend what the author said and meant.

The point of this exercise is to persuade students that they really do have a particular way of saying things. An interesting exercise is to ask students to rephrase a lengthy quotation that has been paraphrased once already (by you, if need be)—without giving them the original. Collect the new versions and print them on one page (or write them on the board) with the original at the top. The result will be a model of individual voice; not a single phrasing will be the same. Discuss differences and similarities among the students' versions. As I've mentioned previously, a family studying in isolation can ask all siblings and parents to do an exercise such as this, or e-mail friends and relatives.

3. Rewrite the following paragraph so that it is coherent and concise. Even though you will be adding transitions, the paragraph should be shorter after revision.

In Taiwan one day we visited the local elementary school where the children in first grade to sixth grade got their education from 9 to 3 each weekday, Monday-Friday. The door was open; we went inside because it was not closed, and we assumed that its being opened meant that we could. The classrooms were big. Also, they were roomy. They were airy also. Fresh air flowed through the windows and doors, as all the windows and doors, not just the outside doors but those into the classrooms, were open. The rooms had dirt on the cement floors but were tidy, and all the desks were neatly lined in rows. There were forty desks in each room. There was one teacher for every forty students, and the teacher had a big desk at the front of the room. Each classroom had a portrait of Sun Yat Sen on the front wall, and there was beside it a list of orders for the children to obey. The school was the pride of the community.

The paragraph contains so many redundant phrases that condensing it should be relatively easy, although students may miss the more subtle repetitions. Comparing the revised paragraphs in class will reinforce the students' expanding awareness of individual voice; it will also give you the opportunity to refine the students' revision techniques.

Whether a class of one or twenty, try this exercise yourself. Don't worry: a "correct" revision doesn't exist (just better or worse ones).

4. On a blank page list the following categories, leaving four to five spaces between each one.

Smelly Words	Morning Words	Vexing Words
Chilling Words	Soft Words	Ugly Words
Dark Words	Sunny Words	Creepy Words

Write at least four words under each category. Be original. Include nouns and verbs as well as adjectives. Get in the habit of consulting the dictionary and *Roget's Thesaurus*. Practice using them in this exercise.

The point of this exercise is for students to experience the power they can exert over word choices in their writing—and to remind them of the fun of writing.

5. In as few additional words as possible, resuscitate the following lifeless paragraph by making it smooth and coherent, by appealing to the senses, and by giving it your voice. Add or change punctuation as needed, correct problems with consistency of voice or tense, and change the passive voice to the active. Replace stiff wording and vague ideas with vivid phrasing and examples. Try to make the piece not only livelier but shorter.

In the student lounge lists of required textbooks were carried about by lost freshmen who didn't know where they were going owing to the fact that it was the first week of classes at college. <u>You</u> feel lost at first and <u>they</u> did. One student stood out from the rest. He carried all his textbooks already in spite of the fact that he had the whole week to buy his books. The reason why is he admired books. There <u>is</u> no doubt that a new book <u>was</u> special to him because it <u>contained</u> a world in itself. A book to him <u>had</u> importance for several reasons, and this <u>was</u> his feeling in being at college with his new books. All his books were new, and not one had been used before. And it was with feelings that they were carried.

Remind students to carry out the revision steps in order, as described in Chapter 6, lest they waste time making specific revisions (such as punctuation changes) that could turn out to be unnecessary once general revisions are completed.

Look out for shifts in voice and tense, especially keeping tense parallel. I have underlined some inconsistencies.

You may want to conduct a practice revision in class before assigning ACT #3 or 5.

6. Go back to your draft from Chapter 6. Make these revisions.

1. Rewrite one sentence so that it sparkles. Add the sentence to your collection of "Notable Quotations" for this chapter.
2. Delete any useless qualifiers.
3. Rewrite two sentences so that the sentence structure varies from other sentences in the paragraph.
4. Change two passive verbs into active verbs. If you don't have any passive verbs, fantastic. Skip to #5.
5. Look for indefinite use of the pronouns *you*, *it*, or *they*. Rewrite so that all references are clear and the voice is consistent.
6. Date your revisions.

You will need to review the students' work for this assignment. Revisions should demonstrate noticeable improvement by this time. If possible, make additional revision suggestions.

"He set out to describe the indescribable. That is the whole business of literature, and it is a hard row to hoe."

G. K. Chesterton, *All I Survey*

eight

Purpose: Reasons to Build

Objectives for This Chapter

After studying this chapter, students should:

•Be able to explain how purpose influences content, and give examples (see answer to SUM UP)
•Be able to name the four writing tasks and explain the purposes of the first three (description, narration, exposition, and persuasion)
•Be able to write descriptive, narrative, and expository essays
•Be able to revise their essays according to the criteria for each one and the revision techniques discussed in Chapters 7 and 8.

Vocabulary

Chapter Vocabulary

extraneous

Enrichment Vocabulary

harl   shamble
nadir   pariah
cowardly/timid/timorous   misconstrue
despair/desperation/despondency/discouragement/hopelessness

Suggested Outside Reading

Ask the class to collect examples in each type of writing. Besides short stories and novels, women's, self-help, fishing, and home-building magazines (such as *Popular Mechanics*) are good sources. Look also at magazines for kids and teens, such as *Dig*, *Kids Discover*, *Boys' Life*, *Zillions* (an e-zine), *Sports Illustrated for Kids*, and *Seventeen*. Each of these addresses a specific audience. Ask the class to explain what elements indicate purpose and to discuss ways that purposes overlap and entwine. You might wish to distribute some writing samples and then ask the students to answer the criteria questions for each type.

The Art of the Personal Essay (edited by Phillip Lopate), Lewis Thomas's *Lives of a Cell*, William Stegner's *Where the Bluebird Sings to the Lemonade Springs*, and John McPhee's *The John McPhee Reader* (edited by William Howarth) offer tremendous models of narrative writing and cover a wide range of subject matter.

Caveats

Typical trouble spots are covered within each section and in the criteria checklists. Doing the above reading and discussing it will help eliminate the main problem with this subject matter, which is the class not understanding how purpose and audience affects what is written (content) and how it is written (style and organization).

Be sure for this chapter and any others that contain examples written multiple ways to go over the differences carefully in class.

Warm Up

For a change of pace, have students sketch the room described in the section on "Descriptive Writing." They should label where each item mentioned would be, including the narrator. Put the drawings up and compare. Were they careful readers? Does the writer need to revise any parts to make the spatial relationships clearer? As a class, rewrite these parts.

SUM UP
1. Write a short summary paragraph of the chapter. Include a list of the four basic writing tasks and the purposes of each.
2. After class discussion add any new points and clarity your original thoughts.

    The paragraph should include the following points:
      1. Purpose influences writing by determining content.
      2. There are four basic writing tasks: description, narration, explanation, and reasoning/persuasion.
      3. Description aims to give readers a vivid picture of a scene, person or persons, situation, object, or idea.
      4. Narration tells a story, describing something in motion through time and/or space.
      5. Expository writing informs and/or provides an explanation.

REACT
1. How does purpose direct your writing? Give examples from outside the text.

    Work with students to figure out reasons for writing beyond the obvious ("you made me"). Insure, through discussion, that students understand how and why purpose influences content.
    For additional examples, look at the writing adults must do at work, in managing a household, or in organizing a homeschool. For instance, in my county, I was required to write my reasons for homeschooling and explain my qualifications. My sister, who has five years of college but no degree, had additionally to prove that she had the skills and knowledge to teach—essentially her letter was a persuasive essay.

2. What are the problems you often experience with each of the writing tasks? Give examples.

    Discuss the various problems that come up. If possible, try to discuss options and solutions the same day.

3. Each writing task has a basic purpose. How does the purpose differ from the thesis?

Purpose is the essential aim of a piece; it is what the writer hopes to accomplish. The thesis is the central idea which the writer attempts to convey. The writer's purpose can influence the thesis, but the thesis does not influence purpose.

4. Why does each writing task have its own criteria? Are any of the criteria the same for the different tasks?

The specific criteria define the guidelines for each task, delineating the ways in which content is—or must be—shaped by purpose. Have students compare the guidelines in the text to see the commonalities and disparities.

5. After class discussion add any new points and clarity your original thoughts.

ACT

1. Add a pair of quotations to "Notable Quotations." Both should be descriptive, but choose one quotation that is rich and lush and a second one that is sparse yet telling. Both should convey a point that moves you emotionally, but in different ways (for example, one makes you feel sentimental and the other angry). Be sure to credit your sources.

Emotionally is the pivotal word in the assignment. The quotations should be ones which make the students feel something. Ask the class to read their quotations aloud. Compare the different styles of the selections. Discuss whether purpose affected the style, and if so, how. Homeschoolers might make up for the lack of peer interaction by making this a weekly assignment and comparing the quotations over the span of a month or more.

Here is an example of a pair of narratives that handle similar subject matter (the students' quotations do not have to) in entirely different styles and with vastly different emotional impact.

> •"Had we lived, I should have had a tale to tell of the hardihood, endurance, and courage of my companions which would have stirred the heart of every Englishman. These rough notes and our dead bodies must tell the tale."
> Robert Falcon Scott, "Message to the Public," *Diary of the Terra Nova Expedition to the Antarctic*

•"And yet—at last a myriad dark arms had let him go; those bonds of his were loosed, as of a prisoner whom they let walk a while in liberty amongst the flowers.

"'Too beautiful,' he thought. Amid the far-flung treasure of the stars he roved, in a world where no life was, no faintest breath of life, save him and his companion's. Like plunderers of fabled cities they seemed, immured in treasure-vaults whence there is no escape. Amongst these frozen jewels they were wandering, rich beyond all dreams, but doomed."

Antoine de Saint-Exupery, *Night Flight*

2. Add two more words to each category in ACT, Chapter 7, #4.

So you don't have to look it up, here is that exercise again: On a blank page list the following categories, leaving four to five spaces between each one. You can do this exercise aloud in class to save time, but it is a fun one to do independently (and then compare answers).

Smelly Words	Morning Words	Vexing Words
Chilling Words	Soft Words	Ugly Words
Dark Words	Sunny Words	Creepy Words

3. Imagine that you're blind. (If you *are* blind, you have an advantage here.) Describe a room that you know well. Appeal to all senses but sight, and use tangible details and figurative language to make your reader "feel" the character of the room—and be able to walk through it without tripping over something. Use one word from your word lists (Exercise #2).

Remember, a prewriting exercise may help you get started and find your focus. A timed writing exercise with an emphasis on touch, for instance, would be a good jumping-off point for this exercise.

This exercise draws upon both imagination and experience. It encourages students to reach past the obvious while staying concrete.

Homeschoolers may want to test the success of this exercise on a friend. Bring the person to the house, and read the directions so the person (blindfolded) must find the way around the room. Or rearrange the furniture in a room and test the student's exercise on another child or parent.

4. Brainstorm about an event in the last year which you consider a personal "rite of passage." Review your ideas, and write your thesis statement. Pin down the points at which the action starts and ends. If you have trouble determining what those points are, create a timeline. Refer to "A Telling

Strategy" for guidelines. Then write a narrative that clearly and evocatively tells the story of your "passage."

As a preliminary to this exercise, you may need to define "rite of passage"—essentially a ceremony or, less formally, any event that indicates a change of status. A Bar or Bat Mitzvah, confirmation, Court of Honor (Scouts), or getting a driver's license are examples of actual ceremonies or events, but consider also experiences which bring a person to a new view of life. For example, the son of a friend of mine took a year off after high school to hike the Appalachian Trail. The experience was far more a rite of passage than his graduation.

5. Explain one of the following:

- •How to plan a budget
- •How to play defense or offense effectively when the other team is better (any relevant sport)
- •How to fix something of your choice (must involve more than seven steps)
- •How to sew a dress, blouse, or pair of pants
- •How to tune up a car
- •How the solar system works
- •How to apply and remove full make-up

Use whatever pattern of order will work best for your subject. Remember that your aim (to explain) must be narrowed to a focus, that is, to explain for a certain reason (for instance, why you should plan for a budget). As always, you need a central idea in the form of a thesis statement.

You may be tempted to skip this exercise because the class must do considerable writing for the chapter as it is. But expository writing is basic to so many "real life" writing needs that students will benefit from trying it while under a teacher's guidance.

6. Review the products of Exercises 3, 4, and 5, asking the appropriate criteria questions. Make revisions as necessary to meet the criteria.

Have students work through this process independently. Then, if possible, have them work with writing partners to make additional revisions before you evaluate their progress and make suggestions of your own.

nine

Another Reason to Build

Objectives for This Chapter

After studying this chapter, students should:

- •Be able to explain the role of reasoning in persuasion
- •Be able to explain, identify, and apply the different types of reasoning
- •Be able to explain why a persuasive essay or letter should show both sides of an argument and any exceptions to a rule
- •Be able to explain, identify, and apply the different types of claims
- •Be able to explain and demonstrate the influences of purpose on content
- •Be able to write and rewrite a persuasive essay following the steps given in the chapter.

Vocabulary

Chapter Vocabulary

machismo   non sequitur
inferences   impel/compel

Enrichment Vocabulary

mitigate	specious
odious	sophistry
principle/canon/rule	compunction
opinionated/biased/prejudiced	
attribute (v.t.)/ascribe/impute	

Suggested Outside Reading

Barbara Minto's *The Pyramid Principle: Logic in Writing and Thinking*, mentioned in the teacher's suggested reading list, is an excellent resource for additional models, ideas, and examples demonstrating the rules of logic.

Bring in examples of persuasive writing from a wide range of sources, and ask students to read and analyse them in class. Don't ignore controversial writings which have nevertheless influenced readers, such as Adolf Hitler's *Mein Kampf* (or any speech), writings by Louis Farrakhan, or Osama bin Laden's writings against the United States. These writers use faulty logic and emotional appeal to make their arguments; if their logic is flawed, why are people sometimes persuaded by them?

Caveats

Students—or for that matter, most people—find it tough to develop and apply a sense of logic. Indeed, often they cannot discern the difference between a logical and illogical argument. Spend as much time on this chapter as possible, and require that students do all the exercises. Review and discuss all homework in class.

If you yourself are weak in logic, read Barbara Minto's book and the chapter carefully. Do as many exercises as you can.

Warm Up

See ACT # 3.

SUM UP

1. In as many paragraphs as needed, write a summary of this chapter's main points. Highlight the chapter's thesis statement.

> 1. <u>Persuasion is the art of convincing someone to accept that a certain position is valid and to act in some way on that belief.</u>
> 2. Reasoning is the logic that makes an argument meaningful.
> 3. Reasoning from example attempts to prove that a position is true because the example holds true in other situations.
> 4. Reasoning from axiom is reasoning from principles.
> 5. Causal reasoning says that certain elements have an impact on one another, and that from this you can assume that general principles are true (inductive reasoning) or that specific conditions or events will occur (deductive reasoning).
> 6. Understanding what reasoning is and how to use it requires practice and observation.
> 7. A proposal is a claim or claims (of policy, fact, or value) that the writer tries to establish in conjunction with the proposed action.
> 8. Persuasion seeks to convince the reader of a certain position and may also seek to spur the reader to a particular action.

2. Write any questions you may have about the chapter.
3. After class discussion add any new points and clarify your original thoughts. In addition, answer any questions you listed in #2.

If students can write answers to their own questions, they have gained understanding of the material. In addition, writing what they have learned will help them retain it.

REACT

1. What are the differences in the way examples are used when reasoning from example and when supporting a general essay?

Examples in general add richness to an essay as well as support for the main points, but an essay may be effectively supported with relevant facts alone. On the other hand, an essay using reasoning by example relies, by its nature, on the examples to validate the major points, and the essay is incomplete without them.

2. Describe the elements of a strong argument. Think about what kinds of argument are likely to persuade you of something. Try ranking them in order of persuasiveness.

Effective persuasion uses clear logic and sound reasoning. It states a position (its thesis) and defends that position with sufficient support framed in precise wording. The argument concludes soon after the key points are made (usually after the strongest point), and it closes forcefully, with a call for action or response of some sort. A compelling argument addresses both sides of an issue, eschews opinion, notes exceptions, tells the full story, and uses succinct wording.

3. Recall a piece of persuasive writing that caused you to change your mind or to do something you wouldn't otherwise have done. (Ads are designed to persuade, and sometimes they do. If you're stymied, you might remember a particularly good ad that impelled you to buy a particular product.) Analyse the piece and try to figure out why the argument was effective. What kind or kinds of argument does the writer use?

The students may not be able to identify the types of methods and claims the author uses if the writer is blending them creatively. Even so, some aspect of the approach should be recognizable.

ACT

1. Add to "Notable Quotations" one demonstrating solid logic and one demonstrating persuasion based on emotional appeal. (Hint: Speeches are a good source for persuasive quotations. Look in the library for daily or weekly speech tabloids.)

Susan B. Anthony, Abigail Adams, Sir William Blackstone, Leonard Pitts, Alexander Hamilton, and Walter Williams are examples of writers, past and present, who build or built their arguments on solid logic but don't ignore emotional appeal.

Franklin D. Roosevelt and Winston Churchill cunningly melded logic and emotion in their speeches. The writings of Martin Luther King, Jr., Etty Hillesum, and Anne Frank were based on emotional appeal.

2. Read through speeches or the editorial section in newspapers and magazines. Check the logic used in the writing, looking for non sequiturs.

Find at least two and explain why the logic is faulty. Rewrite them to make the argument logical.

Any local paper, including school and college newspapers, are excellent sources for non sequiturs. So are election speeches. Students might also turn to television editorials as an additional source. (Taking usable notes of a speech in process will fine-tune listening skills in a hurry.)
Don't kill yourself looking for examples, however. If the students can find some, great, if not, just keep a look-out for the rest of the year.

3. Write a paragraph aimed at convincing traditionally schooled students to homeschool. (If you are in a traditional school, aim your paragraph toward convincing homeschoolers of the merits of a public or private education.)

Students must pick the age group they are writing to—elementary, middle, or high school; each will require different language and sentence structure. Writing to a specific audience is covered in Chapter 11, but considering it now won't hurt. One simple approach to testing the appropriateness for the audience is to try the "Fog Index," a method used to calculate educational and reading level.
Pick out several different articles or examine textbooks written for different ages—say, eight, twelve, and seventeen. You might even compare entries on the same topic, e.g., the first colonial settlement in Jamestown, Virginia. (Homeschoolers, you can mix history and math into this lesson.)

•Count the number of words in the sample (the selection could be as short as one paragraph or as long as one page; just be consistent). Let's say the sample has 148 words.
•Count the number of sentences—in our hypothetical case, 13.
•Count the number of words with three or more syllables—33.
•Calculate the average sentence (divide the number of sentences into the number of words)—148/13 = 11.
•Calculate the percentage of "big" words (*big* being defined as 3 or more syllables; this may be zero); divide the total number of words into the number of "big" words—33/148 = 22%
•Add the average sentence length to the percentage of big words—11 + 22 = 33.
•Multiply the result by .4: 33 x .4 = 13.2
•Fog index = 13.2 (high school plus slightly more than one year of college)

4. Write a persuasive paragraph using reasoning from example. Conclude with a proposal that is a claim of policy, fact, or value. The paragraph should respond to the following problem.

> Two men put a roof on a new house. Each does half. One is an experienced roof-builder; the other has no experience. They each work the same amount of time. The half of the roof that the experienced man built does not leak; the other half does. Do both men get paid? Do both get paid equally? Does effort count as much as result? Does an experienced person have an obligation to correct, educate, or compensate for an inexperienced person?

This exercise tests logic and reasoning skills while forcing students to examine their own values, which is a key facet of persuasive writing. The paragraph may stimulate lively, even heated debate. If the class is large, have students vote which is the best of the opposing arguments and then defend their choices logically.

Homeschoolers, raising this issue at home will give you a stimulating topic for an ethics debate. You might even hold an actual debate, if you're in touch with other homeschoolers, assigning the two viewpoints to two different teams—and then switching them.

A warning about the assignment: Limit the students' written response to the one paragraph stipulated. They have to rewrite it several times, so a restricted length will reduce the time involved, but it will also force the students to restrict their arguments to the most critical points.

5. Rewrite your paragraph using reasoning from axiom. Conclude with a proposal using a different type of claim.
6. Rewrite your paragraph using causal reasoning, either deductive or inductive (or both). Conclude with a proposal using the remaining type of claim.

Students usually find it more difficult to reason from axiom than from example, largely because they try to argue with loose, vague, or irrelevant axioms. Likewise, causal reasoning dizzies them because they link coincidences, confuse cause and effect, consider a limited view of the circumstances, or ignore other causes. Look for these problems during class discussion and when you critique their work.

You may find that their three paragraphs may not be equally effective, or that one student's writing may make the strongest case using reasoning from axiom, while another fares better with causal reasoning. Examine and compare outcomes.

7. Test your logic, reasoning, and persuasion in your three paragraphs by asking yourself the questions in the "Persuasive Causes" and "Reasoning Reasonably" sections. Rate your three arguments as effective, mildly effective, or ineffective. Exchange papers with a writing partner, and rate each other's arguments. Discuss the results and ways to improve each paragraph.

Admittedly, this assignment is a ton of work. The pay-off is great, however, and students who complete all the assignments in this chapter are likely to have a firm grasp on reasoning logically. They will also write better essays, reports, application letters, and term papers.

"...*use original detail in your writing.* Life is so rich, if you can write down the real details of the way things were and are, you hardly need anything else."

Natalie Goldberg, *Writing Down the Bones*

ten

Putting Reasons and Purpose Into Practice

Objectives for This Chapter

After studying this chapter, students should:

- Understand the ways in which the reasons for writing influence content and organization
- Understand how brainstorming about a topic can clarify intent
- Understand how brainstorming about intent can clarify a topic
- Look at the four writing tasks and identify how they affect content
- Be able to explain the differences among the four examples developed in the chapter and explain the choices the author made
- Be able to write four essays on the same subject, varied to meet the criteria of the four different writing tasks.

Vocabulary

Chapter Vocabulary

amoeba   requisite

Enrichment Vocabulary

desultory
bowdlerize
proclivity/aversion
traduce/denigrate

martinet
pander
ignominy/abject
empathy/sympathy

Suggested Outside Reading

Look through popular magazines for examples of the four writing tasks; which magazines tend to carry which kind of writing? Does one kind predominate popular magazines? Is it different for men and women, adults and children? Use the reading to answer REACT #1.

Discussion Points

In class analyse and compare the four essays in the section "Purpose in Action: Brainstorming." Ask students to find the items on the original list that appear in all four columns and to point out the changes made from one essay to another. Discuss the differences and similarities among the essays.

SUM UP
1. In as many paragraphs as needed, write a summary of the chapter's main points. Highlight the chapter's thesis statement.

> 1. <u>Purpose shapes content and organization.</u>
> 2. Purpose affects what details the writer chooses to include.
> 3. Purpose affects how those details are developed.
> 4. The four writing tasks are the main parameters of purpose, but they may be combined in various ways.
> 5. The more precisely you can define the reasons for writing, the clearer the writing will be.

2. Write any questions you may have about the chapter.
3. After class discussion add any new points and clarify your original thoughts. In addition, answer any questions you listed in #2.

REACT

1. Give two examples demonstrating how purpose shapes content and organization. Do not use examples from the text.

ACT

1. Draw four columns on a blank page. Designate one column for each of the four writing tasks. Brainstorm about the same topic for all four tasks, duplicating relevant points as you shift from one column to another. When finished, compare lists. You should see some duplicate points and many original points in each column, and the overall picture should be one demonstrating the influence of purpose on content.

You can do this exercise verbally in class if you're short on time.

This is an especially productive exercise for homeschoolers who can work with other groups. Students will be astonished at how many different ideas can be generated from the same topic.

2. Write a draft on the subject, using your brainstorming work in #1 and picking just one of the writing tasks as your aim.
3. Write a draft on the same topic but for a different purpose.

Teachers who can try these exercises (even if you just write a paragraph for each) will be better equipped to understand the difficulties the class will face. But don't feel guilty if you don't have the time or energy to do so.

"No one can write decently who is distrustful of the reader's intelligence, or whose attitude is patronizing."

E. B. White, as quoted in *Advice to Writers*

eleven

Tone and Attitude: Building for an Audience

Objectives for This Chapter

After studying this chapter, students should:

- Be able to explain how audience influences writing, generally and specifically
- Be able to analyse a piece of writing and make an assessment about its designated audience
- Be able to explain the relationship between controlling tone and attitude and responding to an audience's needs
- Be able to define, give examples of, and control tone
- Be able to define, give examples of, and control attitude
- Be able to recognize and correct inconsistencies in tone or attitude
- Be able to determine their own attitude about any topic.

Vocabulary

Chapter Vocabulary

nuance	connotation
sarcasm	euphemism
allusion	allegory
ironic	salient

Enrichment Vocabulary

piquant   curmudgeon
arcane   bravado
adulterate   astute
happiness/bliss/contentment
innocent/blameless/guiltless

Suggested Outside Reading

Bring in samples (or ask the class to) of writing, non-fiction or fiction, which convey tone and attitude effectively. Discuss the best examples; ask students to point out specific words, phrases, or sentence structures that indicate the spirit behind the words.

Homeschoolers might periodically examine the reading material of everyone in the house, and discuss indicators of tone and attitude.

Discussion Points

Go over the computer example together (instructions to four different age groups). Discuss in detail the similarities and differences, such as in sentence length and structure, complexity of language and content, and inclusions or omissions.

Caveats

Writing for a particular audience demands extensive control over language and organization. While most students cannot at this point demonstrate much control, they can handle this task if broken into short assignments. Instilling in the students a sense of achievement, through positive reinforcement of small successes, will help them master the challenges of the chapter.

It is possible to have a lot of fun with this chapter. It can be entertaining to change sentence style and structure for a different audience, especially if you make room for some absurd responses.

SUM UP

1. Write a short summary paragraph of the chapter. Highlight the chapter's thesis statement.

> 1. <u>What writers say and how they say it is shaped by audience.</u>
> 2. The age of the reader influences vocabulary, sentence structure, length, and complexity of content.
> 3. The reader's background knowledge affects wording, complexity, and content.
> 4. The reader's needs influence direction and style.
> 5. Tone is a tool for controlling the audience's relationship with the material.
> 6. Attitude, the writer's belief about and stance on an issue or idea, affects how readers respond to the material.
> 7. The elements of purpose and audience together give the writer direction which affects content, style, wording, and organization.

2. List the writing you've done in the past year and state who the audience was. See whether you can describe in a few phrases the salient (essential) characteristics of each audience.

Teachers should try this exercise themselves, since their experiences are likely to be far broader than the students' and therefore will better demonstrate the point of the exercise.

REACT

1. What "needs" do you have? Are your basic needs met? How different are your parents' or guardian's needs? What needs are common to all people? How does one discover the needs of others?

For an interesting exercise, apply Maslow's hierarchy to people in vastly different circumstances, as profiled in newspapers or magazines. Doing so will help the students develop perspective about their own lives.

2. What kinds of audiences are there? Give some examples besides the ones in the text.

If students get stumped by this exercise, suggest that they analyse the audiences for different media. Ask who the audiences are for certain genres within the medium. For example, who listens to story broadcasts on the radio, who listens mostly to weather reports or sports, talk shows, or rap? Who watches reruns of "The Golden Girls" and who watches reruns of "Gilligan's Island"? Are they the same people watching MTV?

3. Age and knowledge are but two influences in determining the reader's interests. What are some others? Give some examples demonstrating the impact of other influences.

If the students can create a thorough list of potential influences, they will find some factors they can manipulate. Some other possible influences are occupation, hobbies, culture, ethnicity, current events, and goals.

A quotation that points out one element that shapes the reader is this one by Lawrence Durrell (from *Justine*): "We are the children of our landscape; it dictates behavior and even thought in the measure to which we are responsive to it." Discuss this and consider your own surroundings. How are they shaping you and your class as readers?

4. How can you manipulate tone and attitude? Name some situations in your daily life when controlling tone and attitude would help you cope or communicate.

Tone and attitude can be controlled through wording, sentence structure, voice, literary devices, personal references, imagery, intonation, connotation, rhythm, irony, euphemisms, and pejorative language. This list is generalized, and although the students will probably not mention all the items, they should be able to explain specifically how to manipulate anything they do list and provide examples demonstrating how to do so.

5. What is the overall tone of this book? Does it shift at all? What is the author's attitude toward the reader? Give examples that demonstrate your views.

The tone of the book is personal and familiar but at the same time somewhat formal. Voice (often active and using both the first and second person), intermittent use of contractions, personal anecdotes, and frequent punctuated asides—dashes and parentheses—are some of the devices I used to bring the reader "into my living room." Complex material and sentence structures, passive voice (at times), advanced vocabulary, and formal transitions are some of the devices I used to put the student back "in the classroom."

My attitude toward the reader could be called either objective or positive. I believe that students can and will master the material, and that is a positive attitude, conveyed through the level of the exercises and various comments and asides. Overall, however, the language of the book is neutral (i.e., objective); therefore, either answer is acceptable so long as the students provide telling examples.

6. Think about the writing you are going to be doing in the coming year, and try to form a picture of the audience. Answer the questions in the section, "May I Have This Dance?" for two different audiences.

Remind the class that employers, friends, educational institutions, and relatives are among their future readers.

ACT

1. Add to your "Notable Quotations" some especially clever euphemisms and some particularly ironic remarks. Credit your sources.

•Irony: "I too had thoughts once of being an intellectual, but I found it too difficult." Albert Schweitzer, speaking to someone who refused to perform a mundane chore on the grounds that he was an intellectual

•Euphemism: Age, death, hate, hurt, racism, trouble, exams, divorce, work, taxes, and evil are some topics to consider when searching for euphemisms. Ads and government publications are also sources of creative euphemisms. Where else would an increase in taxes be called "a tax relief bill"?

2. Write a series of sentences concerning the same subject for readers with four different sets of interests. Do this exercise again for a second topic. Almost any subject will do, but here are a few suggestions.

Prayer	Scuba Diving	Computers
Safety	Exercise	Pride
Dating	Competition	Success
Environment	Parenthood	Responsibility
Terrorism	Punctuality	Homeschooling

Warm up by trying this exercise first in class. Ask the students to name the subject first, since it is more challenging to fit a subject to an audience than an audience to a subject. Working through two or three subjects should provide enough practice.

3. Write a sentence in the third person for each tone listed in "Moving to the Inner Rhythm," conveying its mood without saying or demonstrating it directly. Saying, "Excuse me, will you please pass the salt?" will not suffice for "polite," for example. Saying, "The recipient of an invitation is generally requested to reply, even when declining it," would do because the verb choices and sentence structure convey a formal and polite attitude. Control your tone through details, examples, and precise word choices.
4. Write four sentences: one formal, one moderately formal, one familiar, and one personal. Do the exercise twice, once with a single topic (four sentences on the same topic) and once with four different topics. Each sentence in both sets should incorporate a few of the characteristics given as indicating levels of formality.

Again, writing a few sentences first as a class effort (for both assignments) may help students grasp the concept behind these exercises, which are both fun and challenging. Have students read their sentences aloud; encourage some dramatic flair in the presentation.

Henceforth, any time you come across a sentence or passage that provides a striking model of tone, read it to your class. Encourage them to bring in examples any time for the rest of the year.

5. Read the sentences below and note what kinds of readers might strongly agree with the position, strongly disagree, or be neutral. Where do you put yourself on each of these issues?

> 1) All athletes, from the high school to the professional level, should be tested for drug use before every game, and abusers expelled from the team.
> 2) "We are advocates of the abolition of war; we do not want war; but war can only be abolished through war, and in order to get rid of the gun it is necessary to take up the gun." (Mao Tse-Tung, *Quotations from Chairman Mao*)
> 3) "Equality for women doesn't mean that they have to occupy *the same number* of factory jobs and office positions as men, but just that all these posts should in principle be equally open to women." (Alexander Solzhenitsyn, *Letter to Soviet Leaders*)

Teachers should be prepared to state their own views on these subjects, but it's preferable to give the floor to the students as much as possible. If you are a homeschooling parent, be careful not to engage in argument about your student's viewpoints if they differ from yours. A head-to-head conflict will distract from the assignment's benefits.

6. List five or more euphemisms and their pejorative counterparts. Check the listings in *Roget's Thesaurus* to find other possibilities.

Students who need help with this exercise might think about names they have been called or have called others (not obscene, of course), or of slang from previous eras. For instance, I was called "stringbean" as a child because I was so skinny. Now I prefer "svelte."

7. In Chapter Seven's "React" section you rated your "beat." Read aloud writing that you have done since then and rate it. Are you getting closer to a 10?

Have students read aloud a paragraph or several sentences written earlier in the course or last year, along with a recent passage. The latter should demonstrate writing that is much improved. Offer specific, appreciative comments about the improvements students have made, and encourage other listeners to do the same.

If you have been trying some of the exercises, take a look at your own previous efforts, too. You should likewise see improvement.

"Writing good standard English is no cinch, and before you have managed it, you will have encountered enough rough country to satisfy even the most adventurous spirit."

E. B. White, *The Elements of Style*

twelve

Editing: A Usage Checklist

Objectives for This Chapter

After studying this chapter, students should:

- Be able to explain the role of an editor and why they must be thorough editors themselves
- Be able to explain why correct grammar is essential
- Be able to recognize and correct most typical grammatical errors
- Be able to use the textbook and other sources to check and correct their grammar.

Vocabulary

Enrichment Vocabulary

probity	inviolate
inhere	salutary
truculent	sanctimonious
sanguine	ambient
chicanery	laity
inane	yield/submit/surrender

Suggested Outside Reading

The Elements of Grammar by Margaret Shertzer (Macmillan) is a thorough and clear guide suitable for high school or college students. For college students *The Transitive Vampire: A Handbook of Grammar for the Innocent, the Eager, and the Doomed* by Karen Elizabeth Gordon (Times Books) is an entertaining and useful compendium of common grammatical problems. (The examples may at times be too provocative for high school students.)

Encourage college students to buy a complete grammar guide for their reference shelves if they don't already have one. While you're at it, discuss the value of building a reference library for themselves.

I have already mentioned that I think *Warriner's English Grammar and Composition (Complete Course)* is the most useful and accurate of all the grammar textbooks I've reviewed. For students needing practice and daunted by grammar, use lower level textbooks. *Harvey's Elementary Grammar and Composition* (and workbook), published by Mott Media, was originally printed in 1880 but still renders the rules clearly. If you are also homeschooling younger students, they may enjoy the composition exercises.

An outstanding series is *Jensen's Punctuation* (formerly called *Major Punctuation*) and *Jensen's Grammar* by Frode Jensen, published by Wordsmiths. As of January 2002, the grammar books, which used to be published as a series of three, were combined. Jensen also offers a vocabulary series and a book on writing (*Format Writing*) that are worth investigating. Any listings and current prices are best found through his website: www.jsgrammar.com—accurate as of this printing.

Caveats

Students don't study grammar willingly. But while it could be argued (and they might try) that concentrating on grammar early during the learning process impedes development, so it can be argued that ignoring grammar (as well as mechanics and appearance) after a certain stage also impedes development. Once the students have practiced enough to be fairly accomplished at prewriting, writing, and rewriting—as they have at this point—they are ready to push themselves (or to be pushed) into a higher level of discipline. The act of editing, of recognizing and applying the rules of English, is one which shapes up not only the writing but the writer. Future writing will be cleaner and clearer as students learn to edit their own work, opening doors to even higher achievement. Also, while grammar is not innately fun, the examples and exercises can be. Try to make any examples or warm-ups you use in class as entertaining and witty as possible. I have found that the more absurd the example is, the easier it is to recall later.

Warm-Up

From here on out, do as much editing as a class or in groups as possible. A fantastic exercise is to work together (in groups of two or three), editing a sample essay line by line. If you do this exercise before you assign the ACT exercises, students will perform far better.

SUM UP
1. In one sentence write the thesis of this chapter.

The thesis statement should convey the following:

> Through editing, a vital stage of the writing process, the writer revises and corrects the material so that the agreed-upon rules of English are consistently applied.

2. List any rules you need to memorize.

The act of listing the rules is tedious, but the process will help students remember them.

REACT

1. What is editing? Why is it important? How can you improve your editing skills?

Students may have answered the first question when they stated the thesis, above.

Every time the students read, they encounter an opportunity to practice editing, if only in their minds. Suggest that students mentally correct and improve grammar (and later, the wording, mechanics, and appearance) of everything they need. Reading, practice, and working with other "editors," especially skilled ones, are the only ways to improve editing skills.

One exercise I have done with my kids since they could read well is to challenge them to find an error (after I have spotted one) in an article, ad, or book. Now they challenge me.

2. Why should you do your own editing (as opposed to leaving it to a teacher or someone else)? How can you develop an objective attitude toward your own words?

The students must do their own editing because the process sharpens their writing skills. Editing is the fine-tuning of writing. Would Michelangelo have let another artist put the final dabs of paint on the Sistine Chapel?

Developing objectivity is not easy. Taking some time between writing and editing helps writers look at material freshly (one more reason not to complete assignments at the last minute). Concentrating on only one aspect of editing or even just one aspect of grammar at a time can also help.

3. Why is it important to follow the rules of standard usage? Give examples to support your points.

If the class has difficulty with this, have them read a writing sample that demonstrates poor usage. They will see that writing and the writer's intent are simply clearer when the writer adheres to the rules. Street newspapers and sensationalist tabloids are often rife with errors.

4. What is your opinion on the issue of using "he" versus "he or she" or "he/she"? What problems arise when you replace pronouns with nouns to circumvent offending an audience (or yourself)? In what ways can you get

around the problem? Name audiences that might have different opinions about this issue.

English is always changing, and the issue of sexism in language is but one of many reasons why. Most students never consider the idea that the language is "alive." Discuss other ways that English changes and other reasons why. For instance, the use of e-mail has led not only to a host of writing shortcuts and abbreviations ("CUL8R"), but also to writers' foregoing capitalization and punctuation for speed. How will this play out in the language ten years from now? Such shortcuts probably won't show up in formal writing, but could they find their way into business writing?

Writer's Digest puts out a series of books on different time periods to help authors create authentic characters (e.g., *Everyday Life from Prohibition through World War II*). A look at one of these or something similar will reveal to students how fluid language really is. For example, did they know that "jiggery pokery" was a common expression in the 1940s for trickery or deception? Or that the slang word "icky," still in use today to mean "nasty," originally meant sappy or sentimental, but wasn't in use before the 1930s?

5. Learning to be a careful editor will teach you patience, industriousness, and attentiveness to details. What other traits will you need to develop to edit your own copy successfully? How can you apply these traits to other aspects of your life?

A good memory, objectivity, and perseverance are but a few of the possibilities students might name. They might also consider how the traits they list might apply to jobs, college, sports, or relationships.

ACT

1. In "Notable Quotations," record two quotations that contend with ideas that you find difficult to write about yourself but that you think the author explains well. Credit your sources.

Possibilities include theological, economic, mathematical, anthropological, or scientific concepts; and any task, job, or activity that might befuddle one person yet seems elementary to another. For example, understanding how the discovery of quarks has changed scientific views is a snap for my husband but a herculean chore for me. When I find an author who explains such information in a way that I can comprehend it, I cherish the experience.

Collections of essays will likely offer suitable quotations. Loren Eiseley's *The Night Country* explains many complex ideas accessibly. Too lengthy to quote here, but if you have the book you should look it up, is a passage on pages 75-76 (Chapter 4, "The Chresmologue") of the 1971 paperback edition. The two-page narrative describes "where God is" most evocatively. NOTE: Probably not a good choice for fundamentalist Christians.

2. Edit all your journal copy (from the first day to today) for correct grammar. Date your revisions.

If you're short of time, you can just assign part of the journal for editing, but the more the students do, the better. Looking at their own work and the problems therein will help them remember the rules of grammar. It should encourage them to make fewer mistakes in the future, too, because they will discover first hand how grammatical errors interfere with clarity— as well as how much more work it is to go back and correct errors than to do it right in the first place.

3. List the types of errors you've made more than once in your journal. Describe the problems in grammatical terms. Think about ways to fix the rules in your memory so that you don't repeat these errors. If you think of any useful tricks, write them down.

The first two steps of the exercise will help students memorize problematic rules. They still need to develop their own "tricks," however, and the process of doing so will imprint the lessons even deeper. They can simplify the task of tracking errors by making a chart and filling it in as they proof their journals. A chart might have the following abbreviated headings, for example:

sp. / voc. / wrdng / cap. / agree. / punc. / etc.

4. Exchange journals with a writing partner. Edit the partner's previously edited copy while the partner re-edits yours. (Use a pencil or pen of a different color.) List and label any problems you find that the writer didn't. Date and initial your revisions.

This exercise can be revealing to the students. They may feel reassured about their editing skills as a result, or they may discover their indolence. Either way, they will learn a great deal from editing another writer's work and from having someone edit theirs. The chart mentioned above will come in handy here also.

5. Look through the newspaper, a magazine, or a book, scanning for mixed metaphors. Bring at least two examples to class. (You can find mixed metaphors even in some classic works. Shakespeare has Hamlet use a mixed metaphor in his "To be or not to be" speech.)

Mixed metaphors are hard to spot, and you may need to give the students some additional examples before they do this exercise.

6. Listen to yourself and others speaking in class. Can you identify poor speech habits that might become bad writing habits? Try to get through an entire class period speaking correctly. Make it a group effort to correct each other's speech (politely).

Certain problems are easier to hear in speech than to see in writing, such as using "like" as a filler or to mean *as*. Being aware of proper grammar increases the odds of improving it. If you can do so without interrupting a student's train of thought, correct grammar errors as they occur or when the student finishes speaking.

"When you become hopelessly mired in a sentence, it is best to start fresh; do not try to fight your way through against the terrible odds of syntax."

E. B. White, *The Elements of Style*

thirteen

Editing: Checkpoints for Wording and Spelling

Objectives for This Chapter

After studying this chapter, students should:

- Be able to explain why writers must edit both wording and spelling
- Recognize and be able to correct common wording problems
- Be able to improve preciseness and vividness and reduce word count
- Use fewer prepositions and use them more accurately
- Be able to find and correct (using a reference book) all spelling errors
- Be able to use a thesaurus, a quotation reference book, a grammar book, and a dictionary as a supplementary reference.

Vocabulary

Chapter Vocabulary

redundancy/repetition   superfluous

Enrichment Vocabulary

gentle/mild/meek   ingenious/ingenuous
laziness/indolence/lassitude   inculcate
irascible/irritable   augment
coddle   equanimity

Suggested Outside Reading

How to Increase Your Word Power (Writer's Digest Books) is a useful supplement to a writer's reference collection. It provides quizzes and exercises and may give you some ideas for use in class.

Vocabulary from Greek & Latin Roots (Educators Publishing Service Inc.) as well as *Vocabulary Energizers* (Hada Publications) are two terrific vocabulary programs mentioned earlier (also, see Appendix).

Caveats

Warn students who use a computer spelling program that they still need to edit their printed copy for spelling. A program cannot pick out words which are misspelled as another word, such as *he* for *the* or *lean* for *learn*. In addition, the programs I have used will not pick up single letters such as *n* for *in* or *p* for *up*.

Warm-Up

To lighten up the lesson, try this exercise.

A kenning is a conventional and poetic phrase used for or in addition to the usual name for a person or thing; it's a combined description/name found especially in Icelandic or Anglo-Saxon verse. A "wave traveler" is a boat, for example. A kenning for my cat might be, "day sleeper."

Have students write a kenning for each of the following. The kenning cannot use any of the same words or word parts as the original.

a parent   a television
a football game   a hairbrush
a dog   a garden
a shower   themselves

SUM UP

1. In one sentence write the thesis of the chapter.
2. Identify the problems which you find particularly vexing, and record them in your journal under the heading: "Watch out for these."
3. Review your journal for spelling errors. Correct any you find, and then make a list of your "most dangerous" words.

Editing wording is a chance to correct mistakes and hone the copy for preciseness, vividness, and conciseness.

As with the parallel grammar exercises, when the students identify their own recurring spelling problems, they are more likely to recognize and avoid them.

REACT

1. Discuss how your life would change if you had to think, speak, and write in a language of only 2,000 words. Give examples of some ideas that would be unavailable to you.

Given the number of words available to English speakers, it may be hard for students to imagine life with a restricted vocabulary. Ask them how they would explain the ideas in this book to a four- or five-year-old (who typically have, in America anyway, about a 2,000-word vocabulary). How much would have to be abandoned or oversimplified so much as to become meaningless? Ask them to try talking for five minutes using only the prepositions *in*, *on*, or *under* to describe a complex spatial relationship (for something in the room or in town, for instance). Set the timer and try it yourself.

2. Why does precise wording have more impact than vague wording? Give examples.

Although students may have difficulty articulating their answers, their examples should demonstrate the difference for them.

3. Is it fair that a grammar, wording, or spelling error could affect a writer's credibility so much that a job opportunity would be lost? Is it fair that writing ability plays so large a role in college admissions? Support your views. What arguments could be made for the opposite viewpoint? Be sure to answer in full sentences.

Regardless of the students' positions on these issues, discussing them should drive home the point that, fair or not, errors and ability do have a great impact on their lives.

4. Do you think that if you write and speak well you cut yourself off from your friends or from other people in your community? Is it affected or snobbish to speak correctly? Does it have to be?

It may be tempting to lecture the students on the "right" or "wrong" of others' attitudes, but if you use your listening skills while the class discusses the points in #4, you will help them find their own answers.

ACT

1. Add quotations to "Notable Quotations" that demonstrate the power of precise wording. They should be short but dynamic.

> •"One generation passeth away, and another generation cometh: but the earth abideth forever."
> Ecclesiastes

> •"Liberty without learning is always in peril and learning without liberty is always in vain."
> John F. Kennedy, remarks on the ninetieth anniversary of Vanderbilt University

> •"Genius has no taste for weaving sand."
> Ralph Waldo Emerson, "The Scholar," *Lectures and Biographical Sketches*

2. Rewrite the following sentences so that they are not redundant or repetitive.

Some possible revisions are listed after each sentence. Remember, students will revise differently; what matters is that the essence of the sentence remains.

> 1) *It is worth the effort to try one more time again to word with vigor, vitality, energy, verve, and life.*
> Try one more time to word with vigor.

2) *Rewrite your words and sentences when you revise copy while editing.*
Rewrite while you edit.
Revise copy as you edit.

3) *His victory in this race today would mean that he would win a race for the first time.*
This could be his first victory.

4) *In my opinion, I think that, to me, a sense of failure is always qualified by a sense of growth that reduces the feeling of failure.*
Failure is qualified by growth.

5) *According to Tom Robbins, who said it, "Make it work is the only rule."*
Tom Robbins said, "Make it work is the only rule."

3. Rewrite the following sentences so that the prepositions are used accurately. Eliminate unnecessary prepositions and generally improve the sentences.

1) *Cut twenty roses from out in the back gardens.*
Cut twenty roses from the back gardens.

2) *Except with commonly used expressions, there are times where the students' slang confuses the teachers and where the teachers confuse the students.*
Replace *where* with *when*, or revise to drop the preposition: The students' slang sometimes confuses the teachers, and the teachers' language at times confuses the students.

3) *Put the cat that's out on the back porch out besides the fence.*
Put the cat that's on the back porch beside the fence.

4) *She told him of her research showing where prepositions are required for mathematics to make quantitative comparisons among numbers.*
She told him about her research showing that prepositions are required in mathematics to make quantitative comparisons between two numbers. (If it's more than two numbers, than *among* is correct.)

5) *As of this date, the sales department is twenty percent below under the monthly sales quota in which bonuses are given; last month over twelve bonuses were awarded.*
As of this date, the sales department is twenty percent below the monthly sales quota for which bonuses are given; last month more than twelve bonuses were awarded.

6) *The hole filled up with water.*
The hole filled with water.

4. Write a sentence demonstrating correct usage for each of the following:

Accept	Disinterested	Moral
Except	Uninterested	Morale
Affect	Imply	Think
Effect	Infer	Feel
Believe		

See the section, "Checkpoint #6: Are You Using the Right Word?" (page 186 of the text) for casual definitions of the above. Ask students to read aloud a few sentences to verify correct usage, or check the sentences next time you review the journal.

5. Discuss the implications of the difference in meaning of "think," "feel," and "believe."

Think is cognitive, *feel* is emotional or sensory, and *believe* is faith-oriented. As an example of the way mixing these words can affect credibility, consider that saying "I feel" about a cognitive process implies that the speaker has not thought through an idea but is responding from the heart and, perhaps, illogically. The students' attitudes toward speakers misusing these words may not be negative, but at some point someone else may view *them* negatively if *they* are imprecise.

6. Read the editorial page of your daily newspaper and look for errors in wording, grammar, and spelling, especially in the letters to the editor.

Discuss whether the students discredited the authors after finding errors. If they say, "Yes," refer to their responses for REACT #3. Do they still hold the same opinion?

7. Begin collecting errors that appear in your local newspapers and present them in class. How many errors per issue can the members of the class find if they pool their examples? Pay particular attention to those which you did not spot but were caught by a classmate or the teacher. (Chances are you yourself are making those errors.)

Make an "error" board for the class to post examples of glaring errors from any source. Students take great glee in finding that professional writers and editors make mistakes that "even they" can find.

Of course, if you find any errors in my textbook or this guide, let me know, and thanks for the additional proofing! (My eyes are worn out at this point.)

"Often you might read page after page in your notebooks, and only come upon one, two, or three good lines. Don't be discouraged. Remember the football teams that practice many hours for a few games."

Natalie Goldberg, *Writing Down the Bones*

fourteen

Editing for Punctuation, Sentence Structure, and Capitalization

Objectives for This Chapter

After studying this chapter, students should:

•Be able to explain why punctuation, capitalization, and structure must be correct
•Be able to catch and correct the errors described in the chapter
•Be able to read aloud with well-considered pauses and stops for punctuation
•Be able to select punctuation for effect and defend the choice
•Be able to write sentences with correct parallel structure.

Vocabulary

Chapter Vocabulary

acronym

Enrichment Vocabulary

succeed/flourish/prosper/thrive
inflexible/relentless/implacable/inexorable
alluvial   similitude
eidetic   crotchety/cantankerous/persnickety

Warm-Up

See REACT #3.

SUM UP
1. In one sentence write the thesis of the chapter.

The thesis sentence should restate this theme: <u>Studying common errors and frequently forgotten or confused rules of punctuation, capitalization, and sentence structure helps writers find and correct problems.</u>

2. Briefly summarize those rules of punctuation that you break most often. The list should serve as a reminder and a personal caution.

Most students will find at least three rules to list. Writing the rules in their own words will help them understand and memorize them.

REACT
1. Although punctuation must adhere to strict rules to be correct, certain punctuation marks are somewhat interchangeable (such as dashes, colons, and parentheses). What criteria would you use for choosing one mark over another when there are several options? What effect could one mark have as opposed to another? Give examples.

A writer might choose one mark over another to manipulate tone and rhythm. The colon is formal, for instance, as are parentheses (to a lesser degree). Dashes are the most familiar of the three. A colon slows the pace the most, dashes the least. Students might describe the reasons for selecting one over another of these marks, or they might explain why an exclamation point makes a different impression than a period, or what impact arranging a phrase in quotations as opposed to paraphrasing it could have.

For a group exercise, pick a sentence from literature that uses a dash, colon, or parentheses. Write the sentence all three ways on the board. Read aloud, and discuss what difference (if any) changing the punctuation makes.

2. How does incorrect punctuation influence the work and the reader?

Punctuation errors interfere with the smooth flow of a work, and they can also change its meaning or implication. They put the reader's focus on the page itself, away from the content.

3. Do you read punctuation correctly? Practice reading aloud to yourself, using the punctuation as a guide for timing and pacing. Read one of your essays to a writing partner. Does your writing have a good sense of rhythm?

Many students have difficulty reading punctuation correctly. They tend to read right through the punctuation, or they have no sense how to pace the pauses and stops. Have the class take turns reading aloud heavily punctuated material (such as Dickens). Compare their performances.

4. Think about acronyms and how often we use them. Draw up a list of those that you commonly use. Then consider how public and political uses vary. What is the strategy behind coining START (Strategic Arms Reduction Talk) or WIN (Whip Inflation Now)?

Check your daily paper or news magazines for examples.

ACT
1. Add quotations to your "Notable Quotations" that demonstrate complex but fluid sentence structure.

> •"There are three classes of intellects: one which comprehends by itself; another which appreciates what others comprehend; and a third which neither comprehends by itself nor by the showing of others; the first is the most excellent, the second is good, the third is useless."
> Niccolò Machiavelli, *The Prince*

> •"Nothing contributes so much to tranquilize the mind as a steady purpose—a point on which the soul may fix its intellectual eye."
> Mary Shelley, *Frankenstein*

> •"I have borne thirteen children and seen most all sold off into slavery, and when I cried out with a mother's grief, none but Jesus heard—and aren't I a woman?"
> Sojourner Truth, Speech at Women's Rights Convention, Akron, Ohio

2. Test your punctuation sense. Add or delete punctuation marks in the following sentences. When necessary for correctness or smoothness, replace one mark with another.

1) *I couldnt help myself, I wanted to be a "one of a kind person"; a rebelling son*
I couldn't help myself; I wanted to be a "one of a kind person," a rebelling son. (Or, break it into two sentences.)

2) *For movie extras, long days often spent standing around sometimes in hot costumes are, compensated, for when a star performs, nearby.*
For movie extras, long days—often spent standing around, sometimes in hot costumes—are compensated for when a star performs nearby. (The first comma is optional, but it sounds better to me with one; either way is correct.)
You could also put part of the sentence in parentheses: For movie extras, long days (often spent standing around, sometimes in hot costumes) are compensated for when a star performs nearby.

3) *After sitting on the bench for a year; I looked forward to a better year; playing!!*
After sitting on the bench for a year, I looked forward to a better year—playing!
Or: ...year: playing! Or: ...year—playing.

4) *In addition a college education could help Jack the big blowhard claimed to prepare his children for earning an income living life fully and moving out of the house as soon as possible.*
In addition, a college education could help, Jack the big blowhard claimed, to prepare his children for earning an income, living life fully, and moving out of the house as soon as possible.
Or: ...Jack, the big blowhard, claimed....

5) *(In her letter Ellen her mother) said the gift of music, is, in many ways, the gift of love and if I helped you to open up to classical music, then, I have given you a present that will last through life.*
In her letter, Ellen (her mother) said, "The gift of music is, in many ways, the gift of love, and if I helped you to open up to classical music, then I have given you a present that will last through life."
[NOTE: Discuss the clues that this was a quotation—shift in voice; didn't use *that* to introduce the thought.]

3. Test your sense of structure. Rewrite the following sentences so that they contain no structural errors.

1) *Suddenly nervous, self-conscious, and shy, the phone shook in his hand.*
Suddenly nervous, self-conscious, and shy, he held the phone in a shaking hand.

2) *Desperately, others watched as the swimmer crawled in the surf, searching for her lost contact lens.*
While others watched, the swimmer crawled in the surf and searched desperately for her lost contact lens.
Or: Desperately searching for her lost contact lens, the swimmer crawled in the surf while others watched.

3) *His son glued tin foil on the walls spraying black paint on the floors without remorse.*
Without remorse his son glued tin foil on the walls and sprayed black paint on the floors.

4) *After shopping at the grocery store, her choices were to go the bank or resting.*
After shopping at the grocery store, she had the choice to go to the bank or rest.

5) *Neither the locals nor the ones who were touring the country responding well to the travel campaign.*
Neither the locals nor the tourists responded well to the travel campaign.

6) *Although he had inside plumbing. He often used the outhouse instead. Because he preferred the view from there.*
Although he had inside plumbing, he often used the outhouse instead because he preferred the view from there.

7) *While leaping for their lives the keys dropped on the floor the women were terrified.*
While leaping for their lives, the terrified women dropped the keys on the floor.

4.   Recheck your journal looking for punctuation errors. Date your revisions and corrections.

If possible, have students exchange journals for a second review before you look at them. Remind students to date their re-editing notes.

5. Begin a collection of dangling participles—the more outrageous the better. Check your newspaper. If you can't find good examples, create some in class.

ACT #3 provides several examples, should you need a model.

fifteen

Presentation: Appearances Matter

Objectives for This Chapter

After studying this chapter, students should:

> •Be able to explain and give examples to demonstrate why presentation is important
> •Know the rules of format for a formal paper
> •Be able to prepare material for presentation and make the presentation perfect
> •Be able to identify and describe the three types of letter format
> •Be able to use all three formats perfectly
> •Be able to prepare a business envelope in perfect format.

Vocabulary

Chapter Vocabulary

slovenly

Enrichment Vocabulary

acumen   pregnable
evanescent   vagary/caprice
profligate   interlay
forswear   scourge
behoove   contingency
precarious   paradox

Discussion Points

The possibilities for discussion are limited for this chapter. Encourage the class to use the checklist before turning in final copies of letters. If they answer every question and correct any corresponding problems, they should be able to turn in letters that are perfect in format.

I'd give the students time in class to write, rewrite, and edit their essays and letters, but homeschoolers may prefer to arrange the schedule differently.

The final essays and letters should be strong in content, organization, wording, and style, and they should have no errors. If you are grading, count off for every error. If you aren't grading, at least mark every error. You and the students should use the editing marks at the back of the book.

Caveats

Typical problems in appearance are messy corrections, faulty alignment, insufficient margins, and improper blocking. The checklist should help eliminate all these mistakes but the sloppy corrections, and a computer will help eliminate those.

SUM UP

1. Write a paragraph about the role that appearance plays in your life.

Often students are incredulous about the weight that presentation carries in competitive situations. It is true that someone can make mistakes on an application and still get a job at a hot-dog stand or nearly any other low-entry job. But it is also true that many more opportunities are closed than are opened to those who do not take care with the appearance of their writing.

2. After class add any new ideas generated in the discussion.

REACT

1. In what ways does presentation convey attitude? What are the key elements in an effective presentation?

It takes time, patience, and diligence to present a paper acceptably, but a perfect appearance instantly conveys these characteristics as well as a professional attitude. Neatness, good spacing, sufficient margins, consistency, and labeling subsequent pages are key elements in an effective presentation. The class may list more.

2. What is your attitude toward personal appearance? We have all heard the aphorism, "You can't judge a book by its cover," but how often do we judge or are we judged according to a first or superficial impression? Be candid.

Students may hesitate to be frank about their own judgmentalism, or they may not recognize it in themselves. Ask them to consider what about a person's appearance attracts, repels, or offends them. What would it take to carry them past a negative first impression enough to begin a conversation?

3. To create a polished piece of work takes time. You cannot dash off an essay the night before it's due and hope to produce perfect copy. Think about how much time you need to do excellent work. Every person works at a different pace; be realistic in estimating the time you require. Then consider how you budget your time. Do you allow enough time to do what is needed? Can you organize your time better?

By now students should have a realistic picture of the time it takes to write effectively and present perfect copy. Students must plan time for prewriting and outlining as well as writing; time between writing and rewriting to gain perspective; and time to rewrite, edit, and prepare final copy. Budgeting time becomes even more important in the last section of the book. Discuss ways to manage time more efficiently, and try to help students eliminate time wasters and implement time savers in their study routines. This will be more easily accomplished by homeschoolers.

My kids all thought they benefited from reading *The Seven Habits of Highly Effective Teens* by Sean Covey.

4. In our "information age" certain skills are especially useful: use of a typewriter or computer, a library, and the Internet among them. How can you upgrade your skills? What other skills are important to your efficiency as a writer and a student?

Taking classes and workshops, researching and practicing skills, and working with more experienced people will help upgrade skills. Being able to keep accurate records and use data banks are two other helpful skills. The students should name skills important to them now in addition to ones that will be important to them when they are adults.

ACT

1. Consult *The Concise Oxford Dictionary of Quotations* or *Bartlett's Familiar Quotations* for entries pertaining to appearance or beauty. Pick at least three and add them to your "Notable Quotations." Analyse them in class to determine which of them you really believe in practice. For example, we might all agree that "Beauty is only skin deep," but when we react or relate to people, do we place greater value on inner qualities or surface appearances?

The students should be able to find a myriad of quotations which convey societal attitudes about appearance and beauty. They might search through teen, women's, and men's magazines to check current ideas and attitudes about appearance and compare them to those of previous decades.

Students who are inexperienced in research may not realize that they can often look up a topic under more than one heading. For instance, a student might search for the headings *looks* or *beautiful* in addition to *appearance* and *beauty*.

Here are four provocative quotations.

> •"A beautiful woman with a brain is like a beautiful woman with a club foot."
> Bernard Cornfield, *Daily Telegraph Magazine*

> •"Black is beautiful."
> Black Panther slogan (at the time, considered both radical and uplifting, depending on the audience)

•"As a white candle/In a holy place/ So is the beauty/Of an aged face."
Joseph Campbell, *The Old Woman*

•"There is beauty in fitness which no art can enhance."
Norman Douglas, *Siren Land*, "The Cove of Crapiola"

2. Write a short descriptive, narrative, expository, or persuasive essay. You may build it from a paragraph you wrote for a previous exercise, use a "Notable Quotation" as a starting point, or start from scratch. Take the essay through the entire rewriting and editing process. Prepare a final copy that is correct in execution and perfect in presentation (typed if possible).

Whether you have a great deal of time or one week allotted to this chapter, you will need to help students schedule the work for this assignment. If possible, dedicate some in-class time to editing and rewriting in groups or with partners. As with every assignment, this one is meant not only to gauge the students' comprehension and skills but to improve them.

3. Redo the paper in letter format, addressed to your teacher. Include your filled-in envelope (also typed if possible) with the finished assignment.

"A great writer creates a world of his own and his readers are proud to live in it. A lesser writer may entice them in for a moment, but soon he will watch them sling out."

Cyril Connolly, *Enemies of Promise*

sixteen

Bridges to Knowledge

Objectives for This Chapter

After studying this chapter, students should:

- Be able to write an effective book report, synopsis, summary, analysis, or criticism of a literary work
- Be able to write more decisive and more relevant introductions than previously
- Be able to recognize and revise hesitant wording
- Be able to perform better on essay tests
- Be able to select, find a focus for, and create a workable thesis for a research paper
- Be able to conduct research and take effective notes for a paper of any length
- Be able to write, revise, and edit a research paper
- Be able to prepare a research paper for formal presentation.

Vocabulary

Chapter Vocabulary

lackadaisical   verbatim
ascertain   innate
correlate

Enrichment Vocabulary

judicious/judicial	impel
actuate	indecorous
humor/wit	profane
abjure	copse
burnish	active/energetic/strenuous/vigorous

Warm-Up

The last three chapters of the book are so time-consuming that I am not going to include warm-ups. If you have time or are feeling stressed, try some of the warm-ups in earlier chapters or look at other books for ideas.

Caveats

Students often find academic writing strenuous because of the subject matter or the pressures of grades and deadlines. As a result, they forget that what they write can and should be strong in style and potent in wording. You may need to remind the students to write eloquently (but not extravagantly) as they fulfill the ACT assignments for this and the ensuing chapters.

Homeschoolers, use the flexibility inherent in your approach to help your students pick topics they're eager to learn about or that you're covering in a unit study.

Since the assignments in this and the next two chapters will require many hours of work, you may have to restrict the number you assign. If possible, do all of them, as it is likely that at no other time in their education will students have the chance to write every major type of writing assignment just for the purpose of improving their ability to do so.

SUM UP

In one sentence write the thesis of this chapter.

<u>Writers must at some point cease practice and apply their skills to real situations, each with its own guidelines, expectations, and criteria.</u>

REACT

1. Why do writers need readers?

Communication requires three elements: someone to communicate, something to communicate, and someone to communicate to. Writers cannot judge or improve their writing significantly without the attention, interaction, and response that readers bring to the process.

2. Discuss the long-term value of writing assignments.

Lead the students to personally meaningful answers. Gaining an appreciation for the intrinsic worth in what they are doing may inspire them to take more responsibility for their own education (which, after all, should become a lifetime habit).

3. What kinds of information are usable as support in a research paper? Why would one type of support carry more weight than another? Why might one source have more credibility than another?

Statistics, tables, charts, quotations, examples, and even anecdotes may provide acceptable support; useability depends on relevance and on whether the material adds to the content or merely fills the pages. The more direct the support, the more weight it carries. Support from sources with extensive first-hand experience is more believable than information from sources with little background.

4. What are primary and secondary research materials? You'll have to do research to find the answer.

Primary materials are first-hand sources and manuscript materials such as interviews, state archives, diaries, original notes, surveys, accounts by first recorders of an event, parish registers, letters, wills, and an author's own words (published or not). For example, the primary sources for someone doing research on Edgar Allen Poe would be the stories, poems, diaries, and articles written by him; his and his family's letters, and contemporary reviews or interviews (although these may include inaccurate quotations). Secondary sources provide information about a subject and include encyclopedias, reference works, and articles or books that deal with the subject. The distinction between primary and secondary materials is one between first-hand and second-hand reports.

ACT

1. Add to your "Notable Quotations" some quotations dealing with issues that fascinate you. Select from both fiction and nonfiction.

> •Fiction: "What is the conscience? It is the most highly developed part of the human being, the core of the spirit, the most sensitive, the most tender. It is shaped by the mores of a given society, it is developed toward wisdom by individual experience, it is maintained by strength of will."
> Pearl S. Buck, *Come My Beloved*

> •Nonfiction: "[Alexander Hamilton] sought to transform the American people into free, opulent, and law-abiding citizens, through the instrumentality of a limited republican government, on the basis of consent, and in the face of powerful vested interests in the status quo. The others were content merely to effect a political revolution. He set out to effect what amounted to a social revolution."
> Forrest McDonald, *Alexander Hamilton: A Biography*

2. Write a summary or synopsis of a movie you have seen recently. Discuss the success or failure of the plot as a development for the movie's thesis.

A movie works well for this assignment because students must pay enough attention as they watch to analyse and determine development; the exercise develops both critical and memory skills. Students should provide support as concrete and telling as for a plot summary or synopsis of a book. Obviously, if the student can watch a movie with this assignment in mind, it will go more easily. The finished piece may be as short as one page.

3. Write a critical or analytical essay on a book (or story or play) you have read. Choose any theme for your discussion; be sure to tie your paper's theme to the central thesis of the book.

Often students have trouble establishing a theme that is separate from the book's central one and then building an argument that links the two. Some preliminary discussion should alleviate this problem.

Another problem is that students fail to note and record quotations that would lend support to their essay. They must then spend hours thumbing through the book to find characters' names, details about setting, major and minor themes, and suitable quotations. I have developed a "bookmark" system to end this problem.

Using standard typing paper, I created a form that I can reproduce on the computer, print, and fold into a bookmark. The form asks questions which the reader fills in (using longhand or a personal shorthand) with page numbers while reading. My biography form and fiction form are in the appendix. Feel free to copy and modify them to suit your requirements. A version for research papers would also be helpful; I'll leave it to your class to invent one.

4. Practice primary research. Interview an eyewitness or eyewitnesses to an event or time period. Take notes throughout the interview; if possible, use a tape recorder. Write a summary of the interview and include a few choice quotations. (You might ask questions about home entertainment in the early 1900s, for example, or what it was like to survive the Holocaust, to fight in the Gulf War, to survive the attack on the World Trade Center, etc.)

If a student finds the subject of this assignment stimulating, you may want to use it as a basis for a research paper.

5. Write a list of possible research topics that interest you. Go to your library and list potential source material for several topics. Select a topic based on availability of reference material.

If possible, don't allow your class to use the Internet only for this assignment; many of America's students are becoming inept in library research because of their heavy reliance on the Internet. They must learn how to use standard reference books as well (such as *The Reader's Guide to Periodical Literature*; of course, that may be on-line at your library).

6. Use the two methods in the chapter ("Find a Focus" section) to find two different focuses for your topic. Choose one and write your thesis in a single sentence.
7. Write a schedule for a research paper. Plan specific dates to finish each stage, from research to final copy. Write a paper according to the chapter's guidelines and your teacher's criteria. You may be able to write a research paper that meets the requirements of another class, such as history or science.

If you don't have time for ACT #7, try to assign #5 and #6, as well as the scheduling exercise in #7. If students at least have the chance to do preliminary research, select a topic, determine possible focuses, and write a clear, manageable thesis under your guidance, they will be infinitely better prepared for future assignments, as these tasks are chief among those that students find troublesome. Scheduling themselves is also tough (although of course not so tough as actually following the schedule).

8. All finished assignments should meet the criteria for presentation given in Chapter 15.

With the exception of their responses for SUM UP and REACT, along with their quotations, students should present all assignments formally from here on out.

seventeen

Bridges to Opportunity

Objectives for This Chapter

After studying this chapter, students should:

•Be able to explain and give examples of the differences between writing for education and writing for opportunity
•Be able to write a personal narrative that is creative, personal, vivid, organized, and analytical
•Be able to assess a narrative question to determine whether they can answer it effectively or should choose another one
•Be able to form a thesis that answers a narrative question effectively and creatively
•Be able to explain the differences and similarities between a letter of application and a cover letter
•Be able to write an effective letter of application
•Be able to write an effective cover letter and résumé
•Be able to write a letter of promotion
•Be able to ascertain personal strengths and relate them to specific and general requirements
•Be able to assess an ad in relationship to their own skills and qualities to determine whether they are eligible for a particular position.

Vocabulary

Chapter Vocabulary

crux
attribute (n.)
exuberant
barrage
truism

adaptability
peripheral
outlandish
substantiate
enticing

Enrichment Vocabulary

grovel
platitude

replete
pervade

Caveats

Students often falter when asked to select and correlate the details of their lives to the requirements of a narrative, job, or other position. They are not alone; many adults flail about when writing about themselves. The exercises in the chapter should help overcome such difficulties, but if the class is still fumbling, you might have them search for websites geared toward helping people find work.

SUM UP

1. In one sentence write the thesis of this chapter.

    Learning to make the most of who you are and what you have done (or could do) in relationship to a specific goal is the crux of writing for opportunity.

2. Describe the opportunities available to you in the past year and the ones you hope to have available in the future.

    Encourage students to consider not only future educational and job opportunities but openings related to activities, hobbies, or community involvement.

REACT

1. Personal narratives, letters of application, and even résumés are persuasive in purpose; their common goal is to sell your experience and qualities to someone else. How do you feel about having to "sell yourself"? In what ways might the sales pitch change according to audience? What aspects of the "pitch" would be constant?

If the reader is known to the writer, that could influence content, style, and possibly tone. The format of the letter and the formula for content are two elements that would not change regardless of audience, even if applying for a job from a relative.

2. What are values? How do your expectations of yourself affect your perception of your own values? Are your expectations high or low? What impact do you imagine your expectations will have on your life? What impact have they had thus far?

Values in this context are attributes. Many students need inspiration and insights regarding their own worth and potential. At the same time they need help planning realistically how to attain goals. Pushing students past their own predetermined limitations has been a secondary function of this course. Opening their minds to the nearly unlimited options available to them if they are industrious has been another.

3. Successful writing for opportunity depends upon meeting high standards. Is this fair? Should people be given chances to prove themselves even if they cannot communicate their own worth, prove their qualifications, or present their information professionally? In what ways do high standards make you expand your capabilities? In what ways do low standards diminish your capabilities?

This question extends the train of thought begun in #2, above. Some students may argue that high standards are unreasonable and unfair. If they can recognize their own improvement through the hard work of the course, and if they can see more and greater opportunities open to them now than at the beginning, then they should be able to embrace the concept that high standards force capabilities to expand. (This is a subtheme in the text.)

4. What is the difference between qualities and qualifications? What are some desirable qualities in a college student? In an employee? Should someone with poor grades, low test scores, but a high IQ be accepted to

college? Who is the better choice for a job, someone with the qualities which make for a great employee but without the requisite skills, or someone with a lousy attitude but the necessary skills? What is *your* attitude toward work of any kind (homework, work at home, jobs, and so forth)?

Qualities are traits, attributes, or features. Qualifications are requirements or duties. Qualities may or may not fulfill qualifications.

The rest of the questions are meant to stimulate an invigorating discussion. Homeschoolers, be careful to make room for your class to express different opinions than yours; controversial ideas may be offered simply to cause friction. You may want to save this discussion for the dinner hour, especially if you have a large family which could also participate.

5. What distinguishes you from your peers?

What makes one person distinct from another is a key factor in an employer or college admissions committee choosing one applicant over another. Students need to determine what qualities they have that make them special and marketable. To initiate the discussion, you might tell the students what makes you yourself distinguishable from your peers.

6. Why must personal narratives, letters of application, and cover letters have a thesis?

The thesis, in these types of writing, is multi-layered; one is to sell the writer's qualities, the other is the focus for shaping those qualities into a convincing argument. Without a thesis, the essays and letters tend to wander and work against their goal.

7. After class discussion add any new ideas to your notes.

ACT

1. Look up the words *opportunity, possibilities,* and *quality* in *Bartlett's Familiar Quotations*. Add three quotations to your "Notable Quotations" relevant to this chapter and your class discussions.

Bartlett's has a section in the back entitled "Anonymous" where folk sayings can be found, some of which will deal with these topics. Also, the headings *work, possibility,* and *money* are other options which may lead to pertinent quotations.

2. List your personal strengths. Include everything positive you can think about yourself and anything negative you have worked on improving.

Homeschoolers, if your class is struggling with this, you might try writing the list for the students and having the students write the list about you. Then trade off and see what you can each add (or want to change).

Traditional classroom teachers may be able to pair up friends for the same variation of the exercise.

3. Write a personal narrative, choosing your topic from the sample list.

Discuss the narrative questions in class. Pick one topic and go through the process together, writing ideas, focus, and finally the thesis statement on the board so students can experience the process fully before working independently.

4. Find an ad for a job that you could apply for and possibly get. Try to choose a challenging position. Make a two-column chart like the one in the chapter, matching qualifications, obvious qualities, and unstated qualities with your experience.
5. Make an activity/attribute chart such as the one in the chapter.

You can also do either of these assignments together in class. Homeschoolers, you may want to apply this assignment to "real" life and have the class apply for summer work.

6. Write a letter of application for the job or a cover letter and résumé.

If pressed for time, it would be better to write the letter of application and skip the cover letter and résumé.

"First I write one sentence; then I write another. That's how I write. And so I go on. But I have a feeling writing ought to feel like running through a field."

Lytton Strachey, in conversation with Max Beerbohm, as quoted in Virginia Woolf's *A Writer's Diary*

eighteen

Bridges to the World

Objectives for This Chapter

After studying this chapter, students should:

- Be able to describe and give examples of the kinds of writing they will have to do for themselves throughout their lives
- Be able to explain why writing and writing well are important, giving personal as well as general examples for support
- Be able to discuss the ways their writing has improved since the beginning of the course and provide examples
- Be able to explain the purpose of and possible reasons to write a letter of inquiry
- Be able to write a letter of inquiry
- Be able to explain the purpose of and possible reasons to write letters of complaint and adjustment
- Be able to write letters of complaint and adjustment
- Be able to explain the purpose of a letter of opinion and some reasons for writing one
- Be able to write a letter of opinion
- Understand and be able to demonstrate through their own examples why personal letters are important
- Be able to write a thank-you letter, a letter of sympathy, and a letter of friendship and to explain the values of each
- Understand how and why writing can improve thinking.

. Vocabulary

Chapter Vocabulary

bereaved   referendum
forego   intercede

Enrichment Vocabulary

bombastic   tangent
predilection   consternation/trepidation
accede   carp
sublime   obsequious/subservient/fawn (v.i.)
subjugate   supercilious
equivocate   aver/vow

Caveats

The term "letters of opinion" misleads students somewhat, inviting them to "speak their minds" rather than to convince other minds of the validity of a position. Such letters tend to be verbal tantrums. Similarly, novice writers lose common sense when they write letters of complaint, often slipping into informal or even abusive language. In either case, students must remember that an insulting attitude offends; it does not convince. A successful editorial or letter of complaint, on the other hands, is as pointed, well supported, and controlled as any formal persuasive essay.

SUM UP

1. In one sentence write the thesis of this chapter.

   Chapter thesis: <u>Writing skills, chiefly in the form of letters, are needed to communicate your personal concerns to the world.</u>

2. Write, in one sentence, the thesis of this book.

   Essentially, the thesis is as follows: <u>Writing is an ongoing process of communication, a bridge between the writer's mind and the reader's, that enhances the writer's ability to think clearly.</u>

For a challenging discussion, ask students to name and give examples of some of the sub-themes of the book, such as, "High standards force capabilities to expand." See the discussion for Chapter 17, REACT # 2, page 136, for two others.

3. Write a paragraph noting how the book's conclusion ties into its introduction. After class discussion revise your summary as needed.

Students may need to reread the first chapter and the last page of Chapter 18 to see the connection.

REACT

1. Why write? Why write well? Think seriously about the need for writing in your life.

This question has been posed in many ways throughout the book. Take the time to answer it yourself now; both you and the students should eschew pat answers. For example, one of my own reasons for writing and writing well is that the mental exercise is among the most challenging I encounter in my life. I thrive on pushing myself beyond previous limits; writing is the perfect vehicle for that drive.

2. How would you define exemplary writing?

Again, students need to give a genuine answer to this question. During discussion ask students why they responded as they did.

3. Review your journal, bearing in mind the statement, "The more you write, the better you write and the clearer you think." Pull out examples from your writing that support this maxim.

Any student who has done the work required of this course should be able to find many telling examples. If you have been making comments all along in the journal about their improvements, they should also have trail markers for charting their journey to clear thinking and effective writing.

4. Can you apply the statement to other disciplines besides writing? In what ways has this course influenced your work in other classes? Can you apply the principle to other areas of your life? Give examples.

The more you practice anything, the more practiced you become at that thing. If this isn't one of the basic laws of nature, it should be. What the students must glean from the discussions for this chapter are that their industriousness has paid off, that hard work always pays off (although not necessarily in dollar bills), and that it therefore makes sense to work hard at other disciplines and in other areas of their lives.

By the way, the preceding paragraph delineates a couple more of the book's minor themes.

5. Have you changed since you started this class? In even so short a time have you grown, matured, developed? Has your writing also matured?

Doubtless students will have considered many new ideas and re-evaluated old ones during this course. The discussions alone would be enough to stimulate personal growth. When you consider the maturity it takes to research and develop ideas; to prewrite, write, rewrite, edit, and proof; and to prepare copy for final presentation, it will be obvious that a great deal of maturation has taken place since the class began. Ask the students: Could they have written six months ago what they are capable of writing now, and as well?

If you have been doing the assignments along with the class, then ask yourself the same question. Even if not, you have accomplished a great deal simply in teaching this class. Congratulations.

ACT

1. Add some quotations to your "Notable Quotations" that demonstrate exemplary writing. Then review your journal, other writing which you have done, or conversations you have had. Can you add to "Notable Quotations" some of your own best lines?

Suggest that students keep quotation journals henceforth. They could combine them with a list of and comments about books they have read, or they could keep them separate for easy reference. Such a record could provide them with invaluable and surprising insights about themselves twenty, thirty, or forty years down the road.

I have sporadically kept a book/quotations journal since my early twenties. To read through it reveals much about my own intellectual, spiritual, and emotional development over the decades.

If you are teaching in a traditional setting, you might also collect the students' quotations for a record of your own which you can build on and draw from over the years.

2. Write a letter of persuasion about an issue that inflames you. Address the letter to an appropriate—and real—audience. Prepare the letter for presentation and review it in class. Then mail a copy to the right person, whether a newspaper editor, your congressional representative, or a state official.

Students should keep a copy of the letter for their journals and make note of any responses to the letter (e.g., mention publication and include the clipping, or include any letters replying to the original). My son was delighted when his letter to our Congressman was answered personally, and even more so when the law about which he was writing to support was passed. He thought, and rightly so, that he had in some small way influenced his country.

3. What present would you most like to receive on your next birthday, and who would send it? Pretend that your wish comes true, and write a thank-you letter for it. Alternatively, write a thank-you letter for a gift you have actually received recently.

Students should mail the letters that respond to an actual gift (after you have read it, of course). Personal letters need not be formal in appearance, but they should be neat and should follow standard letter format.

4. Write a personal letter—to yourself. In it describe the changes that you have undergone in the past semester or year. End by voicing your aspirations. Seal the letter and put it in a safe place. Let it be a private time capsule to be opened ten years from now.

If the students want to share this letter, fine. Thank them for the opportunity to read it. Otherwise, let it go. Do the assignment yourself.

If a homeschooler, you may want the whole family to undertake this activity. On the eve of the millennium, everyone in my household wrote letters to themselves, and I sealed them in a big can along with pictures of us from that time (taken next to some newly planted trees for comparison later). We plan to open it in 2030.

5. Remember in the first chapter, when I said I had never written to thank the woman who helped me so much when I was in high school? After

telling you that, I felt so guilty that I found her address and wrote a long letter explaining how much she had helped me. I thanked her sincerely, and then I told her some about how I have felt her influence over the years. I heard back from her soon thereafter; she couldn't thank me enough, in return, for the impact that the letter had had on her, especially now that her children had grown up and she had been widowed. It was a rewarding response.

So now it's your turn. Write a thank-you letter to some person who has genuinely contributed to your life. (Why wait? When someone is dead, it's too late to say thank you.) You can be brief, but you should include enough detail to show your sincerity. Go ahead and mail the letter.

One possibility for this and the previous letter is to read them aloud in class, not to edit, but to appreciate. The students must be willing, however, and the letter for ACT #5 should be mailed (if the recipient is still alive; students might pick someone they wish they had written to).

6. Discuss what you have learned about writing from reading this book. Evaluate yourself. In what ways have you most improved your writing? Do you need to attend to any specific areas? If so, in what ways can you continue on your own to improve your writing?

The students should consider these questions in a written draft; discuss them in class, and then rewrite their responses. The resulting paper need not be long, but it should be honest and specific.

7. Write a letter to me, the author, via the publisher. The address is in the front of the book. Let me know what you liked or didn't like about the book, and what (if anything) you'd like to see added. If I've made any errors, point them out (tell me the page number too, please). Send me an example of your writing at the beginning of the course and at the end; let me see how you have improved.

This assignment is optional, but I shall certainly enjoy any letters I get. You might also note, as the teacher, what I could do in future editions that would have helped you, along with any warm-ups or assignments that were particularly successful (or a bomb).

If you include permission to use your or the class's comments, I may include them in a future edition or in a column on the Popular Weasel Press website (popularweaselpress.com).

Thank you for the hard work, energy, and enthusiasm that this course required; if even one of your students writes more effectively now, the world is a better place for it.

"It is a great gift to have a good teacher."

Natalie Goldberg, *Long Quiet Highway*

Trust in yourself, listen to your students—really listen—and be passionate about your subject. You will be that teacher.

APPENDIX

EDITING SYMBOLS

MARK	EXPLANATION
ℓ	Delete character or characters indicated.
stet	Let a previously deleted character or characters stay.
#	Insert space.
‿	Close up space.
tr ⁀	Transpose; switch places. Place switches.
caps or ⸗	Use capital letters. washington
lc or /	Use lower case letters. the Giraffe
∧	Insert something that has been omitted.
gr	Error in grammar.
ref	Error in pronoun reference.
t or tense	Error in verb tense.
p or punc	Error in punctuation.
ital or ___	Use italic type or underline.
⊙	Put in period.
ss	Error in sentence structure.
frag	Sentence fragment.
rs	Run-on sentence.
w or wording	Problem in wording.
nc or ?	Not clear; question to author.
sp	Spelling error.
spell out	Spell out an abbreviation or acronym.
¶	Start paragraph.
no ¶	No paragraph break; run together.
ms or format	Problem in manuscript form or neatness.
⁞⁞	Even out lines.
⊢ or ⊏	Move the line left.
⊣ or ⊐	Move the line right.

Comprehensive Vocabulary List

abjure
accede
acronym
active/energetic/strenuous/vigorous
actuate
acumen
adaptability
adulterate
aggregate (v.t.)
allegory
allusion
alluvial
ambient
amoeba
analysis
anathema
anecdote
anemic
arcane
arraign
ascertain
assay
astute
attribute (n.)
attribute (v.t.)/ascribe/impute
augment
aver/vow
bailiwick
baneful
barrage
behoove
bereaved
bombastic
bowdlerize

bravado
burnish
carp
chicanery
coddle
cogency
coherence
compassion
compunction
congruence
conjecture/surmise
connotation
consternation/trepidation
contingency
copse
correlate
cowardly/timid/timorous
credibility
crotchety/cantankerous/persnickety
crux
curmudgeon
debilitate
decry
delineate
denunciate
denunciation
despair/desperation/despondency/discouragement/hopelessness
desultory
diligence
ebullient
echelon
eclectic
eidetic
emaciation
empathy/sympathy
enmity
enticing
equanimity
equivocate
eschew
euphemism
evanescent

expurgate
extraneous
extrinsic/intrinsic
exuberant
feasible
fetter
forego
forswear
fractious
frail
froward
fulminate
gentle/mild/meek
gobbledygook
grovel
hackneyed/trite/banal
happiness/bliss/contentment
harbinger
harl
hierarchy
honor/honesty/integrity/sincerity
humor/wit
ignominy/abject
impel
impel/compel
inane
inculcate
indecorous
inequity
infallible
inferences
inflexible/relentless/implacable/inexorable
ingenious/ingenuous
ingratiate/cavil
inhere
inherent
innate
innocent/blameless/guiltless
insipid/jejune
insurgent
interlay
inveigle

inviolate
invoke
involute
ironic
jargon
judicious/judicial
kith
lackadaisical
laity
laziness/indolence/lassitude
machismo
make/construct/manufacture
martinet
misconstrue
mitigate
mitigate
moil
nadir
nadir
nascent
non sequitur
nuance
obfuscation
obsequious/subservient/fawn (v.i.)
obtuse
odious
opinionated/biased/prejudiced
orator
outlandish
palatable
pandemic
pander
paradox
paraphrase/sum up
pariah
peripheral
perspicuous/manifest
pervade
phlegmatic
piquant
platitude
plight

poltroon
potency
precarious
precise/concise
predilection
pregnable
preliminary/introductory
principle/canon/rule
probity
proclivity/aversion
profane
profligate
propitious
puerile
recant
recondite
redundancy/repetition
referendum
replete
requisite
rescind
resilient
roil
salient
salutary
sanctimonious
sanguine
sarcasm
scourge
secular
serendipity
serendipity
shamble
similitude
slew (n.)
slovenly
sophistry
sparsely
specious
spume
spume
stint

subjugate
sublime
substantiate
succeed/flourish/prosper/thrive
succor
supercilious
superfluous
surmise
synthesis
tangent
testament
thwart/frustrate/baffle
tractable
traduce/denigrate
truculent
truism
truncate
unrefined
vacuous/vacant/blank
vagary/caprice
verbatim
winnow
yield/submit/surrender

"The one real object of education is to leave a man in the condition of continually asking questions."

Bishop Creighton, as quoted in *Things Ancient and Modern*, by C. A. Alington

EVALUATION/CRITIQUE GUIDE

This is the same guide as in the textbook, but it may help you to have an extra ne here. You may copy it or retype it (allowing yourself more space for omments) to use alongside a draft, or just use it to direct your comments while you rite on the draft itself (in pencil, please). It may help to number the paragraphs so at you can refer to them without confusion (for example, ¶ 3, insufficient pport). If you find yourself refining this guide, please send me your nprovements to incorporate in future editions. Thank you.

ntroduction:
   Clear?
   States thesis?
   Sets up development"
   Starts with a strong "hook"?
OMMENTS:

ody:
   Each idea presented clearly?
   One idea per paragraph?
   Uses logical development?
   Develops all points stated
       in introduction?
   Supports each major idea with
       at least two points?
   Includes supportive examples?
   Uses supportive quotations?
   Uses supportive anecdotes?
   Needs additional support?
OMMENTS:

onclusion:
   Restates thesis in new way?
   Sums up key points?
   Ends with a "clincher"?
OMMENTS:

Writing: The Bridge Between Us--156

Style (add after Ch. 7):
　　Flows smoothly?
　　Varies sentences?
　　Appeals to senses?
COMMENTS:

Purpose and Audience
　　(add after Ch. 10):
　　Purpose clear and focused?
　　Tone and attitude appropriate
　　　　for audience?
COMMENTS:

Wording (add after Ch. 12):
　　Uses concrete language?
　　Any points ambiguous?
　　Any points unclear?
　　Any points redundant?
　　Any points repetitive?
　　Could wording be more
　　　　concise?
　　Could wording be more
　　　　precise?
COMMENTS:

Grammar, mechanics, and appearance (add after Section 4):
COMMENTS:

BIOGRAPHY "BOOKMARK"

I suggest that you retype this so you can reproduce it readily. Print it on the front and back of an 8 1/2" by 11" paper. Divide the page into two columns, and leave more space between sections. Add any questions that pertain to your studies. Make a page break where I do, and print the next page on the back of the sheet rather than on a separate piece of paper. Then fold the paper in half for use as a bookmark and note-taking system. Because my pages are smaller than I'm recommending, the proportions will be off.

All notes should be accompanied by a page number. Direct quotations should give the full citation.

Likewise spread the fiction Notes/Bookmark between two pages, also printed front and back.

BIOGRAPHY NOTES/BOOKMARK

One of the most compelling aspects if the subject is (include page number of examples)

Title:
Author:
Date published:
Publisher:

Dates subject lived:
Where born and raised:

Family & influence of family:

Summary:

Opinion: I liked/didn't like the author's approach; why/why not

Author's slant on the subject (major and minor themes):

What are some unusual traits of the subject?

As a child, the character of the subject showed when he or she (or developed because of):

BACK SIDE OF BOOKMARK

Pages w/ important info.:

Pages that show critical incidents in subject's youth

Key influences on the subject:

What were some of the greatest disappointments in the person's life? Did they influence why the person became great?

Greatest achievements?

To achieve greatness, the person had to overcome:

Impact on society:

Any nicknames or trademarks?

I identified/didn't identify w/ this person because:

Anecdotes that demonstrate the subject's character or attitude

I would/wouldn't recommend the book because:

Anecdotes or quotations that demonstrate how others viewed this person

FICTION NOTES/BOOKMARK

Fiction Notes/Bookmark

The most compelling
aspects of the story (include
page number of examples)
(or if not compelling, quotations
demonstrating why)

Title:
Author:
Date published:
Publisher

Time period:
Setting:

Major and minor themes:

Background info.:

Major conflicts or setbacks:

Protagonist(s)—give name &
describe:

Minor conflicts or setbacks:

What does the main character
want? What is in the way?

How the setting affects the story
(if at all)/ time and place

Antagonist(s)—give name,
description, and relationship
to protagonist

How does the antagonist
influence the course of the story?

What does the antagonist
want? What is in the way?

How does the helper character(s)
influence the course of the story?

Name & describe helper
characters & relationships to
other characters:

What is the climax, or turning
point of the story?

What are some unusual traits
of the main character that help
identify his/her nature? Of the
antagonist?

How is the major conflict resolved?

Pages w/ important info.:

Quotations that support the
major theme of the book:

I would/wouldn't recommend the book
because:

Quotations that support the
minor themes of the book:

"We shouldn't teach great books; we should teach a love of reading."

B. F. Skinner, as quoted in *B. F. Skinner: The Man and His Ideas*, by R. Evans

SUPPLEMENTARY READING

uggested Readings for Teachers

OTE: Undoubtedly, there are more recent editions of many of these books. Check ith your library, book store, or with the publisher directly. Many of these are entioned in the text or elsewhere in this guide.

ernays, Anne. *What If?* New York: HarperCollins College Publishers, 1995. This ontains many great ideas for fiction exercises, which will also improve the vidness of your students' nonfiction writing. Many examples are from students d could be used for critiquing exercises, especially when the class is limited to e student. In the back is a worthy collection of short stories.

olton, Robert. *People Skills.* New York: Simon & Schuster, 1979. This is a book out communication skills—listening and responding effectively—and even ough the book talks a great deal about relationships, its tips for breaking through mmunication barriers are useful for anyone in any setting.

alkins, Lucy McCormick. *The Art of Teaching Writing.* Portsmouth: Heinemann ducational Books, 1986. Although the focus of this book is on elementary rough junior high school students, it offers many insights into the writing process d the challenges that writing teachers face. Well worth skimming through.

ard, Orson Scott. *Characters & Viewpoint.* Cincinnati: Writer's Digest Books, 988. This book is written to help fiction writers, but students will become better aders if they study Card's ideas about what makes a strong character in fiction.

heney, Theodore A. Rees. *Getting the Words Right: How to Rewrite, Edit, & evise.* Cincinnati: Writer's Digest Books, 1990. An excellent book on rewriting hich has terrific examples. The book's three sections clearly delineate the main pproaches to revision: "Revision by Reduction," "Rethink and Rearrange," and Revise by Rewording."

Fowler, H. W. *A Dictionary of Modern English Usage*. Revised and edited by S Ernest Gowers. New York: Oxford University Press, 1983. An excellent referenc for the finer points of grammar, syntax, wording, and style. Along with a standar dictionary and a bad speller's dictionary, this is a great manual to keep on your des for students to use during class writing periods.

Gibson, Walker. *Persona: A Style Study for Readers and Writers*. New Yorl Random House, 1969. A brief study of voice, tone, and attitude, it contair effective examples.

Goldberg, Natalie. *Writing Down the Bones*. Boston: Shambhala Publication 1986. A slightly zany but liberating approach to writing freely and creatively wit many stimulating writing exercises. Goldberg is a champion of "practice writing May contain some profanity, so homeschoolers, review first (while standing in th bookstore, perhaps).

Gordon, Karen Elizabeth. *The Transitive Vampire: A Handbook of Grammar fc the Innocent, the Eager, and the Doomed*. New York: Times Books, 1984. This a funky but somewhat limited guide to grammar, not suitable for conservativ homeschoolers. For others, it offers a wacky approach that may help studen remember rules of grammar.

Jensen, Frode. *Jensen's Grammar, Jensen's Punctuation; Format Writing*. Gran Pass: Wordsmiths. Described on page 100. My son and my sister's children lov his books and did the exercises without nagging; what better endorsement do yc need? Here's one: a year later, my son still remembers all the rules from th punctuation book. Books and prices: www.jsgrammar.com

Kaplan, David Michael. *Revision: A Creative Approach to Writing and Rewritin Fiction*. Cincinnati: Story Press, 1997. For fiction writers, obviously, but offel some good tips for all writers. Worth skimming for ideas.

Minto, Barbara. *The Pyramid Principle: Logic in Writing and Thinking*. Londor Minto International, 1982. A nuts-and-bolts approach to logic, using a variation c the "hourglass" principle (described in Chapter 4 of the text). If your class is havin trouble with organizational concepts, this book may provide additional support.

Rico, Gabriele Luffer. *Writing the Natural Way*. Los Angeles: J. P. Tarcher, 198: Offers intriguing and successful techniques for breaking through writer's bloc increasing a sense of confidence and experimentation in writing. A good source fc warm-up exercises.

hertzer, Margaret. *The Elements of Grammar*. New York: Macmillan Publishing ompany, 1986. The author lays out the rules simply and clearly. This is a good sic reference book and less expensive than the guide by Warriner (below).

arriner, John E. *English Grammar and Composition: Complete Course*. New ork: Harcourt Brace Jovanovich, Inc., 1982. This is the most thorough, accurate, d accessible grammar book I have ever used. The complete course is better than e versions for lower grades. The exercises are staid but effective.

ideo

For a follow-up course to this—if your homeschooler isn't graduating yet—I commend that you investigate the video course, "The ABZs of Writing," by ichael McClory. I have not previewed this course, but I have talked with the thor and studied the information on his website. It seems likely that the course ould broaden the base of skills developed in my textbook.

Suggested Readings for Students

What follows is a highly personal and somewhat eccentric list which I expec would supplement standard anthologies and the classics. The main criterion was n so much whether I liked the book as whether the author demonstrated a distincti voice. Books that vividly portray a particular lifestyle or time period also made th list, which could be nearly infinite.

I am not much one for censorship past middle school, but I respect that th sensibilities of homeschooling families may differ from mine. I recommend th parents read or at least scan a book before assigning it. If nothing else, it will gi you a base for discussing it with your child.

Encourage your students to read daily, and ask them to read all kinds literature and non-fiction. Every story, essay, play, or book they read will broad the spectrum of words, styles, and ideas available to them.

FICTION

Baldacci, David: *Wish You Well*
Baldwin, James: *Go Tell It On the Mountain*
Berquist, Laura M. (Ed.): *The Harp & Laurel Wreath* (an excellent poetr anthology)
Bradbury, Ray: *The Martian Chronicles*; *The Illustrated Man*; *Fahrenheit 451*; nearly anything else he has written
Buck, Pearl S. *Come My Beloved*
Card, Orson Scott: *Ender's Game* (the whole series)
Carlson, Lori M. (Ed.): *American Eyes* (short stories by Asian Americans)
Cather, Willa: *My Antonia*
Curtis, Christopher Paul: *The Watsons Go to Birmingham—1963* (this is a midd grade reader, but an excellent story for any age)
Earley, Tony: *Jim the Boy*
Ellison, Ralph: *Invisible Man*
Ford, Richard: *Wildfire*
Gibbons, Kaye: *Ellen Foster*
Hamill, Pete: *Snow in August*
Heinlein, Robert: *Strangers in a Strange Land*
Heller, Joseph: *Catch-22*
Hurston, Zora Neale: *Their Eyes Were Watching God*
Kennedy, William: *Ironweed* (contains harsh language and sexual references)
Marquez, Gabriel: *100 Years of Solitude*
Marquis, Don: *archy and mehitabel*
Maugham, W. Somerset: any short story collection

McCullers, Carson: *A Member of the Wedding; The Heart Is a Lonely Hunter*, or a short story collection

McGammon, Robert R.: *Boy's Life* (some sexual references)

Morrison, Toni: *Beloved* (some profanity, sexual references)

Oates, Joyce Carol: *Because It Is Bitter, Because It Is My Heart* (some profanity, sexual references)

O'Connor, Flannery: any short story collection

Sachar, Louis: *Holes* (a kids' book, but a fun, well-constructed story for any age)

Sams, Ferrol: *Run with the Horsemen; Whisper of the River*

Shakespeare, William: try some of his lesser known works

Stegner, Wallace: *Crossing to Safety*

Tan, Amy: *The Joy Luck Club*

Theroux, Paul: *The Mosquito Coast*

Thurber, James: *The Thurber Carnival*

van der Post, Laurens: *A Story Like the Wind; A Far Off Place* (the style is exceedingly difficult, especially at first, but the stories are more than worth the effort)

Walker, Alice: *The Color Purple* (profanity, sexual references)

Welty, Eudora: any short story collection

Westlake, Donald: *Jimmy the Kid; Bankshot* (any of the early Dortmunder series; some profanity)

Wodehouse, P. G.: *Psmith, Journalist; The Uncollected Wodehouse* (and almost anything else)

NON-FICTION

Bragg, Rick: *All Over But the Shoutin'; Ava's Man* (some profanity in both)

Bulfinch, Thomas: *Bulfinch's Mythology* (so many writers draw from mythology that every student should be familiar with it)

Callahan, Steven: *Adrift*

Cheever, John: *The Letters of John Cheever*

Conway, Jill Ker: *The Road from Coorain*

Dawson, George; Glaubman, Richard: *Life is Good*

Eiseley, Loren: *The Night Country*

Gotfryd, Bernard: *Anton the Dove Fancier & Other Tales of the Holocaust*

Grealy, Lucy: *Autobiography of a Face*

Keyes, Ralph: *The Courage to Write: How Writers Transcend Fear* (frank language)

de Saint-Exupery, Antoine: *Night Flight; Flight to Arras*

King, Jr., Martin Luther: any collection of speeches or letters

Lamb, Brian: *Booknotes*

Lincoln, Abraham: any collection of speeches or letters
Lomax, Eric: *The Railway Man*
Lopate, Phillip (Ed.): *The Art of the Personal Essay: An Anthology from the Classical Era to the Present*
Markham, Beryl: *West with the Night*
McBride, James: *The Color of Water* (well-told, moving memoir; some profanity)
McCourt, Frank: *Angela's Ashes* (same as above)
McDonald, Forrest: *The Boys Were Men*
Min, Anchee: *Red Azalea* (an excellent memoir about growing up in China during the Cultural Revolution; sexual references)
Moyers, Bill: *A World of Ideas*
Ravitch, Diane (Ed.): *The American Reader: Words That Moved a Nation*
Raybin, Patricia: *My First White Friend*
Sowell, Thomas: *Ethnic America*
Steffens, Lincoln: *The Autobiography of Lincoln Steffens*
Strunk Jr., William, and White, E. B.: *The Elements of Style* (teachers should also read this)
Terkel, Studs: *American Dreams: Lost & Found*
Thomas, Lewis: *The Lives of a Cell: Notes of a Biology Watcher*
Thurber, James: *The Letters of James Thurber*
White, E. B.: *Essays of E. B. White*
Zinsser, William: *Writing to Learn*
Representative American Speeches (published by H. W. Wilson Co.; use any collection)

INDEX

"Delightful task! to rear the tender thought,
To teach the young idea how to shoot."

James Thompson

"...teach us all to have aspiring minds...."

Christopher Marlowe, *Tamburlaine the Great*

ORDER FORM

Fax orders: 434-955-2479. Send this form.
Telephone orders: Call 866-268-1361 (toll-free). Have your credit card read
Website orders: www.popularweaselpress.com
Postal orders: Popular Weasel Press, P.O. Box 247, South Hill, VA 23970,
USA. Telephone: 434-955-2478.

Please send the following:

_____ copies of Writing: The Bridge Between Us, @ $22.95 each
_____ copies of Teacher's Manual, @ $14.95 each

_____ Total copies   _____ **Total Cost of copies**

Shipping: U.S.: Add $4.00 for the first book and $2.00 for each additional
product. Virginia residents multiply by .045 for sales tax.
Tax: $ _____
Total enclosed: $ _____

Ship to:
Name: _____

Address: _____

City, State, & Zip: _____

Telephone: _____

email address: _____

Payment: Check _____   Visa _____   MasterCard _____

Card number: _____

Name on card: _____ Exp. date: ___/___

Please send information about upcoming publications:
Yes _____   **No** _____

"The aim of education is the knowledge not of fact but of values."
W. R. Inge

Heart Failure

Evaluation and Care of Patients with Left-Ventricular Systolic Dysfunction

Commentary on the Agency for Health Care Policy and Research Clinical Practice Guideline #11

Editor:

Edward K. Kasper, M.D.
Assistant Professor of Medicine
Director, John Hopkins
Cardiomyopathy and Heart Transplant Service
The Johns Hopkins Hospital
Baltimore, Maryland

CHAPMAN & HALL

I T P® International Thomson Publishing

New York • Albany • Bonn • Boston • Cincinnati • Detroit • London • Madrid • Melbourne
Mexico City • Pacific Grove • Paris • San Francisco • Singapore • Tokyo • Toronto • Washington

Cover Design:
Andrea Meyer, emDASH, Inc.
Copyright © 1997
Chapman & Hall

A service of I(T)P ®

Printed in the United States of America

For more information, contact:

Chapman & Hall
115 Fifth Avenue
New York, NY 10003

Thomas Nelson Australia
102 Dodds Street
South Melbourne, 3205
Victoria, Australia

International Thomson Editores
Campos Eliseos 385, Piso 7
Col. Polanco
11560 Mexico D.F.
Mexico

International Thomson Publishing Asia
221 Henderson Road #05-10
Henderson Building
Singapore 0315

Chapman & Hall
2-6 Boundary Row
London SE1 8HN
England

Chapman & Hall GmbH
Postfach 100 263
D-69442 Weinheim
Germany

International Thomson Publishing
Hirakawacho-cho Kyowa Building, 3F
1-2-1 Hirakawacho-cho
Chiyoda-ku, 102 Tokyo
Japan

1 2 3 4 5 6 7 8 9 10 XXX 01 00 99 98 97

Original material from Konstam M, Dracup K, Baker D, et al. Heart Failure: Evaluation and Care of Patients With Left-Ventricular Systolic Dysfunction. Clinical Practice Guideline Number 11 (amended) AHCPR Publication No. 94-0612. Rockville, MD: Agency for Health Care Policy and Research and the National Heart, Lung, and Blood Institute, Public Health Service, U.S. Department of Health and Human Services. June 1994.

Library of Congress Cataloging-in-Publication Data

Kasper, Edward K. (Edward Kevin) 1957–
    Heart failure : evaluation and care of patients with left-ventricular systolic dysfunction: commentary on the Agency for Health Care Policy and Research Clinical practice guidelines #11 / Edward K. Kasper.
        p.   cm.—(Clinical practice guidelines series)
    Includes bibliographical references and index.
    ISBN 0-412-11261-2 (alk. paper)
        1. Heart failure—Handbooks, manuals, etc.   2. Heart—Left ventricle—Diseases—Handbooks, manuals, etc.   I. United States. Agency for Health Care Policy and Research.   II. Titile.   III. Series.
        [DNLM: 1. Heart Failure.   2. Heart Failure, Congestive—diagnosis.
    3. Heart Failure, Congestive—therapy.   4. Ventricular Dysfunction, Left.   WG 370 K185h 1996]
    RC685.C53K37   1996
    616.1´29—dc20
    DNLM/DLC
    for Library of Congress

96-9561
CIP

British Library Cataloguing in Publication Data available

To order this or any other Chapman & Hall book, please contact **International Thomson Publishing, 7625 Empire Drive, Florence, KY 41042**. Phone: (606) 525-6600 or 1-800-842-3636. Fax: (606) 525-7778. e-mail: order@chaphall.com.

For a complete listing of Chapman & Hall's titles, send your requests to **Chapman & Hall, Dept. BC, 115 Fifth Avenue, New York, NY 10003**

Contents

TABLES

FIGURES

Preface

This Agency for Health Care Policy and Research published this Clinical Practice Guideline in June of 1994. It provides recommendations for the evaluation and care of patients with heart failure due to systolic dysfunction. The Heart Failure Panel Members and the Project Staff should be congratulated for the thoughtful and useful guideline they created.

This guideline will be periodically revised by The Heart Failure Panel. We have not attempted to completely update their work. Rather, we have provided comments from the Directors of four active heart failure units who were not involved in the original publication. Why publish a text of commentary on heart failure guidelines? It was our goal to provide practical advice on how we use the content of this guideline in our daily care of patients with heart failure. We have pointed out several areas of disagreement and many areas of agreement.

It is our hope that houseofficers, primary care practitioners, cardiology fellows, cardiologists, nurses, and others who care for patients with heart failure will find our commentary a useful adjunct to the original guideline. We have updated the reference list and have tried to include recently published information germane to heart failure. We have also made every effort to maintain the simple format used in the original guideline. This falls far short of a complete revision.

I would like to thank the Contributors Providing Commentary for their efforts.

Edward K. Kasper, M.D., F.A.C.C., Editor
Director, The Johns Hopkins Cardiomyopathy and Heart Transplant Service
Baltimore, Maryland

Contributors Providing Commentary

G. William Dec, Jr., M.D.
Associate Professor of Medicine
Medical Director, Cardiac Transplantation Program
Division of Cardiology
Massachusetts General Hospital
Boston, Massachusetts

Edward K. Kasper, M.D.
Assistant Professor of Medicine
Medical Director, Cardiomyopathy and Heart Transplant Program
Johns Hopkins Hospital
Baltimore, Maryland

Barry Rayburn, M.D.
Assistant Professor of Medicine–Cardiology
Assistant Professor of Surgical Sciences–Cardiothoracic Surgery
The Bowman Gray School of Medicine
Winston-Salem, North Carolina

Richard Rodeheffer, M.D.
Associate Professor of Medicine
Director, Congestive Heart Failure Clinic
Division of Cardiovascular Disease
Mayo Clinic
Rochester, Minnesota

Guideline Development and Use

Guidelines are systematically developed statements to assist practitioner and patient decisions about appropriate health care for specific clinical conditions. This guideline was developed by an independent, multidisciplinary panel of private sector clinicians and other experts convened by the Agency for Health Care Policy and Research (AHCPR). The panel, with the assistance of the RAND Corporation, employed an explicit, science-based methodology and expert clinical judgment to develop specific statements on patient assessment and management for the clinical condition selected.

Extensive literature searches were conducted, and critical reviews and syntheses were used to evaluate empirical evidence and significant outcomes. Peer review and pilot testing were undertaken to evaluate the validity, reliability, and utility of the guideline in clinical practice. The panel's recommendations are primarily based on the published scientific literature. When the scientific literature was incomplete or inconsistent in a particular area, the recommendations reflect the professional judgment of panel members and consultants.

The guideline reflects the state of knowledge, current at the time of publication, on effective and appropriate care. Given the inevitable changes in the state of scientific information and technology, periodic review, updating, and revision will be done.]

We believe that the AHCPR-assisted clinical guideline development process will make positive contributions to the quality of care in the United States. We encourage practitioners and patients to use the information provided in this *Clinical Practice Guideline*. The recommendations may not be appropriate for use in all circumstances. Decisions to adopt any particular recommendation must be made by the practitioner in light of available resources and circumstances presented by individual patients.

Linda K. Demlo, Ph.D.
Acting Administrator
Agency for Health Care Policy and Research

Publication of this guideline does not necessarily represent endorsement by the U.S. Department of Health and Human Services.

Clinical Practice Guideline

Number 11

Heart Failure:
Evaluation and Care of
Patients With Left-Ventricular
Systolic Dysfunction

Marvin A. Konstam, MD (Co-chair)
Kathleen Dracup, DNSc, RN (Co-chair)
David W. Baker, MD, MPH
Michael B. Bottorff, PharmD
Neil H. Brooks, MD
Robert A. Dacey
Sandra B. Dunbar, DSN, RN
Anne B. Jackson, MA, RN
Mariell Jessup, MD
Jerry C. Johnson, MD
Robert H. Jones, MD
Robert J. Luchi, MD
Barry M. Massie, MD
Bertram Pitt, MD
Eric A. Rose, MD
Lewis J. Rubin, MD
Richard F. Wright, MD
David C. Hadorn, MD

U.S. Department of Health and Human Services
Public Health Service
Agency for Health Care Policy and Research
Rockville, Maryland

AHCPR Publication No. 94-0612

Panel Members

Marvin A. Konstam, MD
Co-chair
Professor of Medicine
Tufts University
Director, Heart Failure
 and Cardiac Transplant Center
New England Medical Center
 Hospitals
Boston, Massachusetts
Specialty: Cardiology

Kathleen Dracup, DNSc, RN
Co-chair
Professor
School of Nursing
University of California
Los Angeles, California
Specialty: Cardiovascular Nursing

Michael B. Bottorff, PharmD
Associate Professor and Chairman
Division of Clinical and Hospital
 Pharmacy
University of Cincinnati
 College of Pharmacy
Cincinnati, Ohio
Specialty: Clinical Pharmacy

Neil H. Brooks, MD
The American Academy of Family
 Physicians
Rockville, Connecticut
Specialty: Family Practice

Robert A. Dacey
Former President
The Mended Hearts, Inc.
Boulder, Colorado
*Specialty: Consumer
 Representative*

Sandra B. Dunbar, DSN, RN
Associate Professor
Emory University
Nell Hodgson Woodruff School
 of Nursing
Atlanta, Georgia
Specialty: Critical Care Nursing

Anne B. Jackson, MA, RN
American Association
 of Retired Persons
 National Legislative Council
Sarasota, Florida
*Specialty: Nursing, Consumer
 Representative*

Mariell Jessup, MD
Associate Professor Medicine
University of Pennsylvania
 School of Medicine
Director, Heart Failure Unit,
 Risk Reduction Center
Presbyterian Medical Center
Philadelphia, Pennsylvania
Specialty: Cardiology

Jerry C. Johnson, MD
Associate Profressor of Medicine
University of Pennsylvania
 Chief, Geriatric Medicine
 Division, Veterans Affairs
Medical Center
Philadelphia, Pennsylvania
*Specialty: Geriatrics and Internal
Medicine*

Robert H. Jones, MD
Mary and Deryl Hart
Professor of Surgery
Duke University Medical Center
Durham, North Carolina
Specialty: Cardiothoracic Surgery

Robert J. Luchi, MD
Chief, Geriatrics Section
Director, Huffington, Center
    on Aging
Baylor College of Medicine
ACOS Geriatrics and
    Extended Care
Veterans Affairs Medical Center
Houston, Texas
Specialty: Geriatrics,
    General Internal Medicine

Barry M. Massie, MD
Professor of Medicine
University of California,
    San Francisco
Director, Hypertension Clinic
Director, Coronary Care Unit
Veterans Affairs Medical Center
San Francisco, California
Specialty: Cardiology

Bertram Pitt, MD
Professor of Internal Medicine
    and Associate Chairman of
    Academic and Industrial Programs
Department of Internal Medicine
University of Michigan
    Medical Center
Ann Arbor, Michigan
Specialty: Cardiology

Eric A. Rose, MD
Chief, Cardiothoracic Surgery
Columbia Presbyterian
    Medical Center
New York, New York
Specialty: Cardiothoracic Surgery

Lewis J. Rubin, MD
Professor of Physiology
    and Professor of Medicine
University of Maryland
    School of Medicine
Baltimore, Maryland
Specialty: Pulmonology

Richard F. Wright, MD
Research Director
Pacific Heart Institute
Assistant Clinical Professor
University of California
Los Angeles, California
Specialty: Cardiology

Project Staff, RAND

David C. Hadorn, MD
Project Director

David W. Baker, MD, MPH
Associate Project Director
Literature Review Manager

James Hodges, PhD
Project Statistician

Carole Oken, MA
Administrative Coordinator

Caren Kamberg, MSPH
Editor

Roberta Shanman, MLS
Research Librarian

Project Secretaries
Lauren Camhi
Karla Danford
Yasmin Facey
Amy Tauber

FOREWORD

Heart failure is a clinical syndrome or condition characterized by (1) signs and symptoms of intravascular and interstitial volume overload, including shortness of breath, rales, and edema, or (2) manifestations of inadequate tissue perfusion, such as fatigue or poor exercise tolerance. These signs and symptoms result when the heart is unable to generate a cardiac output sufficient to meet the body's demands. This guideline uses the term "heart failure" in preference to the commonly used "congestive heart failure" because many patients with heart failure do not manifest pulmonary or systemic congestion.

Heart failure is a major public health problem. The National Heart, Lung, and Blood Institute has estimated that more than 2 million Americans have heart failure and that about 400,000 new cases of heart failure are diagnosed each year. Total treatment costs for heart failure—including physician visits, drugs, and nursing home stays—were more than $10 billion in 1990.

The Agency for Health Care Policy and Research (AHCPR) sponsored development of this *Clinical Practice Guideline.* It provides recommendations for the evaluation and care of patients with heart failure due to reduced left-ventricular systolic function, which is the most common type of heart failure. It touches only briefly on the management of patients with heart failure occurring despite normal ventricular systolic performance, and it does not address the management of patients with surgically correctable valvular disease. Except as noted, the recommendations in this guideline apply to both inpatient and outpatient settings. Specialized techniques used only in the hospital setting—such as right-heart catheterization and cardiac assist devices—are not discussed.

The recommendations in this guideline are based on evidence obtained through extensive literature reviews. Where such evidence was lacking, consensus opinion of a panel of selected experts and consumers was used to formulate recommendations. Details of the literature reviews and related analyses are reported in a companion *Guideline Technical Report,* available from the National Technical Information Service. The panel obtained the advice and guidance of about 50 experts and clinicians concerning both the content of the guideline recommendations and the usefulness of the guideline in clinical practice.

This is the first edition of the *Clinical Practice Guideline* on heart failure. It will be updated to reflect advances in science and technology. Comments on the guideline are welcomed by AHCPR. Please address comments to the Director, Office of the Forum for Quality and Effectiveness in Health Care, AHCPR, Willco Building, 6000 Executive Boulevard, Suite 310, Rockville, MD 20852.

Heart Failure Guideline Panel

EXECUTIVE SUMMARY

Heart failure is a serious condition affecting an estimated 2 million Americans and resulting in average mortality rates of 10 percent at 1 year and 50 percent after 5 years. In addition, quality of life is reduced for many heart failure patients, who often experience physical symptoms and reduced functional status. Because the incidence of heart failure rises substantially beyond age 65, the prevalence of this condition is likely to increase as the population ages.

Heart failure also places a significant economic burden on society, consuming more than $10 billion in health care expenditures each year. More than $7 billion was spent on the 1 million hospitalizations that took place for this condition in 1990. The Heart Failure Guideline Panel believes that many of these hospitalizations could have been prevented by improved outpatient care. In addition, many of the tests and treatments currently provided to heart failure patients are of dubious value. In other cases, appropriate services are underutilized.

This guideline describes the range of diagnostic and management strategies that the guideline panel considers appropriate for heart failure patients with left-ventricular systolic dysfunction. This guideline addresses only briefly management of patients whose heart failure has occurred despite normal ventricular systolic performance and does not address management of patients with surgically correctable valvular disease. This guideline contains recommendations that are applicable for use in inpatient and outpatient settings but does not consider interventions that can be applied only in the hospital setting (e.g.; cardiac assist devices). The recommendations described in the guideline are based where possible on evidence obtained from extensive literature reviews. Where evidence was lacking, recommendations were based on the consensus opinion of the panel, as formulated after receiving input and suggestions from dozens of consultants around the country.

This guideline is intended for use by a broad range of health care practitioners, including family physicians, internists, cardiologists, cardiac surgeons, clinical nurse specialists, nurse practitioners, and physician assistants. The guideline panel recommends that consultation be obtained whenever practitioners find that

> This guideline represents an ambitious attempt to outline in a clear, concise fashion the diagnosis and management of heart failure due to left-ventricular systolic dysfunction. The Executive Summary describes in brief the recommendations contained within the main body of the document.

management is difficult or complicated, or when invasive management is contemplated.

This Executive Summary describes the most significant recommendations contained in the guideline. To place these recommendations within a logical framework, this summary is organized around a clinical algorithm (Attachment). The algorithm is designed both to depict the scope of the guideline and to provide assistance with decisionmaking strategies for patients and practitioners on a case-by-case basis. The guideline's key recommendations are organized as annotations to this algorithm, which combines four additional, more focused algorithms presented as figures in the guideline text.

The recommendations are presented here in very abbreviated form. Readers should refer to the guideline text for supporting discussion, including citations and levels of evidence for each recommendation.

The first topic addressed below is the prevention of clinical heart failure in patients with asymptomatic left-ventricular systolic dysfunction. Because these patients do not yet manifest heart failure, a prevention node is not included in the management algorithm.

Prevention in Asymptomatic Patients

Asymptomatic patients who are found to have moderately or severely reduced left-ventricular systolic function (ejection fraction [EF] <35–40 percent) should be treated with an angiotensin-converting enzyme (ACE) inhibitor to reduce the chance of developing clinical heart failure.

Probably the largest number of such patients will be those who have recently sustained a myocardial infarction (MI). For this reason, EF should be determined in most patients following an MI unless they are at low risk for significant systolic dysfunction—that is, unless they meet all of the following criteria:

- No previous MI.
- Inferior infarction.
- Relatively small increase in cardiac enzymes (i.e., <2–4 times normal).
- No Q-waves develop on electrocardiogram (ECG).
- Uncomplicated clinical course (e.g., no arrhythmias or hypotension).

Other asymptomatic patients without MIs may be found to have reduced EF on evaluation of heart murmurs or cardiomegaly. These patients should also be treated with ACE inhibitors.

Patient Evaluation
Symptoms of Heart Failure

All patients who complain of paroxysmal nocturnal dyspnea, orthopnea, or new-onset dyspnea on exertion should undergo evaluation for heart failure

Physicians, in general, have not been exceptional at following recommendations in previously published guidelines. Ellerback showed that standard acute myocardial infarction (MI) therapies are under utilized in many Medicare patients who are ideal candidates.[1] What are we to make of this finding? There are several interpretations if we assume the validity of the data. First, practicing physicians are not as current with the evolving medical literature as hoped. All states have Continuing Medical Education requirements for relicensing, and we currently have access to many medical journals both online and on paper. Second, academic physicians have neglected to disseminate advances vigorously. It is difficult for the practitioner to place each new advance into the proper context. A good example would be the current debate about the use of beta blockers in patients with left-ventricular dysfunction. Finally, physicians know of the advances but are unwilling to change practice patterns for a number of reasons. Practice guidelines such as this are a direct response to the above problems. They are an attempt to compile the known information into a form that can be readily digested and used.

The results of this work should not be confused with "cookbook medicine." It should be recognized that we are not treating heart failure or even left-ventricular dysfunction. We are, instead, treating people. Dr. Tumulty expressed this well in his book *The Effective Clinician*.[2]

> *A pair of kidneys will never come to the physician for diagnosis and treatment. They will be contained within an anxious, fearful, wondering person, asking puzzled questions about an obscure future, weighed down by responsibilities of a loved family, and with a job to be held, and with bills to be paid.*

Patients are not widgets and cannot be treated as such. Guidelines, therefore, are not meant to replace the astute clinician. They are available to help us become better physicians in the same fashion that textbooks and journal articles improve our ability to manage patients.

Guidelines are not designed to be the final word on every patient. There are good reasons why all of the guidelines contained within this text are not appropriate for every patient. Judgment by the individual physician in direct contact with the patient remains the paramount skill of good medical care. In comparison to the judgment of a skilled, master clinician, guidelines will always fall short.

unless history and physical examination clearly indicate a noncardiac cause for their symptoms, such as severe pulmonary disease.

Initial Evaluation

The physical examination can provide important information about the etiology of patients' symptoms and about appropriate initial treatment. However, physical signs are not highly sensitive for detecting heart failure.

Patients with symptoms that are highly suggestive of heart failure should undergo echocardiography or radionuclide ventriculography to measure left-ventricular EF (see below) even if physical signs of heart failure are absent.

Evaluation for Alternative Diagnoses

Practitioners should perform a chest x-ray; ECG; complete blood count (CBC); serum electrolytes, serum creatinine, serum albumin, liver function tests; and urinalysis for all patients with suspected or clinically evident heart failure. A T4 and thyroid-stimulating hormone (TSH) level should also be checked in all patients over the age of 65 with heart failure and no obvious etiology, and in patients who have atrial fibrillation or other signs or symptoms of thyroid disease.

Need for Hospital Management

Presence or suspicion of heart failure and any of the following findings usually indicates a need for hospitalization:

- Clinical or ECG evidence of acute myocardial ischemia.
- Pulmonary edema or severe respiratory distress.
- Oxygen saturation below 90 percent (not due to pulmonary disease).
- Severe complicating medical illness (e.g., pneumonia).
- Anasarca.
- Symptomatic hypotension or syncope.
- Heart failure refractory to outpatient therapy.
- Inadequate social support for safe outpatient management.

Patients with heart failure should be discharged from the hospital only when:

- Symptoms of heart failure have been adequately controlled.
- All reversible causes of morbidity have been treated or stabilized.
- Patients and caregivers have been educated about medications, diet, activity and exercise recommendations, and symptoms of worsening heart failure.

■ Adequate outpatient support and followup care have been arranged.

Patients who have been hospitalized for heart failure should be seen or contacted within 1 week of discharge to make sure that they are stable in the outpatient setting and to check their understanding of and compliance with the treatment plan.

Assessment of Volume Overload and Initial Therapy

During initial evaluation, the clinician should determine whether the patient manifests symptoms or signs of volume overload.

Symptoms of volume overload include orthopnea, paroxysmal nocturnal dyspnea, and dyspnea on exertion. Signs of volume overload include pulmonary rales, a third heart sound, jugular venous distension, hepatic engorgement, ascites, peripheral edema, and pulmonary vascular congestion or pulmonary edema on chest x-ray.

Patients with heart failure and signs of significant volume overload should be started immediately on a diuretic. Patients with mild volume overload can be managed adequately on thiazide diuretics, whereas those with more severe volume overload should be started on a loop diuretic.

Assessment of Left-Ventricular Function

Patients with suspected heart failure should undergo echocardiography or radionuclide ventriculography to measure EF (if information about left-ventricular function is not available from previous tests).

Most patients with heart failure will have EF less than 35–40 percent. Patients with EF of 40 percent or greater may still have heart failure on the basis of valvular disease or diastolic dysfunction.

Patient Management

Patient and Family Counseling and Education

After a diagnosis of heart failure is established, all patients should be counseled regarding the nature of heart failure, drug regimens, dietary restrictions, symptoms of worsening heart failure, what to do if these symptoms occur, and prognosis.

It is vital that patients understand their disease and be involved in developing the plan for their care. In addition, family members and other responsible caregivers should be included in counseling and decisionmaking sessions.

Regular exercise such as walking or cycling should be encouraged for all patients with stable heart failure.

There is insufficient evidence at this time to recommend the routine use of formal rehabilitation programs for patients with heart failure, although patients who are anxious about exercising on their own or are dyspneic at a low work level may benefit from such programs.

Dietary sodium should be restricted to as close to 2 grams per day as possible. In no case should sodium intake exceed 3 grams daily. Alcohol use should be discouraged. Patients who drink alcohol should be advised to consume no more than one drink per day. One drink equals a glass of beer or wine, or a mixed drink or cocktail containing no more than 1 ounce of alcohol.

It is vital that patients receive accurate information concerning prognosis in order to make decisions and plans for the future. Practitioners should discuss patients' desires regarding resuscitation, and all patients should be encouraged to complete a durable power of attorney for health care or another form of advance directive.

Because noncompliance is a major cause of morbidity and unnecessary hospital admissions in heart failure, educational programs or support groups should be a routine part of the care of patients with heart failure.

Practitioners should be aware of the problem of noncompliance and its causes and should discuss the importance of compliance at followup visits and assist patients in removing barriers to compliance (e.g., cost, side effects, or complexity of the medical regimen).

Initial Pharmacological Management

As noted above under Assessment of Volume Overload and Initial Therapy, diuretics should be started immediately when patients present with symptoms or signs of volume overload.

Patients with heart failure due to left-ventricular systolic dysfunction should be given a trial of ACE inhibitors unless specific contraindications exist: (1) history of intolerance or adverse reactions to these agents, (2) serum potassium greater than 5.5 mEq/L that cannot be reduced, or (3) symptomatic hypotension. Patients with systolic blood pressure less than 90 mmHg have a higher risk of complications and should be managed by a physician experienced in utilizing ACE inhibitors in such patients. Caution and close monitoring are also required for patients who have a serum creatinine greater than 3.0 mg/dL or an estimated creatinine clearance of less than 30 mL/min; half the usual dose should be used in this setting.

ACE inhibitors may be considered as sole therapy in the subset of heart failure patients who present with fatigue or mild dyspnea on exertion and who do not have any other signs or symptoms of volume overload. Diuretics should be added if symptoms persist.

Isosorbide dinitrate and hydralazine is an appropriate alternative in patients with contraindications or intolerance to ACE inhibitors.

Digoxin can prevent clinical deterioration in patients with heart failure due to left-ventricular systolic dysfunction, although its effect on exercise toler-ance and mortality is not clear. Digoxin should be used routinely in patients with severe heart failure and should be added to the medical regimen of pa-tients with mild or moderate heart failure who remain symptomatic after op-timal management with ACE inhibitors and diuretics.

Patients with mild-to-moderate heart failure who become asymptomatic on op-timal doses of ACE inhibitors and diuretics do not require digoxin.

Routine anticoagulation is not recommended. Patients with a history of sys-temic or pulmonary embolism, recent atrial fibrillation, or mobile left-ven-tricular thrombi should be anticoagulated to a prothrombin time ratio of 1.2–1.8 times each individual laboratory control time (International Normalization Ratio 2.0–3.0).

Evaluation of Patients for Revascularization

Coronary artery disease is currently the most common cause of heart failure in the United States, and some heart failure patients may benefit from revasculariza-tion.

Contraindications to Revascularization

There are no absolute contraindications to revascularization except if the pa-tient refuses surgery or is unable to give informed consent. However, a number of factors may preclude intervention or raise the risk above any expected benefit:

- Patient is unwilling to consider surgery.
- Severe comorbid diseases, especially renal failure, pulmonary disease, or cere-brovascular disease (e.g., severe stroke).
- Very low EF (i.e., <20 percent).
- Illnesses that imply a limited life expectancy less than or equal to 1 year, in-cluding advanced cancer, severe lung or liver disease, chronic renal disease, ad-vanced diabetes mellitus, and advanced collagen vascular disease.
- Technical factors, including previous myocardial revascularization or other car-diac procedure, inadequate vascular conduit, history of chest irradiation, and diffuse distal coronary artery atherosclerosis.

Patient Counseling and Decision

Patients without contraindication to revascularization should be advised of the possibility of revascularization, including its potential benefits and harms.

Three parameters are important: (1) likelihood of surgically correctable lesions, (2) expected benefits of revascularization, and (3) expected risks and potential harms of revascularization. Counseling should be based on patients' individual characteristics, particularly on an assessment of patients' risk factors for coronary artery disease. Patients can be classified into three major subgroups: (1) patients who have neither angina pectoris nor a history of MI, (2) patients who have no significant angina but have a history of MI, and (3) patients who have significant angina.

Patients Without Angina or History of MI

It is unclear whether patients without a history of MI or significant angina should be routinely evaluated for ischemia. Patients should be counseled concerning the expected benefits and risks of evaluation for ischemia, including the fact that there is no evidence from controlled trials to show that revascularization benefits heart failure patients in the absence of angina.

The likelihood of coronary disease in heart failure patients without angina or history of MI varies with patient risk factors (e.g., age, sex, smoking history, hyperlipidemia, hypertension, family history of premature coronary artery disease, and diabetes).

Patients Without Angina but With History of MI

Patients without significant angina but with a history of MI should be advised to undergo a physiologic test for ischemia, followed by coronary artery angiography if ischemic regions are detected.

Available evidence suggests that about 40–45 percent of patients who suffer an MI have clinically important myocardial ischemia in areas supplied by other coronary arteries. There are no data, however, to show that revascularization of these areas is beneficial (in terms of increased life expectancy or enhanced quality of life) if angina or anginal equivalent is not present. Nevertheless, patients with large areas of ischemia may possibly benefit from revascularization.

Physiologic Testing

Although there are a number of acceptable physiologic tests for ischemia, the most widely available and accepted procedure for determining the presence of ischemic myocardium is myocardial perfusion scintigraphy, such as thallium scanning, with post-stress, redistribution, and rest reinjection imaging.

Patients With Significant Concomitant Angina

Heart failure patients without contraindications to revascularization who have exercise-limiting angina, angina that occurs frequently at rest, or recurrent episodes of acute pulmonary edema should be advised to undergo coronary artery angiography as the initial test for operable coronary lesions.

The potential benefit of revascularization is clearest and probably highest in individuals with severe or limiting angina or angina equivalent (e.g., recurrent acute episodes of pulmonary edema despite appropriate medical management).

Some patients may need physiologic testing for ischemia to interpret the significance of the findings from coronary artery angiography.

Patient Counseling and Decision

Based on the results of physiologic testing and/or coronary artery angiography, the physician should give the patient a refined estimate of the risks and benefits of revascularization. The patient can then decide whether he or she desires revascularization.

Continued Medical Management

The medical therapy started at Initial Pharmacological Management should be continued if (1) a patient is not a candidate for revascularization, (2) studies show insufficient evidence of reversible ischemia, or (3) surgery has been performed but the patient has residual left-ventricular dysfunction.

Revascularization

Coronary artery bypass grafting (CABG) is the only revascularization procedure that has been shown to prolong life in patients with heart failure and angina. The effect of percutaneous transluminal coronary angioplasty (PTCA) on survival has not been studied. The choice between CABG and PTCA will depend on numerous considerations, including multiple technical factors (e.g., coronary anatomy), relative risk of the two procedures in individual patients, and patient preferences.

Approaches to Patient Monitoring and Followup Evaluation

Careful history and physical examination should be the main guide to determining outcomes and directing therapy. A thorough history should include questions regarding physical functioning, mental health, sleep disturbance, sexual function, cognitive function, and ability to perform usual work and social activities.

The panel recommends against the routine use of invasive or noninvasive tests, such as echocardiography or maximal exercise testing for monitoring patients with heart failure.

Patients should be encouraged to keep records of their daily weights and to bring those records with them when visiting their practitioners. Patients should be instructed to call their practitioners if they have experienced an unexplained weight gain greater than 3–5 pounds since their last clinical evaluation.

Additional Pharmacological Management

If patients remain symptomatic on a combination of a diuretic, an ACE inhibitor, and digoxin, a consultation should be obtained with a practitioner who has expertise in the management of heart failure, if this has not been done previously.

Patients with persistent volume overload despite initial medical management may require more aggressive administration of the current diuretic (e.g., intravenous administration), more potent diuretics, or a combination of diuretics.

Patients with persistent dyspnea after optimal doses of diuretics, ACE inhibitors, and digoxin should be given a trial of hydralazine and/or nitrates.

Beta-adrenergic blockers may improve functional status and natural history in patients with heart failure, but this form of treatment should be considered investigational at this time.

Consideration of Heart Transplantation

Consideration should be given to cardiac transplantation in patients with severe limitation or repeated hospitalizations because of heart failure despite aggressive medical therapy in whom revascularization is not likely to convey benefit.

Patients with severe symptoms should be referred to a cardiologist to ensure that medical therapy is optimized before referral for possible transplantation. Practitioners should refer to existing documents concerning heart transplantation for further information concerning patient selection criteria.

1

Overview

Commentary by Edward K. Kasper, M.D.

Introduction

On December 19, 1989, the Omnibus Budget Reconciliation Act (Public Law 101-239) added a new Title IX to the Public Health Service Act establishing the Agency for Health Care Policy and Research (AHCPR). AHCPR's goal is to enhance the quality, appropriateness, and effectiveness of health care services and access to such services. Section 911 of the Act establishes within AHCPR the Office of the Forum for Quality and Effectiveness in Health Care. Section 912 directs the Forum to facilitate the development and periodic review and updating of:

Clinically relevant guidelines that may be used by physicians, educators, and health care practitioners to assist in determining how diseases, disorders, and health care conditions can most effectively and appropriately be prevented, diagnosed, treated, and managed clinically.

Following this mandate, AHCPR selected heart failure as a topic for guideline development and as one of the first three guidelines to be developed under contract. Unlike the first seven guidelines, which were developed by private-sector panels convened directly by AHCPR, these contract guidelines were created by panels of experts and consumers selected (with the concurrence of AHCPR) and staffed by a private contracting organization. In the case of the heart failure guideline, the contracting agency was RAND, a nonprofit public policy and research organization in Santa Monica, California.

Heart failure is a clinical syndrome or condition characterized by (1) signs and symptoms of intravascular and interstitial volume overload, including shortness of

Heart failure is a particularly important topic for guideline development. This chapter provides an overview of the topic. Patients with heart failure are often elderly and have multiple comorbidities. With the graying of the American population, we can expect the incidence and prevalence of heart failure to increase as well.

breath, rales, and edema, or (2) manifestations of inadequate tissue perfusion, such as fatigue or poor exercise tolerance. These signs and symptoms result when the heart is unable to generate a cardiac output sufficient to meet the body's demands. This guideline uses the term "heart failure" in preference to the commonly used "congestive heart failure" because many patients with heart failure do not manifest pulmonary or systemic congestion.

The definition of heart failure is problematic. Emphasis must be placed on the term "syndrome": the constellation of signs and symptoms associated with a morbid process. In this guideline, the underlying process is left-ventricular systolic dysfunction. While this is far and away the most common cause of heart failure syndrome in the developed world, it is not the only cause and may not be the most common cause in the Third World. Correction of the underlying cause is the most direct and proximate means of treating patients with heart failure. The term "heart failure" is itself a problem in that some causes of this syndrome may have nothing to do with a failing heart. A good example would be volume overload from a large arteriovenous fistula. The proximate cause of the syndrome is the fistula. The heart is but an innocent bystander.

More than 2 million Americans suffer from the effects of heart failure, and about 400,000 new cases are diagnosed each year. Mortality is high, with 5-year mortality rates in the range of 50 percent. In addition, quality of life is often adversely affected by symptoms and reduced functional capacity.

The evaluation and care of patients with heart failure exacts a high economic price from society, with more than $10 billion in resources going to treatment of patients with heart failure each year. Table 1 provides estimates of total national expenditures of all patients with this condition based on the most recent evidence available.[3-7]

According to information supplied by the Health Care Financing Administration, Medicare paid $2.4 billion in 1992 for 654,000 hospital admissions for patients with a principal diagnosis of heart failure. Actual hospital charges for Medicare patients were more than double this amount, totaling $5.6 billion (mean charge: $8,500). Thus, heart failure represents an important component of uncompensated hospital care. The in-hospital mortality rate for Medicare patients in 1992 was about 7 percent, which contrasts with 30-day mortality rates of about 15 percent for heart failure patients observed in three large studies of Medicare admissions from the 1980s.[8-10] Part of this discrepancy may be accounted for by the difference between in-hospital and 30-day mortality rates, but it is also possible that in-hospital mortality rates have improved over the past few years.

Because of the high prevalence of heart failure and the resulting high cost of caring for these patients, improvements in the quality of care—and in the practice of cost-effective care—could have a tremendous impact on costs and outcomes. Proper management of heart failure can reduce both morbidity and mortality from this condition, as summarized in Table 2. The greatest difference in mortality (about a 16 percent to 18 percent adjusted mortality reduction) has been observed with coronary artery bypass graft (CABG) surgery in patients with angina and impaired left-ventricular function and with use of the angiotensin-converting enzyme (ACE) inhibitor enalapril in patients with severe heart failure.[11,12] The mortality reductions observed with other interventions have been smaller. However, when

Table 1. Estimated Total Direct Economic Cost of Heart Failure in the United States

Type of Service	Number[a] (thousands)	Costs[b] (millions)
Hospital days	5,800[c]	$7,500
Physician office visits	3,000[d]	690
Nursing home days (1985)	17,000[e]	1,900
Drugs	Not applicable	230
Total direct costs	Not applicable	10,320

[a]Estimated from total national numbers in each category multiplied by the proportion devoted to heart failure (based on International Classification of Diseases, 9th Revision [ICD-9] codes).[3]
[b]Estimated from totoal national expenses in each category[4] multiplied by the proportion of expenditures devoted to heart failure (based on ICD-9) codes).[3]
[c]National Hospital Discharge Survey, National Center for Health Statistics (NCHS) 1990.[5]
[d]National Ambulatory Medical Care Survey, NCHS, 1989.[6]
[e]National Nursing Home Survey, NCHS, 1985.[7]

Table 2.   Effects of Treatment on Mortality in Patients With Left-Ventricular

Study Author, Year	Study Population	N	Duration of Followup (years)
Surgical Management of Heart Failure or Left-Ventricular Dysfunction			
Bounous et al., 1988[11]	First cardiac catheterization; EF ≤40%	710	3.0
Medical Management of Left-Ventricular Dysfunction			
Pfeffer et al. (SAVE), 1992[18]	3–16 days after MI; EF ≤40%; no current heart failure	2,231	3.5[d]
SOLVD Investigators (SOLVD Prevention Trial), 1992[19]	EF ≤35%; no heart failure	4,228	3.1[d]
Medical Management of Heart Failure			
Cohn et al. (VHeFT I), 1986[20]	Chronic heart failure, cardiac enlargement or EF < 45%, and MVO$_2$ <25 mL/Kg/min	642	3.0
CONSENSUS Trial Study Group, 1987[12]	New York Heart Association Class IV heart failure	253	1.0
SOLVD Investigators (SOLVD Treatment Trial), 1991[21]	Chronic heart failure; EF ≤35%	2,569	3.5[d]
Cohn et al. (VHeFT II), 1991[22]	Same as VHeFT I	804	2.5[d]

[a]All mortality differences are significant at p <0.05 except where indicated (NS).
[b]Symptomatic hypotension requiring termination of the study drug.
[c]Adjusted for baseline prognostic factors.
[d]Mean duration of followup.

Dysfunction or Clinical Heart Failure

Treatment	Mortality Rate (percent)	Absolute Mortality Difference[a] (percent)	Symptomatic Hypotension[b] (percent)
CABG	14[c]	18	--
Medical	32[c]	(Operative mortality NR)	--
Captopril	20.4		
Placebo	24.6	4.2	0.7
Enalapril	14.8		
Placebo	15.8	NS	NR
HYD/ISDN	36.2		
Placebo	46.9	10.7	NR
Enalapril	36.2		
Placebo	52.4	16.2	5.5
Enalapril	35.2		
Placebo	39.7	4.5	2
Enalapril	32.8		
HYD/ISDN	38.2	5.4	4.5

Notes: NR = not reported, NS = not significant, HYD/ISDN = hydralazine and isosorbide dinitrate, CABG = coronary artery bypass graft, EF = ejection fraction, MI = myocardial infarction, MVO_2 = maximum oxygen uptake, SAVE = Survival and Ventricular Enlargement, SOLVD = Studies of Left-Ventricular Dysfunction, VHeFT = Veterans Affairs Vasodilator Heart Failure Trial.

one considers the millions of people with heart failure or left-ventricular dysfunction, even the smaller reductions in mortality depicted in Table 2 (see page 4) may translate into hundreds of thousands of lives extended.

> The reasoning behind the choice of heart failure as one of the first guidelines to be developed is clear. This is a common syndrome with high associated morbidity and mortality. The cost of caring for these patients is high. Small changes in practice patterns may result in major improvements in clinical outcomes for these patients at minimal expense to society.

Conversely, poor quality care has been shown to have a negative impact on outcomes. Patients hospitalized with heart failure who received poor quality care, as defined by explicit, validated process criteria, experienced increased death rates in the 30 days following hospital discharge.[13] Despite improvements in the quality of care in recent years, this group of investigators found that 12 percent of patients hospitalized with heart failure received poor or very poor quality care. In addition, 7 percent of patients were thought to have been discharged too soon, and those discharged in unstable condition were found to have a 16 percent mortality rate at 90 days after discharge compared with 10 percent in those who were discharged in stable condition.[14]

Deficiencies have also been found in the quality of outpatient care. Retchin and Brown[15] found that less than half the patients they studied were advised to follow a salt-restricted diet. Many patients were found to have uncontrolled hypertension, but medications were initiated or modified in only 62 percent of fee-for-service (FFS) patients and 36 percent of patients in the health maintenance organization (HMO) groups. Twenty-seven percent of patients in the FFS group had a followup visit within 1 week of discharge from the hospital; 42 percent of HMO patients were seen within this period. Improved management of outpatients could reduce morbidity and mortality and decrease hospitalizations.

> Physicians in general have been better at managing the acute syndrome of pulmonary edema than the chronic syndrome of heart failure. It has been difficult to develop the necessary infrastructure to systematically monitor outpatients with severe heart failure symptoms. The resultant lack of frequent monitoring allows early heart failure decompensation to be missed. Patient compliance is also influenced by the lack of consistent enforcement and encouragement. With hospital stays becoming shorter, this leaves less inpatient time to devote to teaching heart failure patients and adjusting medications. A vicious cycle of admission and readmission ensues.

Practice Variations

Fleg et al.[16] found differences in self-reported practice styles in the utilization of laboratory procedures to monitor outpatients with heart failure. In comparison with internists or family physicians, cardiologists were more likely to follow outpatients with heart failure by using echocardiography, radionuclide ventriculography, or exercise testing. The estimated yearly cost of following a patient with New York Heart Association (NYHA) Class II heart failure was $303 for the quartile of physicians with the lowest utilization of procedures compared with $1,167 for the highest quartile. If the average costs of such tests could be reduced by $250 per year, more than $500 million could be saved annually on a national basis.

> It should not be surprising that practice patterns for the management of heart failure should vary. Patients with heart failure are often complicated and have multisystem disease. It is difficult enough to get physicians to agree on the diagnosis and management of relatively simple problems. It will be important to analyze the impact of this guideline, as well as other recently published guidelines,[17] on the diagnosis and management of patients with heart failure.

Common Errors in Management

As a way to organize the panel's thinking and to help ensure that the guideline has a positive impact on quality of care, the panel identified several aspects of the care of heart failure patients that are often not managed appropriately. This list was circulated to about 20 project consultants, who concurred on almost all points and added others. The complete list follows.

Errors in Diagnosis

> This is a particularly good way of emphasizing patient management objectives for patients with heart failure syndrome. Much of this will be detailed in later chapters.

- Patients with symptoms suggestive of heart failure are often not thoroughly evaluated to rule out noncardiac causes before treatment for heart failure is instituted.
- Symptoms of heart failure may be attributed to chronic obstructive pulmonary disease (COPD) and treated inappropriately.

> It is the rule rather than the exception that young patients with the onset of heart failure symptoms are diagnosed as having bronchitis and are often treated with multiple antibiotics before the correct diagnosis is made.

- Reversible causes of heart failure are not always identified, or if identified, they may be undertreated.

> A search for reversible causes of heart failure should always be undertaken. A reversible cause, however, is infrequently identified. Most patients with left-ventricular dysfunction will not have a correctable cause found even after a complete evaluation.[23]

- Patients with peripheral edema may be inappropriately labeled as having heart failure when there is another cause for the edema.
- An initial measurement of left-ventricular function is not always obtained.

> This error in diagnosis should never be made.

- Concurrent angina or other evidence of ischemia is not always properly evaluated.

Errors in Evaluation and Testing

- Chest x-ray, electrocardiography, echocardiography, and radionuclide studies are commonly used for monitoring patients' progress, rather than symptom- or activity-based measures.
- Holter monitoring is overutilized, leading to unjustified treatment of asymptomatic ventricular arrhythmias.

Errors in Management

- Coexistent hypertension is often not treated aggressively enough.
- Patient, family, and caregiver education is often inadequate.
- Patients with heart failure that is not due to systolic dysfunction may be treated inappropriately.

- Practitioners may not instruct patients to monitor their weight closely.
- Patient noncompliance and its causes are often not recognized and dealt with appropriately.
- The possibility of revascularization is often not considered in patients who have severe coronary artery disease with left-ventricular systolic dysfunction.
- Patients with severe heart failure are often referred too late for heart transplantation, after severe decompensation and the development of secondary multisystem organ failure.
- Exercise prescriptions are underutilized.
- ACE inhibitors are often not initiated or are prescribed at suboptimal doses because of clinicians' concerns about possible side effects.
- Physicians frequently prescribe inadequate doses of diuretics in patients who continue to have overt volume overload despite modest doses of diuretics.
- Practitioners may fail to appreciate the potentially deleterious effects of certain pharmacological agents in heart failure (e.g., calcium blockers, nonsteroidal anti-inflammatory agents, beta-agonist inhalers).

Each of these areas is addressed by this *Clinical Practice Guideline.*

Scope of Guideline

This guideline focuses on the practical aspects of management of patients with heart failure due to reduced left-ventricular systolic performance (ejection fraction [EF] <35–40 percent). This area of heart failure management offers a great opportunity for improved clinical practice and, accordingly, for improved survival and health-related quality of life. The guideline panel elected not to address in detail the management of heart failure associated with diastolic dysfunction (i.e., heart failure associated with normal or elevated EF). This category of patients is quite heterogeneous, and there are very few data concerning the appropriate approach to these patients. Similarly, the guideline does not address medical management strategies specific to the in-hospital setting (e.g., pulmonary artery catheters or intra-aortic balloon pumps) or heart failure caused by surgically correctable valvular disease, aneurysm, or identifiable myocardial disease (e.g., amyloidosis, sarcoidosis). These topics may be suitable for future guidelines.Figure 1 depicts the overall organization and topics covered by this guideline.

> The scope of the guideline was ambitious even though several important areas were not addressed. Diastolic dysfunction, inpatient management, surgically correctable lesions other than ischemia, and specific cardiomyopathies were not addressed. The authors chose to address the most common reason for heart failure syndrome, and they chose to address this syndrome in the outpatient setting. It is in the outpatient setting where the greatest cost saving is likely to occur largely through the prevention of hospital admission.

Methodology for Guideline Development

> The process for guideline development was extensive. The members chosen to serve on the expert panel are recognized as such in their respective fields. The appropriate literature was thoroughly reviewed. Before publication, the guideline was critiqued by multiple outside groups. This represents a mammoth undertaking and a real service to patients with heart failure and those who care for them.

The. guideline development process used during this project followed the evidence-based approach recommended by AHCPR. A 16-member expert panel was constituted to interpret and supplement the evidence available in published literature. Panelists were selected after a broad range of input was obtained from professional and health careconsumer organizations and individuals. At least one professional or consumer organization nominated or endorsed each panel member. The panel consisted of five cardiologists, two cardiac surgeons, one internist-geriatrician, one general internist, one family physician, one pulmonologist, one clinical pharmacist, two nurses with expertise in cardiac care and research, and two consumer representatives. To help define and circumscribe the scope of the guideline and associated literature reviews, the panel co-chairs and project staff first developed a draft clinical algorithm. The algorithm is designed both to depict the scope of the guideline and to provide assistance with decisionmaking strategies for patients with heart failure and practitioners on a case-by-case basis. This draft algorithm was then considered by the full guideline panel at its first meeting, in February 1992.

To refine the guideline topic, the panel decided to focus the scope of the guideline on the evaluation and care of patients with left-ventricular systolic dysfunction and to exclude consideration of interventions specific to the inpatient setting (e.g., right-heart catheterization, mechanical assist devices).

To further focus the scope of the guideline and to ensure maximal impact of the guideline in actual clinical practice, the panel next developed a list of commonly seen errors in the outpatient management of heart failure, as already described. Project staff were charged with ensuring that the guideline addressed these areas of management. Because of the potentially very large number of topics available for review within the selected domain, and because time and budgetary restrictions prohibited an all-inclusive literature review, the panel rated topics to determine their priority for literature review.

Project staff then conducted comprehensive literature reviews in the selected areas, including (1) the use of echocardiography and radionuclide ventriculography for measuring left-ventricular function, (2) the use of revascularization, (3) the use of ACE inhibitors and other pharmacological agents, (4) patient education

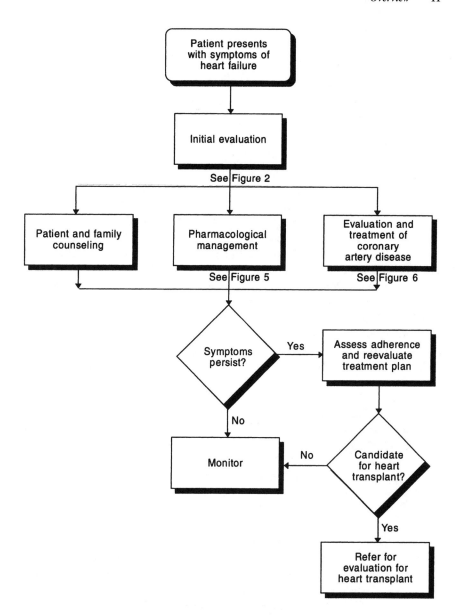

Figure 1.   Overview of Evaluation and Care of Patients With Heart Failure

and compliance issues, and (5) followup monitoring. More than 1,000 articles were examined during this review. Of these, 237 were specifically used to develop the recommendations in this guideline and are cited in this document. Another 70 articles are cited in the annotations to the guideline. A quality-assessment system (discussed below) was developed to rate methods used in these studies.

The literature reviews focused on the clinical benefits and harms (in terms of life expectancy and effects on quality of life) associated with each possible intervention and management strategy. Panelists weighed the expected benefits and harms of diagnostic and treatment strategies in order to derive their management recommendations. Costs of treatment were not explicitly taken into account when these recommendations were formulated, although the panel recognized the potential systemwide financial implications of those recommendations.

Results of the literature reviews were described in several reports prepared by project staff and distributed to panelists before the May 1992 panel meeting. Based on these reports, the panel formulated initial management recommendations for the diagnosis and treatment of heart failure patients.

On June 26, 1992, before its regular meeting, the panel convened a public open forum to give interested parties an opportunity to comment on any aspect of heart failure management of interest to them. Several organizations and individuals offered oral or written testimony that the panel considered during its subsequent deliberations. In subsequent meetings, the panel revised its management recommendations on the basis of continued evaluations of the literature, panel discussion, and input from project consultants.

During January and February 1993, a formal round of peer review was conducted in which the guideline document was circulated to about 40 professional organizations and individuals. Twenty-nine formal responses were obtained. The recommendations and suggestions contained in these responses were summarized for the panel, which considered them during its February 1993 meeting. The guideline was revised after this meeting.

Finally, a pilot review was conducted on the revised document in August 1993 to evaluate the usefulness, clarity, and feasibility of the *Clinical Practice Guideline, Quick Reference Guide for Clinicians,* and *Patient and Family Guide.* These documents were sent to 30 organizations and individuals representing primary care practitioners. Twenty responses were obtained. The strong consensus of reviewers who tried using the documents with patients was that the algorithm format provided a useful framework for applying the recommendations contained in the *Clinical Practice Guideline* and *Quick Reference Guide for Clinicians* to individual patients, particularly in complicated cases. Reviewers also believed that the structure of the documents was reasonably clear and user friendly. In addition to comments concerning the utility of the guideline in actual clinical settings, pilot reviewers also offered additional comments and recommendations. These were considered by the panel, and changes were made as appropriate.

Literature Quality-Rating System

In developing an evidence-based guideline, the quality of the studies used by the panel to guide its recommendations is important. Project staff defined seven levels of evidence for the panel's use. The levels depended on the study design, the quality of the studies (discussed below), sample sizes, and the consistency of results across centers and studies. The seven levels were:

   I.   Evidence from large, well-conducted randomized controlled trials (RCTs).
  II.   Evidence from small, well-conducted RCTs.
 III.   Evidence from well-conducted cohort studies.
 IV.   Evidence from well-conducted case-control studies.
  V.   Evidence from uncontrolled or poorly controlled studies.
 VI.   Conflicting evidence, but tending to favor the recommendation.
VII.   Expert opinion.

A quality-rating system was developed based on the large body of work done in the area of meta-analysis.[24–28] The following principles were incorporated:

- The main focus of the rating system should be on the detection of methodologic flaws that might introduce enough bias to threaten the validity of a study's results. (These were considered major flaws.)
- Those elements that are unlikely to have a major influence on validity and may represent poor reporting or editing (minor flaws) should be recorded separately rather than being incorporated into a global score of quality.
- The criteria used for grading studies should be as explicit as possible.
- If the data from a study were analyzed incorrectly by the author and enough information is given to analyze the data correctly, the corrected results should be used.

Studies were assessed on eight aspects of method: patient selection, allocation of patients to treatments, description of the therapeutic regimen, study administration, withdrawals, patient blinding, outcome measurement, and statistical analysis. Specific criteria were defined for major and minor flaws in each aspect of method.

The classification scheme for the guideline document was later simplified into a three-level system for strength of evidence:

A   Good evidence: Evidence from well-conducted RCTs or cohort studies (Levels I-III).
B   Fair evidence: Evidence from other types of studies (Levels IV-VI).

C   Expert opinion (Level VII).

I would not underestimate the value of expert opinion. While I firmly agree with the literature rating scale used in this guideline, expert opinion may have to suffice in many instances. Certain management strategies, such as loop diuretics, will probably never be studied in mortality-based randomized clinical trials, and yet we know they effectively relieve symptoms. If heart failure is a clinical syndrome with many causes, so is left-ventricular dysfunction. We currently do not have a complete understanding of the multiple causes of left-ventricular dysfunction. Randomized clinical trials may serve to mask some important differences in how certain patients respond to treatment. An example might be the treatment of megaloblastic anemia. If the various causes of megaloblastic anemia had not yet been defined, a randomized clinical trial of vitamin B_{12} in such patients might not yield positive results. Expert opinion, however, might recognize that certain patients with megaloblastic anemia responded to vitamin B_{12} administration.

Recommendations for Future Research

The heart failure guideline panel identified several areas related to diagnosis and treatment that were not addressed, or that were inadequately studied, in available literature. These topics constitute important areas for future research that could be addressed to the extent possible in updates of the guideline. Guideline updates are currently planned for this and other AHCPR-sponsored clinical practice guidelines.

Guidelines such as this will only remain useful if they are routinely updated. Otherwise, they will shortly become documents of historic interest outlining the favored management of a disorder at a defined point in time. Research continues and advances are rapidly made. The useful life of a guideline such as this is likely to be short.

Questions identified by the panel as in need of research were:

1. What are the current practice patterns for patients with heart failure?

    - How often are ACE inhibitors used?
    - How often are heart failure patients hospitalized over the course of a year?
    - How many office visits do heart failure patients make during a year?
    - How often are various medications employed?
    - How often are echocardiograms and other noninvasive tests performed?
    - How often are heart failure patients revascularized?
    - Are there geographic variations in management practices?

> Surprisingly little is known about current practice patterns for patients with heart failure. What data are available tend to come from tertiary centers.[29] If little is known about practice patterns, even less is known about cost. Part of this is the difficulty of getting at actual cost in a payment system where the money billed often has little to do with the actual cost and almost nothing to do with the amount reimbursed by third party payers.

2. What are the costs associated with current patterns of treatment for heart failure patients?

    - Costs of office visits and hospitalizations.
    - Costs of testing.
    - Costs of medications.
    - Costs of revascularization.
    - Geographic variation in costs.

3. What are the sensitivity, specificity, and predictive values of noninvasive testing for ischemia in patients with heart failure? (For example, how often are positive noninvasive tests predictive of significant coronary lesions appropriate for revascularization?) Existing published data are based on patients with angina as their primary symptom.

4. What are the outcomes (e.g., mortality, functional status, quality of life) of revascularization (CABG versus percutaneous transluminal coronary angioplasty [PTCA]) in patients with heart failure, with or without significant angina? Again, most published data on revascularization apply to patients with angina as the predominant symptom. In addition, surgical techniques have changed since the time of most available studies.

5. Can patients play a more active role in their own management? Several panelists are interested in developing and testing a patient-centered self-management protocol that would incorporate patient preferences. One aspect of this protocol would

probably address drug dose titration techniques according to patient-measured end-points (e.g., daily weights). Protocol evaluation would address the outcomes (e.g, hospitalization, patient-reported health and functional status), costs, and patient satisfaction associated with the experimental intervention versus control.

> Recently published data suggest that patients can be taught to self-monitor if this is combined with careful followup.[30]

6. What is the best way to initiate and titrate drug therapy? A study of the cost, patient acceptance, and outcomes associated with sequential versus combined administration of common pharmacological agents (e.g., diuretics, ACE inhibitors, digoxin) would be desirable.
7. What is the value of anticoagulation in heart failure patients?
8. What are patient preferences and expectations for several key areas of management?

> Patient preferences are almost never taken into account when guidelines are developed. Nease showed that angina patients differ substantially in their willingness to tolerate similar levels of functional impairment.[31] There is no reason to believe that patients with heart failure are any different.

- Medical versus surgical management approaches.
- Rehabilitation and exercise programs.
- Compliance with salt- and alcohol-restricted diets.
- Quality-of-life aspects of living with heart failure and its treatments.

9. How can the built-in biases of tertiary center data bases be overcome in analyzing practice patterns, outcomes, and associated costs? Panelists have suggested that a national heart failure patient registry should be established at several different practice environments. A standard set of variables would be coded, including descriptions of the presence/absence/degree of concomitant angina, management strategies pursued, costs, and outcomes.
10. What criteria should be used to follow patients and determine their response to treatment? Current evidence suggests that available clinical tests (e.g., echocardiogram) do not provide information pertaining to changes in patient prognosis or quality of life. Development and testing of functional health status and quality-of-life measures for use in the heart failure population could prove extremely valuable by providing endpoints for monitoring patient response to treatment.

11. Given the poor prognosis associated with heart failure and the lack of donor hearts, what is the role of new and innovative forms of treatment (e.g., mechanical assist devices)?

12. What is the impact of heart failure on patients' families? How do family members or other caregivers respond to the burden of caring for these patients?

13. What interventions improve compliance with low-sodium diets, exercise or activity recommendations, and medication regimens?

14. What nonpharmacological interventions (e.g, family and patient support groups, strategies to improve psychosocial status) improve patients' and families' ability to cope with heart failure?

15. What will be the impact of this and other guidelines on clinical practice and outcomes?

These are fifteen of the many questions that remain about the diagnosis and management of patients with heart failure. For such a common and devastating disorder, we have much to learn about "best therapy" for patients with the heart failure syndrome.

2

Prevention in Asymptomatic Patients

Commentary by Richard Rodeheffer, M.D.

Asymptomatic patients who are found to have moderately or severely reduced left-ventricular systolic function (EF <35–40 percent) should be treated with an ACE inhibitor to reduce the chance of developing clinical heart failure. (Strength of Evidence = A.)

The prevention of clinically evident heart failure represents one of the most important opportunities for decreasing mortality and morbidity from this often fatal condition. The most effective preventive interventions are probably the treatment of hypertension and the prevention of MI through the reduction in risk factors for coronary vascular disease. Thrombolytic therapy to minimize the size of an MI and prevention of second infarctions are also important. A description of these interventions lies outside the scope of this guideline.

The concept of "secondary prevention" in patients with established mild left-ventricular systolic dysfunction raises some fundamental questions which are not addressed in the Clinical Practice Guideline. The first basic question regards the prevalence of left-ventricular systolic dysfunction. The existing literature on heart failure has focused on patients whose symptoms have brought them to medical attention. These patients may be "the tip of the iceberg." Asymptomatic patients, by their very nature, will be difficult to detect.

(Continued)

(Continued from previous page)

The historical epidemiologic literature, comprising data gathered from 1960 to 1985, suggests that the prevalence of symptomatic congestive heart failure among adults is approximately 2–3%[32–35] Since the methods of case ascertainment in these studies were based on symptoms and signs of ventricular dysfunction, they necessarily failed to measure the prevalence of asymptomatic cases in whom preventive interventions might be applied. Recent preliminary data from a population-based study which employed objective measurement of ventricular function (echocardiography) suggest that as many as 62 percent of adults with systolic dysfunction, defined as EF ≤35 percent, are asymptomatic.[36] This study was conducted in a population with a known high coronary disease prevalence and further studies will be important to confirm and refine this observation in other populations. However, it is important in that it suggests that the asymptomatic base of the ventricular dysfunction iceberg may be larger than the symptomatic tip.

The Clinical Practice Guideline describes well what we know about the preventive value of ACE inhibition in asymptomatic patients with EF ≤35% (the SOLVD Prevention Study) and patients with recent MI and EF ≤40% (the SAVE Trial). Aside from the recommendation to assess ventricular function in high risk post-MI populations, the guideline is unable to provide adequate information on how to most effectively identify asymptomatic patients who might benefit from treatment. Although there is a need for an accurate and cost-effective method of detecting patients with asymptomatic ventricular dysfunction, we are left at this time with maintaining a high index of suspicion. Selected patients who have mild nonspecific symptoms and sign such as dyspnea, edema, supine cough, ectopic beats, partial or complete bundle branch block, or mild radiographic cardiomegaly may benefit from echocardiographic assessment. This is particularly true if they have other risk factors for ventricular dysfunction such as hypertension, smoking, hyperlipidemia, diabetes, or a family history of cardiomyopathy or coronary artery disease.

Even after patients have sustained an MI and developed moderate-to-severe left-ventricular systolic dysfunction, it is still possible to slow or prevent the progression to symptomatic heart failure. In the Survival and Ventricular Enlargement (SAVE) trial, patients with an MI in the preceding 3–16 days and EFs of 40 percent or less were treated with captopril titrated to 50 mg TID as tolerated.[18] Overall mortality during the 2- to 5-year study period (average followup: 42 months) was 20 percent in those treated with captopril, compared with 25 percent in those treated with placebo. The proportion of patients developing heart failure that required open-label treatment with ACE inhibitors was reduced from 16 to 11 percent, and the proportion of patients hospitalized for heart failure was reduced from 17 to 14 percent. The Cooperative New Scandinavian Enalapril Survival Study (CONSENSUS) II[37] found a reduction (from 30 to 27 percent) in the incidence of symptomatic heart failure when enalapril was used after MI, but no reduction in mortality was observed. However, the methods used in this study differed from those of other studies in that (1) early intravenous dosing was used post-MI, (2) therapy was not limited to patients with left-ventricular dysfunction, and (3) patients were followed for only 6 months postinfarction—a time when benefits in the SAVE study were only beginning to be apparent.

EF should be determined before discharge (e.g., 3–7 days post-MI) in patients following an MI to determine whether an ACE inhibitor would be beneficial. This may not be necessary, however, for patients at low risk for significant systolic dysfunction—that is, patients who meet all of the following criteria:

- No previous MI.
- Inferior infarction.
- Relatively small increase in cardiac enzymes (i.e., <2–4 times normal).
- No Q-waves on ECG.
- Uncomplicated clinical course (e.g., no arrhythmias or hypotension).

Asymptomatic patients with moderate-to-severe left-ventricular dysfunction may also be discovered during the evaluation of other problems, such as a heart murmur or cardiomegaly on a chest x-ray. These patients may also benefit from ACE inhibitors. The Studies of Left-Ventricular Dysfunction (SOLVD) prevention trial found that enalapril (titrated to 10 mg BID) could reduce the development of symptomatic heart failure to 21 percent in asymptomatic patients, compared with 30 percent in those treated with placebo.[19] The average duration of followup was 3 years. No significant effects on total mortality or cardiovascular mortality were observed. These results are encouraging, but they do not justify screening asymptomatic patients for left-ventricular dysfunction unless they have a history of previous Q-wave MI and EF was not measured after the infarction. The majority of patients with asymptomatic left-ventricular dysfunction will have had a previous MI, and they may be taking aspirin or a beta blocker. Adding ACE inhibitors to these medications is generally safe and effective.

The Clinical Practice Guideline correctly recommends ACE inhibition for patients who fit the profiles of the SOLVD Prevention and SAVE Trials. This is a conservative interpretation of the data appropriate to a rigorous scientific analysis. It reflects the way we should think about data when we assess a completed therapeutic trial or plan a new one. In the clinical care of patients, however, we often seek to help patients who do not precisely meet the entry criteria of published trials. A physician must use clinical judgment, and this frequently means extrapolating from data gathered in well-defined trial cohorts to individual patients who may not fit trial criteria. Using this more flexible approach to the interpretation of the data, we say that the SOLVD Prevention and SAVE Trials established the principle that ACE inhibition attenuates the inexorable progression of ventricular systolic dysfunction, delays the onset of heart failure symptoms, reduces heart failure hospitalizations, and reduces recurrent MI. When faced with patients having left-ventricular dysfunction and an EF ≥35–40 percent, it may also be reasonable and appropriate to use ACE inhibitors. It is understood that such a decision is not based on proven benefit or known cost-effectiveness in this group of patients. Further studies are needed. Indeed, a large trial is currently underway to address the question of the value of ACE inhibition in patients with coronary disease and EF >40 percent (the PEACE Trial).

Initial Evaluation

Commentary by Richard Rodeheffer, M.D.

Symptoms Suggestive of Heart Failure

All patients who complain of paroxysmal nocturnal dyspnea (awakening from sleep with shortness of breath), orthopnea (shortness of breath upon lying down), or new-onset dyspnea on exertion should undergo evaluation for heart failure unless history and physical examination clearly indicate a noncardiac cause for their symptoms, such as severe pulmonary disease. (Strength of Evidence = B.)

The guideline supports assessment for heart failure when paroxysmal nocturnal dyspnea, orthopnea, or new-onset exertional dyspnea occurs "unless history and physical examination clearly indicate a noncardiac cause." The example of severe pulmonary disease is given. The guideline then follows with a discussion emphasizing the inadequate sensitivity and specificity of the history and physical examination in diagnosing heart failure. Given the inaccuracy of the history and physical, and the ever-present potential for a patient to have two coexistent disorders which could cause dyspnea, it would be reasonable to lower the threshold for evaluating ventricular function in patients with paroxysmal nocturnal dyspnea, orthopnea, or new-onset exertional dyspnea to include those with noncardiac causes of these symptoms. Indeed, conditions often associated with chronic obstructive pulmonary disease, such as smoking or atrial fibrillation/flutter, may also be risk factors for ventricular dysfunction. To pursue this example further we might also recall that serious pulmonary disease is a chronic condition.

(Continued)

(Continued from previous page)

The new onset or the worsening of dyspnea in such a patient should prompt concern about why symptoms are changing in the setting of a chronic disease. Has the patient with long-standing pulmonary disease now developed left- or right-ventricular dysfunction, atrial arrhythmias, pulmonary emboli, or respiratory infection? The failure to recognize ventricular dysfunction in the setting of chronic pulmonary disease is a well known clinical oversight.

Symptoms suggestive of heart failure include the following:

- Paroxysmal nocturnal dyspnea.

Paroxysmal nocturnal dyspnea may be expressed as a supine cough.

- Orthopnea.
- Dyspnea on exertion.
- Lower extremity edema.
- Decreased exercise tolerance.
- Unexplained confusion, altered mental status, or fatigue in an elderly patient.
- Abdominal symptoms associated with ascites and/or hepatic engorgement (e.g., nausea or abdominal pain).

Many patients with severely impaired left-ventricular function have no symptoms of heart failure. Marantz et al. reported that 20 percent of patients with EFs less than 40 percent met no clinical criteria for heart failure,[38] and Mattleman et al. found that only 42 percent of patients with left-ventricular EFs less than 30 percent had dyspnea on exertion.[39]

The estimate of Marantz that 20 percent of patients with EF <40 percent had asymptomatic left-ventricular dysfunction may reflect referral bias and may be a substantial underestimate. Recent preliminary population-based echocardiographic data suggest that 62 percent of persons with EF ≤35 percent may be asymptomatic.[36]

When clinical heart failure develops, dyspnea on exertion appears to be the earliest symptom. In a study of patients with known coronary disease undergoing coronary artery angiography, two-thirds of patients with elevated pulmonary capillary wedge pressures had dyspnea on exertion.[40] Only 31 percent had paroxysmal nocturnal dyspnea, 23 percent had a history of leg edema, and 21 percent had orthopnea. However, many patients with normal pulmonary capillary wedge pressures also had dyspnea on exertion (specificity: 52 percent), whereas the other symptoms were unusual unless the wedge pressure was elevated (specificity: 76–81 percent).

> The guideline notes that exertional dyspnea is often the earliest symptom of heart failure. The elicitation of the history of dyspnea warrants expansion. Patients who develop ventricular dysfunction gradually are similar to patients with angina or stenotic valvular disease. They often engage in the subtle and slowly incremental modification of daily physical activities in order to avoid producing symptoms. One reason why patients with advanced ventricular dysfunction report few symptoms is that they become gradually more sedentary. The examiner must press for a more detailed history. A patient who denies symptoms when he climbs a flight of steps may admit to symptoms if asked how he feels when he climbs steps at a normal pace, or when he climbs steps next to a healthy person. The history provided by a spouse may also suggest more profound limitation. In general, one should try to quantify the patient's history where possible. Both as a discipline and as a means of communicating more effectively with colleagues, clinical notes should include a description of the NYHA classification of patients with heart failure.

Although the presence of any one of the symptoms listed above is sufficient to warrant consideration of heart failure as the underlying cause, orthopnea, paroxysmal nocturnal dyspnea, and progressive dyspnea on exertion are of greatest concern. The other symptoms listed above are less likely to represent heart failure if they occur in isolation. A history of previous MI, poorly controlled hypertension, or other heart disease, in conjunction with the preceding symptoms, points strongly toward a diagnosis of heart failure in patients with compatible symptoms.

It is important to note that the symptoms listed above are not always due to heart failure. Dyspnea (whether at rest or on exertion) can be caused by a wide range of conditions, including most pulmonary diseases, obesity, deconditioning, volume overload from nephrotic syndrome or renal failure, intermittent cardiac ischemia, anxiety, and acute lower respiratory infections. Patients with these conditions may not require evaluation for heart failure unless the symptoms are more severe than can be accounted for on the basis of those conditions.

Dyspnea on exertion is particularly common in patients with COPD, interstitial lung disease, chronic pulmonary thromboembolic disease, and primary pulmonary hypertension. It is usually possible to distinguish between cardiac and pulmonary causes of dyspnea on the basis of history, physical examination, and chest x-ray.

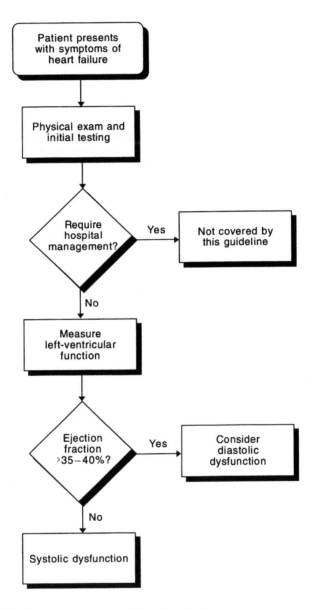

Figure 2a.   Initial Evaluation of Patients With Heart Failure

Absence of cardiomegaly on chest x-ray weighs against the diagnosis of heart failure due to systolic dysfunction except when pulmonary hyperinflation may mask an enlarged heart.[41,42] Patients with evident pulmonary disease generally do not require a full evaluation for heart failure unless their symptoms are out of proportion to the severity of their lung disease.

In addition to obtaining information about symptoms suggestive of heart failure, it is important that a complete medical history be obtained during the initial evaluation. In particular, information should be sought concerning previous MI; angina or equivalent (e.g., flash pulmonary edema); diabetes; renal, pulmonary, thyroid, or gastrointestinal disease; and medications.

Physical Examination

The physical examination can provide important information about the etiology of patients' symptoms and about appropriate initial treatment. However, physical signs are not highly sensitive for detecting heart failure. Therefore, patients with symptoms that are highly suggestive of heart failure should undergo echocardiography or radionuclide ventriculography to measure EF even if physical signs of heart failure are absent. (Strength of Evidence = C.)

Conversely, many physical findings of heart failure are not highly specific. Elevated jugular venous pressure, a third heart sound, and a laterally displaced apical impulse are the most specific and are virtually diagnostic in a patient with compatible symptoms. Pulmonary rales or peripheral edema are relatively nonspecific findings, however. The presence of these signs, therefore, does not require measurement of EF if other symptoms, signs, and radiographic findings of heart failure are absent. (Strength of Evidence = B.)

The guideline rightly emphasizes the low sensitivity and specificity of the physical examination for the diagnosis of heart failure but concludes that nonspecific signs such as pulmonary rales and peripheral edema do not require assessment of ventricular function if "other symptoms, signs, and radiographic findings of heart failure are absent." This interpretation suggests that the presence of "other symptoms, signs, and radiographic findings" is specific to some unknown but presumably useful extent. In patients with chronic pulmonary rales or edema of sufficient severity to attract medical attention, the possibility of ventricular dysfunction should be entertained. If the condition is persistent and not obviously explained by some other cause (lower extremity venous thrombosis or insufficiency, introduction of a calcium-channel blocker, lymphatic obstruction), evaluation for ventricular dysfunction is appropriate.

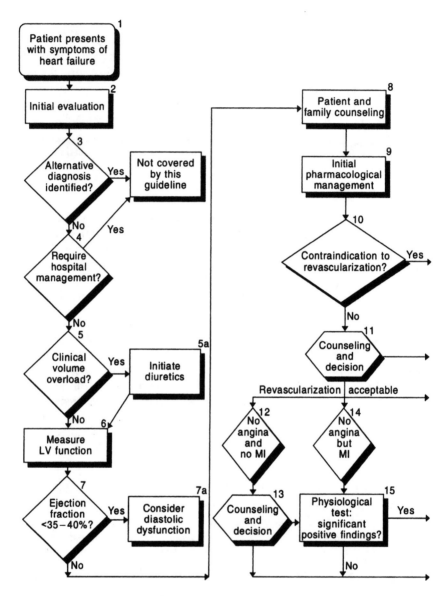

Figure 2b. Clinical Algorithm for Evaluation and Care of Patients With Heart Failure
Note: See Executive Summary for annotation. LV = left-ventricular, MI = myocardial infarction.

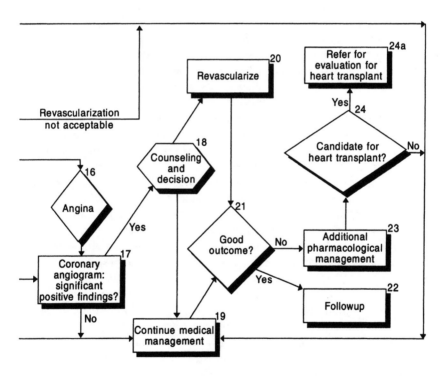

The initial workup of patients with symptoms suggestive of heart failure begins with a careful physical examination. Abnormal physical findings that tend to support a diagnosis of heart failure include the following:

- Elevated jugular venous pressure or positive hepatojugular reflux.
- A third heart sound.
- Laterally displaced apical impulse.
- Pulmonary rales that do not clear with cough.
- Peripheral edema not due to venous insufficiency.

Many patients with moderate-to-severe left-ventricular systolic dysfunction or early symptoms of heart failure have no physical findings. The most sensitive physical finding is the third heart sound. A third heart sound was found in 68 percent of patients with EFs below 30 percent.[39] Rales and a displaced apical impulse were present in only 37 and 42 percent of patients, respectively. Jugular venous distention and peripheral edema appear to be the least sensitive signs.[40] Studies of patients with severe heart failure undergoing cardiac catheterization before transplantation have also shown that physical findings are frequently absent even in patients with pulmonary capillary wedge pressures as high as 35 mmHg.[43]

The specificity of physical findings is less well defined because this has not been studied in a patient population without known or suspected heart disease. Elevated jugular venous pressure (as manifested by elevated jugular vein pulsations) and third heart sound are the most specific signs of heart failure. Rales in a patient with compatible symptoms and no known pulmonary disease are highly suggestive of heart failure. Lower extremity edema is a relatively nonspecific finding common in patients without heart failure. The most common cause of peripheral edema is venous insufficiency, not heart failure. Other causes of lower leg edema include lymphatic obstruction, conditions associated with hypoalbuminemia, deep venous thrombosis, and treatment with a calcium-channel blocker.[43,44] Leg edema is unlikely to be caused by heart failure if there is no elevation in the jugular venous pressure and no orthopnea, paroxysmal nocturnal dyspnea, or dyspnea on exertion.

As mentioned, physical examination findings may not be highly sensitive indicators of heart failure. Some patients with heart failure do not manifest any of these signs, so the absence of physical findings should not dissuade the clinician from undertaking a thorough evaluation of patients with unexplained symptoms of heart failure.[43,44] Care must be taken in assessing clinical signs of heart failure, because several studies suggest that intra- and interrater reliability of physical signs is often lower than would be desirable.[45,46]

Diagnostic Testing

Practitioners should perform a chest x-ray; ECG; complete blood count (CBC); serum electrolytes, serum creatinine, serum albumin, liver function

tests; and urinalysis for all patients with suspected or clinically evident heart failure. A T4 and thyroid-stimulating hormone (TSH) level should also be checked in all patients over the age of 65 with heart failure and no obvious etiology and in patients who have atrial fibrillation or other signs or symptoms of thyroid disease. (Strength of Evidence = C.)

Assessment for thyroid dysfunction should be considered when a patient with known but stable ventricular dysfunction exhibits worsening symptoms. This is especially true for patients taking amiodarone.

A chest x-ray should be obtained as an early diagnostic test. Cardiomegaly in symptomatic patients is highly suggestive of heart failure especially when accompanied by pulmonary venous congestion.[39,41,42] As discussed earlier, a normal chest x-ray weighs against a diagnosis of heart failure but does not rule it out. Besides helping to distinguish cardiac from pulmonary causes of dyspnea, chest x-rays can also provide information concerning pulmonary disease, calcified heart valves, left-atrial size, and right-ventricular versus left-ventricular enlargement.

An ECG should also be performed. Among the possible findings of interest are acute ischemia, arrhythmias, prior MI, left-ventricular hypertrophy, and conduction abnormalities. However, the ECG is usually nonspecific in patients with heart failure.[47]

Among electrocardiographic conduction abnormalities which may suggest left-ventricular dysfunction, AV block or bundle branch block deserve special emphasis. Left bundle branch block may be the consequence of a large anterolateral MI, or may be a premonitory sign for the development of dilated cardiomyopathy, particularly familial dilated cardiomyopathy.[48,49]

In some patients it may be difficult to distinguish between symptoms due to cardiac and pulmonary dysfunction. Screening spirometry may be helpful in these cases although measurement of EF may be equally (or more) illuminating.

An initial exercise test may occasionally be useful to determine a patient's exercise tolerance when the history regarding dyspnea on exertion is difficult to evaluate. This situation can occur in patients who (1) are sedentary, (2) are unable to provide an accurate history, (3) usually deny or minimize symptoms, or (4) have histories that conflict with those of family members. Patients with unexplained decreases in exercise tolerance without apparent cause should also be evaluated for heart failure.

The utility of exercise testing in the setting of an ambiguous history of fatigue and dyspnea should be emphasized. The value of the exercise test is greatly enhanced if the physician is present to observe the test, to auscultate for pulmonary rales during exercise-induced dyspnea, and to observe for other features such as orthopedic limitations, evidence of deconditioning, or signs and symptoms of hyperventilation syndrome.

A search for precipitating, complicating, or primary causative factors should be undertaken in every patient with suspected new-onset heart failure. Table 3 summarizes the tests that should generally be undertaken to assess patients with symptoms or signs of heart failure, including possible findings and suspected di-

Table 3. Recommended Tests for Patients With Signs or Symptoms of Heart Failure

Test Recommendation	Finding	Suspected Diagnosis
Electrocardiogram	Acute ST-T wave changes	Myocardial ischemia
	Atrial fibrillation, other tachyarrhythmia	Thyroid disease or heart failure due to rapid ventricular rate
	Bradyarrhythmias	Heart failure due to low heart rate
	Previous MI (e.g., Q-waves)	Heart failure due to reduced left-ventricular performance
	Low voltage	Pericardial effusion
	Left-ventricular hypertrophy	Diastolic dysfunction
Complete blood count	Anemia	Heart failure due to or aggravated by decreased oxygen-carrying capacity
Urinalysis	Proteinuria	Nephrotic syndrome
	Red blood cells or cellular casts	Glomerulonephritis
Serum creatinine	Elevated	Volume overload due to renal failure
Serum albumin	Decreased	Increased extravascular volume due to hypoalbuminemia
T4 and TSH (obtain only if atrial fibrillation, evidence of thyroid disease, or patient age >65)	Abnormal T4 or TSH	Heart failure due to or aggravated by hypo/hyperthyroidism

Note: TSH = Thyroid-stimulating hormone, MI = myocardial infarction.

> In patients with features of dilated cardiomyopathy, serum ferritin should be measured, particularly if there is skin pigmentation or evidence of hepatic dysfunction.

agnosis. Routine chemistry examinations (including serum electrolytes, blood urea nitrogen [BUN], and measures of renal and liver function) should be obtained on all patients for baseline purposes and to assist in subsequent decisionmaking regarding management (e.g., elevated potassium may preclude use of ACE inhibitors).

> The search for precipitating or complicating factors should also be undertaken when there has been a significant clinical deterioration in a previously stable patient with known left-ventricular dysfunction. Common intercurrent events which produce decompensation include new rhythm disturbance (e.g., atrial fibrillation or flutter), a new MI, a pulmonary embolism, an infection, the development of anemia, renal or thyroid dysfunction, or nonadherence to medication and dietary recommendations.

Probably the most common complicating factor for heart failure is hypertension. In patients with hypertension and clinically evident heart failure, every effort should be made to control blood pressure.

Hematocrits of 25–35 percent may aggravate underlying heart failure; patients with anemia in this range should be managed as appropriate (e.g., with iron supplements for patients with iron deficiency anemia, or with transfusion if there is evidence of ongoing ischemia) while receiving continued evaluation and management of their heart failure. Hematocrits below 25 percent can produce signs and symptoms of heart failure without underlying cardiac abnormalities; patients with anemia in this range should be re-evaluated after correction of anemia to determine whether additional workup for heart failure is required. Extreme caution should be exercised if transfusion becomes necessary, as this process may exacerbate symptoms of heart failure. Use of packed red blood cells is recommended when transfusion is necessary.

Renal insufficiency or failure may cause volume overload that mimics heart failure or exacerbates underlying left-ventricular dysfunction. These patients should generally be treated with diuretics or dialysis and reassessed after correction of volume overload to determine whether further evaluation for heart failure is necessary. Decreased serum albumin may also mimic or exacerbate heart failure.

Screening for Arrhythmias

Screening evaluation for arrhythmias, such as ambulatory electrocardiographic (Holter) recording, is not routinely warranted. (Strength of Evidence = A.)

Patients with a history of syncope possibly due to ventricular arrhythmias should be referred immediately to a practitioner with expertise in arrhythmias. (Strength of Evidence = C.)

A full discussion of the treatment of arrhythmias in patients with heart failure is beyond the scope of this guideline, which addresses only the issue of screening for arrhythmias. Ventricular arrhythmias are common in patients with heart failure, and death is sudden in up to half of patients.[22,50,51] Patients with nonsustained ventricular tachycardia, as identified by ambulatory electrocardiographic monitoring, have a worse prognosis than patients without this finding.[52] However, the observed increase in mortality is due in part to an increased rate of death from heart failure.[53] Thus, for an individual patient, the finding of frequent premature ventricular depolarizations or nonsustained ventricular tachycardia may be a poor predictor of sudden death. Arnsdorf and Bump concluded that "ambulatory ECG monitoring helps define the average risk of death in a group of people but is of limited value in defining the risk for the individual patient."[50] Even if a high-risk group could be accurately identified, there is no treatment available at this time that has been shown to decrease the mortality rate of patients with asymptomatic, nonsustained ventricular tachycardia. Studies of amiodarone in this setting have shown conflicting results.[54–58] A large, placebo-controlled trial was scheduled for completion in March 1994.

The results of this trial suggested that no mortality benefit was achieved by amiodarone treatment in patients with EF ≤40 percent.[59] Amiodarone may, however, have contributed to an improvement in EF and a trend toward better survival in a nonischemic heart failure subgroup.

A controlled trial, Sudden Cardiac Death in Heart Failure: Trial of Prophylactic Amiodarone or Implantable Defibrillator Therapy vs. Placebo (SCD-HeFT), is scheduled to begin in 1996 to assess the impact of the use of implantable cardiac defibrillator/pacemaker devices in patients with symptomatic heart failure, EF ≤35 percent, who have not had sustained ventricular arrhythmias. If this trial demonstrates a benefit from such a therapy, new impetus would be given to efforts to identify risk factors for sudden death in heart failure and to prevent it with a proven intervention.

Patients with heart failure should be questioned about symptoms suggestive of sustained ventricular tachycardia, such as syncope or near syncope. Patients with these symptoms should be referred immediately to a practitioner with expertise in the management of arrhythmias. Patients lacking such symptoms should not be subjected to a search for arrhythmias using ambulatory ECG recording. Such testing will often detect less serious forms of ventricular ectopy, including premature ventricular contractions.[60-66] These findings are often worrisome to both the patient and clinician and may provoke physicians into using antiarrhythmic agents that have no proven value and carry a significant risk of proarrhythmic effects and death. Antiarrhythmic drugs worsen arrhythmias in 5–20 percent of patients with normal left-ventricular function,[67-72] and patients with left-ventricular dysfunction are at higher risk for this effect.[73-75] The Cardiac Arrhythmia Suppression Trial[76,77] found an increased mortality rate in patients with EFs of 40 percent or less and 6 or more ventricular premature depolarizations per hour and who were treated with the antiarrhythmic agents moricizine,[76] encainide,[77] and flecainide.[77] These findings raise serious concerns about treating all but the most serious arrhythmias in patients with left-ventricular dysfunction.

Atrial Fibrillation

Atrial fibrillation is present in 10–15 percent of patients with heart failure.[21-22] It may occur in up to 50 percent of patients with more severe heart failure.[12] If atrial fibrillation causes sudden, severe worsening of heart failure, immediate cardioversion may be necessary. However, most patients can be stabilized by using digoxin to control the heart rate. Once stable, all patients should be considered for cardioversion.

> Digoxin is helpful to control ventricular response rate in atrial fibrillation or flutter, but beta-blocking agents may be more effective and should be considered when digoxin does not provide good rate control. If utilized, beta blockers may be given in addition to digoxin and should be initiated at low doses under close physician monitoring.

Patients with left-atrial diameters of less than 50 mm and less than a 1-year history of atrial fibrillation should be cardioverted. Patients should be anticoagulated for 3 weeks before cardioversion. (Strength of Evidence = C.)

Because of the risks of antiarrhythmic drugs, electrical cardioversion is probably the preferred therapy. If this is successful, patients should be continued on anticoagulants for 6–12 months and monitored for recurrence of atrial fibrillation. If atrial fibrillation recurs, then the risks and benefits of repeat cardioversion must be weighed again. If atrial fibrillation does not recur, then anticoagulation can be discontinued at the discretion of the clinician.

Patients with left-atrial diameters greater than 50 mm or with chronic atrial fibrillation for more than 1 year are unlikely to remain in sinus rhythm without antiarrhythmic therapy. Because the risk of provoking ventricular arrhythmias with type I antiarrhythmic drugs is increased in patients with heart failure, patients should be placed on these agents only if there are clear-cut benefits from the resumption of sinus rhythm (i.e., improved hemodynamics or decreased risk of embolism in a patient with contraindications to chronic anticoagulation). Amiodarone may be the preferred agent. If a patient tolerates the atrial fibrillation well, has no contraindication to anticoagulation, and is unlikely to remain in sinus rhythm without antiarrhythmic drugs, it may be best to allow the patient to remain in atrial fibrillation and to start anticoagulation.

It is stated that some patients may be left in atrial fibrillation with appropriate anticoagulation if the rhythm is well tolerated. This course may be taken after appropriate attempts have been made to restore sinus rhythm. In selected patients who tolerate atrial fibrillation poorly due to the inability to achieve good rate control, consideration should be given to AV node ablation and pacemaker implantation. Poorly controlled atrial fibrillation rate, like other forms of incessant tachycardia, may itself be a cause of reversible left-ventricular systolic dysfunction.[78]

Hospital Admission and Discharge Criteria

The presence or suspicion of heart failure and any of the following findings usually indicates a need for hospitalization. (Strength of Evidence = C.)

- Clinical or electrocardiographic evidence of acute myocardial ischemia.
- Pulmonary edema or severe respiratory distress.
- Oxygen saturation below 90 percent (not due to pulmonary disease).
- Severe complicating medical illness (e.g., pneumonia).
- Anasarca.
- Symptomatic hypotension or syncope.
- Heart failure refractory to outpatient therapy.
- Inadequate social support for safe outpatient management.

Most of the guideline's evaluation and care recommendations can be accomplished in either an inpatient or outpatient setting. The guideline does not address strategies specific to inpatient settings (e.g., pulmonary artery catheter, cardiac assist devices) but does make some statements concerning the transition between outpatient management and inpatient care.

Specifically, practitioners should be aware of the appropriate indications for hospitalization and for discharge from hospital. The above recommendations are made in the absence of specific data, although studies of predictors of hospital mortality were useful in formulating these recommendations.[8,10,79] Some patients with the above findings may be managed at home or in an assisted living or nursing home setting if, in the physician's carefully considered opinion, it is safe to do so and adequate outpatient monitoring and followup visits can be arranged.

Patients with heart failure should be discharged from the hospital only when (Strength of Evidence = C):

The guideline appropriately recognizes the potential for the outpatient management of marginally compensated patients in certain "carefully considered" situations. Although the guideline does not address issues of terminal care, it should be recognized that many patients with severe heart failure are elderly, some are managed in nursing home or home care environments, and that for many such patients heart failure will be the cause of death, despite our best therapy. It is incumbent upon the physician to develop an appreciation for the patient and family wishes in such cases. The physician should provide an intensity of care appropriate to the medical needs of the patient and which is respectful of the wishes and dignity of the patient.

- Symptoms of heart failure have been adequately controlled.
- All reversible causes of morbidity have been treated or stabilized.
- Patients and caregivers have been educated about medications, diet, activity and exercise recommendations, and symptoms of worsening heart failure.
- Adequate outpatient support and followup care have been arranged.

Proper discharge planning is an essential component of managing patients with heart failure. Heart failure is one of the most common causes for recurrent admission to hospitals, and many of these admissions may be avoidable. Readmission rates as high as 57 percent within 90 days have been reported in patients over the age of 70 years.[80] Vinson et al. found that the factors associated with readmission to hospitals were: failed social support systems (21 percent), inadequate followup (20 percent), failure to seek medical attention promptly when symptoms recurred (20 percent), noncompliance with diet (18 percent), noncompliance with medication (15 percent), and inadequate discharge planning (15 percent).[80] Gooding and Jette found that 36 percent of 147 patients were readmitted within 6 months.[81] Patients were more likely to be readmitted if the initial discharge site was home rather than a secondary facility (39 and 19 percent, respectively). These authors highlighted the importance of securing compliance for medication and dietary regimens and called for better home care after discharge and better coordination of care between secondary and primary care providers.

Rosenberg demonstrated that better patient education decreased hospital admissions for patients with heart failure.[82] Perlman et al. demonstrated that public health nurses could detect deterioration in heart failure at a stage early enough to allow intervention that avoided admission to the hospital.[83] Patients should usually have a followup contact within 7 days after discharge to (1) make sure that medications are being taken properly, (2) assess compliance with reduced salt diet, (3) ensure that patient's weight is stable, (4) adjust the dosage of diuretics and other medications if necessary, and (5) determine that the patient, family, and caregivers understand when and how to contact the practitioner. Electrolytes, BUN, and creatinine should also be checked about 1 week following discharge, and medications adjusted as necessary.

Note: Figure 2 shows the content and organization of this chapter.

The need for patient and family education, as well as the need for close coupling between hospital discharge and outpatient followup, should be emphasized. A recent report underscores the importance of well coordinated long-term management of heart failure by committed personnel in a dedicated heart failure clinic.[30] This multidisciplinary approach was shown to reduce hospital readmission for heart failure, improve quality of life, and reduce the overall cost of medical care.

Patients should become actively involved in monitoring their own clinical status. It is valuable for the patient to maintain a diary to record daily weight, the use of extra doses of diuretic, and changes in symptoms. The patient should bring this diary along to be reviewed at office visits.

Assessment of Left-Ventricular Function

Commentary by G. William Dec, Jr., M.D.

Patients with suspected heart failure should undergo echocardiography or radionuclide ventriculography to measure EF (if information about ventricular function is not available from previous tests). (Strength of Evidence = B.)

Measurement of left-ventricular performance is a critical step in the evaluation and management of almost all patients with suspected or clinically evident heart failure. The combined use of history, physical examination, chest x-ray, and electrocardiography cannot be relied on to distinguish between the major etiologies of heart failure: left-ventricular systolic dysfunction (i.e., EF <35–40 percent), left-ventricular diastolic dysfunction (i.e., heart failure occurring despite EF ≥40 percent), valvular heart failure disease, or a noncardiac etiology.

Emphasizing the importance of quantifying left-ventricular EF by noninvasive techniques, should not imply that the clinical approach to the patient with new-onset heart failure has no value.[84] The presence of a diffuse, laterally displaced point of maximal impulse or an audible third heart sound should point the clinician toward a diagnosis of systolic dysfunction. Likewise, the presence of a prominent fourth heart sound and a normal apical impulse should raise the possibility of diastolic dysfunction. Nonethe-

(Continued)

(Continued from previous page)

less, the sensitivity and specificity of physical findings in diagnosing heart failure of either etiology remain low. Many patients with compensated systolic dysfunction have clear lungs despite significant elevation in left-sided filling pressures sufficient to create exertional dyspnea. Further, a third heart sound may be absent despite severe depression of systolic function (LVEF <30 percent) in patients who are clinically well-compensated. Despite its lack of sensitivity, an audible third heart sound is relatively specific in identifying systolic dysfunction.Atrioventricular regurgitation is commonly heard in patients with ventricular dilatation. These so-called "functional" murmurs are seldom greater than II/VI in intensity. The presence of a murmur of greater intensity should lead the clinician to suspect primary valvular disease. One caveat requires special emphasis. Since the murmur is related to velocity of flow, critical lesions such as aortic stenosis may present with a surprisingly soft murmur when forward flow is severely impaired.

The chest film and ECG may provide additional diagnostic clues to heart failure etiology. Significant cardiomegaly on chest film should suggest a-diagnosis of systolic dysfunction. Likewise, the presence of clear-cut QS-waves is helpful in defining etiology and pointing toward ischemic left-ventricular systolic dysfunction. Nonetheless, physical findings are often inconclusive, and accurate differentiation of systolic from diastolic heart failure generally requires echocardiography or radionuclide ventriculography.

A substantial proportion (up to 40 percent in some studies) of patients with signs and symptoms of heart failure have EFs greater than 50 percent.[38,41,42,85,86]

Accurate assessment of left-ventricular function following acute MI requires echocardiography or radionuclide ventriculography. It is well recognized that up to 40 percent of patients will have at least 24 hours of transient heart failure during the early stages of acute MI; many such individuals may be left with normal or near-normal function following completion of their ischemic event.

These patients generally have valvular disease, intermittent ischemia, or ventricular diastolic dysfunction. If measurement of ventricular performance is not obtained in these patients, inappropriate treatments may be instituted (e.g., digoxin, which has not been shown to be effective in patients with normal ventricular systolic function).[86]

Echocardiography or radionuclide ventriculography can substantially improve diagnostic accuracy in distinguishing between systolic and diastolic dysfunction.[39,41–42,86–92]

Noninvasive assessment of ventricular function is the most clinically relevant and cost-effective approach to the initial evaluation of a heart failure patient.[17] Information provided from this single study allows differentiation of systolic from diastolic heart failure, aids in predicting prognosis, which is highly dependent on the degree of left-ventricular dysfunction, and can aid in treatment.

Patients whose symptoms are fully accounted for by an underlying noncardiac condition (see above) or who have previously documented decreased ventricular performance (e.g., recent echocardiogram or contrast ventriculogram) do not require determination of EF.

Although elderly patients with mild symptoms are often managed without measurement of ventricular performance, this practice is discouraged for the following reasons:

- The elderly are the very individuals in whom it may be most difficult to make the diagnosis of heart failure and to determine whether failure is due to systolic or diastolic dysfunction.

- Although mild diuretic therapy may cause little harm in patients with fluid retention of any etiology, use of other medications—such as ACE inhibitors, digoxin, or nitrates—has significant risks and no established benefit unless they are specifically indicated. These agents may even worsen the condition of patients with heart failure secondary to left-ventricular diastolic dysfunction.

Heart failure is, in fact, a syndrome of the elderly. It is the most common discharge diagnosis for patients greater than 65 years of age. Based upon the Framingham Heart Study, disease incidence and prevalence are highly age-dependent, increasing in a curvilinear fashion from age 50 to 80 years.[17] A nonaggressive approach to older patients with heart failure appears unjustified since at least 80 percent of all newly diagnosed cases occur in older patients.

Both echocardiography and radionuclide ventriculography are appropriate measures for the evaluation of left-ventricular performance. Although EF measured by radionuclide ventriculography may have a higher correlation with cineangiography than that measured by echocardiography ($r = 0.88$ versus $r = 0.78$, respectively),[93] echocardiography has good reproducibility ($r = 0.89$)[94] and accuracy for measuring EF ($r = 0.78–0.89$).[93-95] The use of quantitative techniques has been found to improve measurement of EF in some studies.[93,95] However, Stamm et al. found that real-time estimation by the echocardiographer was more accurate than any of several algorithms tested.[94]

In general, the panel considered echocardiography to be the preferred test because of its ability to assess valvular function and left-ventricular hypertrophy, but selection of a diagnostic test should depend on the capabilities of individual clinical centers. Between 8 and 18 percent of patients will have technically inadequate echocardiograms, in which case radionuclide ventriculography should be performed.[96-98]

The echocardiogram is, indeed, the preferred procedure for noninvasively defining ventricular function. It is available in virtually all hospitals, and the frequency of a technically inadequate study has declined during the past decade. Fewer than 5 percent of echocardiograms are typically unsuitable for providing at least qualitative information regarding overall cardiac function. The echocardiogram provides substantial additional information beyond that of systolic performance. It reliably quantifies cavity size, which is closely related to prognosis in heart failure patients. The larger the left-ventricular end-diastolic dimension, the poorer the long-term prognosis. Functional mitral regurgitation is often quite soft or even inaudible on physical examination but may be of moderate severity by Doppler echocardiography. This information is of clinical relevance since recent data demonstrate that vasodilator therapy is most effective in relieving symptoms when significant AV regurgitation exists. Echocardiography is also generally reliable in assessing right-ventricular size and function. This author disagrees with the information in Table 4 which suggests that a radionuclide ventriculogram can provide a better assessment of right-ventricular function. Two-dimensional echocardiography provides similar information regarding contractility and is more reliable in defining right-ventricular size and quantifying the degree of tricuspid regurgitation.

There is no question that radioventriculography is more accurate in providing precise quantification of left-ventricular EF than echocardiography. Echocardiographic studies are notoriously dependent upon reader assessment, and interobserver variability may result in a 5 to 10 percent variation in overall EF. Nonetheless, the overall semiquantitative assessment is usually more than adequate for proper diagnosis and management.

The echocardiogram is unquestionably superior to radionuclide ventriculography in differentiating the cause of diastolic dysfunction (Table 4). It can reliably detect hypertrophic cardiomyopathy and is also reasonably useful in excluding pericardial disease.

The transesophageal echocardiogram can provide very high definition images but is invasive, requires sedation, has increased cost, and is associated with a higher risk than a transthoracic surface study. A radionuclide ventriculogram is the preferred procedure in this population when a technically inadequate echocardiogram is obtained.

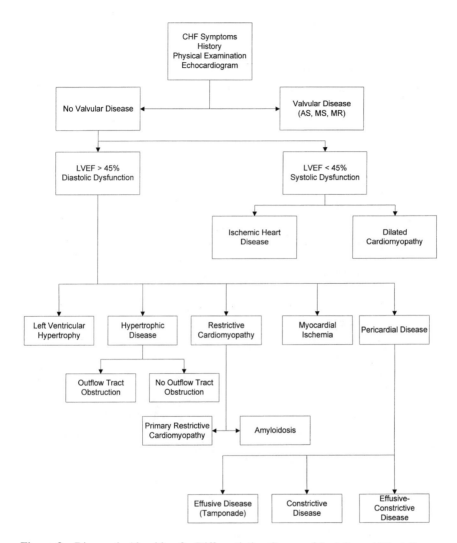

Figure 3.   Diagnostic Algorithm for Differentiating Causes of Systolic and Diastolic Heart Failure by Two-Dimensional Echocardiography
Note: CM = Cardiomyopathy.

Although there are no studies in the literature on the quality of echocardiography and radionuclide ventriculography in community practice, the panel perceives significant quality problems in the performance and interpretation of both tests. When referred to a specialist, patients should be encouraged to bring a video of the actual images of their echocardiogram with them, rather than a written report. In this way, the quality of the study can be determined directly. Advantages and disadvantages of echocardiography and radionuclide ventriculography are summarized in Table 4.

Role of Serial Assessment of Left-Ventricular Ejection Fraction

It is generally not recommended that LVEF be determined on a regular basis. However, serial assessment may be useful in a number of situations. It is useful in acute-onset dilated cardiomyopathy, which has a high rate of both spontaneous improvement and rapid progression. Reassessment of function after several months of treatment is generally quite helpful in this population.[99] Reassessment of ventricular size and function is also important when a major change in clinical status has occurred. Typically, it is re-employed when a patient who had previously been stable develops worsening heart failure signs and symptoms. The echocardiogram can rapidly assess whether there has been further deterioration in ventricular function, worsening mitral regurgitation, or development of another structural lesion. Reassessment of ventricular function following extensive MI is also frequently useful to assess the extent of ventricular remodeling and dilatation. The remodeling process may begin within the first 2 weeks but often takes several months before it becomes evident. Serial echocardiography is not infrequently used to reassess the degree of left-ventricular dilatation. Progressive dilatation is often used to guide more aggressive escalation in vasodilator treatment. Unfortunately, data are currently lacking that support the hypothesis that this echocardiographically-guided approach to treatment is physiologically beneficial. Serial studies in patients with asymptomatic left-ventricular dysfunction are frequently performed, but their utility in guiding long-term prognosis and management remains uncertain. Finally, serial echocardiography is often useful in patients with hypertrophic disease to determine response of dynamic outflow tract obstruction to treatment. Serial studies are essential in children and adolescents with symptomatic disease and in asymptomatic first degree relatives when a history of the familial form of hypertrophic disease is present. Progressive ventricular hypertrophy not infrequently develops during growth spurts, and adolescence and serial studies are necessary to detect such changes.

Table 4. Echocardiography and Radionuclide Ventriculography Compared in Evaluation of Left-Ventricular Performance

Test	Advantages	Disadvantages
Echocardiogram	Permits concomitant assessment of valvular disease, left-ventricular hypertrophy, and left-atrial size	Difficult to perform in patients with lung disease
	Less expensive than radionuclide ventriculography in most areas	Usually only semiquantitative estimate of EF provided
	Able to detect pericardial effusion and ventricular thrombus	Technically inadequate in up to 18% of patients under optimal circumstances
	More generally available	
Radionuclide ventriculogram	More precise and reliable measurement of EF	Requires venipuncture and radiation exposure
	Better assessment of right-ventricular function	Limited assessment of valvular heart disease and left-ventricular hypertrophy

It is important to note that although echocardiography or radionuclide ventriculography is essential for determining the presence and degree of left-ventricular dysfunction, these tests are less useful in determining the etiology of that dysfunction.Specifically, the presence or absence of regional wall motion abnormalities is of limited value in determining whether a patient's disease is due to coronary artery disease or to idiopathic dilated cardiomyopathy.[96,97,100,101] For example, Diaz et al. found that 56 percent of patients with idiopathic dilated cardimyopathy had regional wall motion abnormalities rather than global hypokinesis.[97]

Segmental wall motion abnormalities do occur in dilated cardiomyopathy and are surprisingly more common than might be anticipated. Up to 50 percent of patients with documented dilated cardiomyopathy will demonstrate segmental dysfunction.[102] Although such regional variation in contractile function was initially attributed to chronic alterations in wall stress, recent data using positron emission tomography suggest that segmental dysfunction may be due to diminished regional oxidative metabolism.[105] Although segmental dysfunction has been stated to be associated with a better prognosis than global hypokinesis, this retrospective observation has not been validated in large prospective studies.

Conversely, 35 percent of patients with coronary artery disease had global hypokinesis without regional wall motion abnormalities.

When global left-ventricular hypokinesis occurs in ischemic heart disease it is most commonly associated with severe multivessel coronary disease and results from balanced ischemia and widespread myocardial hibernation. It is uncommonly observed in single- or double-vessel coronary disease.

It should not be misconstrued that noninvasive assessment of regional variation of ventricular function is completely without value in differentiating ischemic from nonischemic cardiomyopathy. The finding of a ventricular aneurysm, marked scarring, or calcification within a region of myocardium can reliably establish an ischemic etiology. Further, echocardiography is never performed in isolation. Both history and electrocardiographic findings generally point toward an ischemic etiology when present.

Similarly, right-ventricular dilatation is not helpful in distinguishing idiopathic dilated cardiomyopathy from ventricular dysfunction due to ischemia or prior MI.[97,104] Thus, the findings from echocardiography or radionuclide ventriculography should not be used to determine the etiology of a patient's cardiomyopathy or the need for further evaluations of coronary artery disease, such as coronary artery angiography.

This author disagrees with the statement that noninvasive assessment should not be used to determine heart failure etiology or to guide further evaluation of coronary disease. While echocardiography or radionuclide ventriculography should not be viewed as providing the definitive answer to disease etiology in most cases, it may help differentiate ischemic from nonischemic disease in many situations.[105] As a general rule, right-ventricular function is somewhat better preserved in heart failure due to ischemic disease than primary dilated cardiomyopathy. Further, severely depressed left-ventricular function (LVEF <15 percent) will often obviate the need for coronary angiography since surgical intervention is usually not feasible. Accurate assessment of right-ventricular function is also useful since patients with biventricular dysfunction (regardless of its etiology) are more likely to die during long-term followup than individuals with preserved right-ventricular function.[106]

(Continued)

(Continued from previous page)
Left-ventricular EF is quite helpful in determining prognosis. The predicted value of EF in chronic heart failure populations is not as good as in patients following acute MI. Although the relation is not linear, prognosis can be predicted by considering broad ranges of systolic dysfunction. Long-term prognosis is clearly better for patients whose EF exceeds 45 percent, is intermediate for EF between 20 and 45 percent; and is worst when EF falls below 20 percent. For homogeneous groupings of patients, no additional prognostic information is provided by EF (i.e., survival does not differ for an EF of 16 percent versus 20 percent). It is also useful to note that, for a given degree of depression in EF, patients with underlying ischemic heart disease have a higher mortality than those with primary cardiomyopathy. This survival difference presumably relates to the higher likelihood of subsequent ischemic events leading to fatal arrhythmias or further loss of functional myocardium.

Left-Ventricular Ejection Fraction and Symptoms

There is a very poor correlation between EF and day-to-day symptoms or functional capacity. Patients who respond well to medications or who can vasodilate and distribute adequate blood supply to skeletal muscles during exercise may have few heart failure symptoms (NYHA Class I or II). Those patients with marked peripheral vasoconstriction that fails to respond to medical therapy will have poor exercise tolerance and marked functional limitation (NYHA Class III or IV). The limitation in physical activity experienced by heart failure patients is typically more closely related to peripheral adaptations to chronic systolic dysfunction and impaired cardiac output than to the actual depression in myocardial contractility as measured by EF.

Ejection Fraction and Response to Treatment

Serial measurement of left-ventricular EF is not useful in guiding drug dosing or judging response to medical therapy. Digoxin and ACE inhibitors will typically increase EF by only 2 to 3 percent but may substantially enhance exercise capacity and improve day-to-day symptoms.

Interpretation of Left-Ventricular Function Testing

The majority of patients with heart failure have moderate-to-severe left-ventricular systolic dysfunction and EFs of <35–40 percent.

This statement is somewhat misleading. The etiology of heart failure is critically dependent on the population studied. Chronic diastolic dysfunction rarely produces symptoms in patients under the age of 50 years but is quite common in patients above 65 years of age.

This guideline is directed at the management of such patients. However, patients with symptoms of heart failure and EFs greater than 40 percent may still have heart failure due to left-ventricular diastolic dysfunction, valvular disease, or pericardial disease. The majority of these etiologies will be discernable with echocardiography. A full discussion of the diagnosis and treatment of these conditions is beyond the scope of this guideline, although a few comments on diastolic dysfunction are necessary because of its high prevalence.

Diastolic Dysfunction

As many as 40 percent of patients with a clinical diagnosis of heart failure have preserved left-ventricular systolic function and no evidence of valvular heart disease.[38,41,42,85,86]

> The prevalence of diastolic dysfunction as a cause for symptomatic heart failure was found to be approximately 10 percent in studies of middle-aged men compared to 30–35 percent for patients above 65 years of age.[107]

Most of these individuals have left-ventricular diastolic dysfunction. In these cases, the left ventricle has increased diastolic stiffness (reduced compliance) and cannot fill adequately at normal diastolic pressures.[108] The elevated pressures required for filling result in symptoms of pulmonary congestion. In addition, the reduced left-ventricular filling volume leads to lowered stroke volumes and symptoms of poor cardiac output.

Most diastolic dysfunction results from coronary artery disease or hypertension.

> Other less common causes of diastolic dysfunction and chronic heart failure are hypertrophic and restrictive cardiomyopathies. These two entities account for approximately 10–15 percent of all cases of diastolic dysfunction.
>
> Although chronic heart failure symptoms are the most common clinical manifestation, acute pulmonary edema may be the initial manifestation of disease in a minority of patients.
>
> Pulmonary edema that develops in a patient with documented normal contractile function (and in the absence of valvular heart disease) should suggest either severe uncontrolled hypertension or, more commonly, significant myocardial ischemia. Such patients need not have typical anginal symptoms even during episodes of severe ischemic left-ventricular dysfunction. This potentially life-threatening presentation requires complete diagnostic evaluation which often will include coronary angiography.

Because ischemia can produce diastolic dysfunction before systolic dysfunction develops, physiologic testing for ischemia should be considered in patients with diastolic dysfunction, particularly when dyspnea on exertion is a prominent symptom.[108] Hypertension is also a common cause of diastolic dysfunction,[109–112] which can develop even in the absence of left-ventricular hypertrophy.[109,113]

> Hypertension is the most common cause of pure diastolic dysfunction, since many patients with underlying ischemic heart disease also demonstrate mild-to-moderate depression in function (in the 40 percent range). The extent of impairment in diastolic ventricular filling is not dependent upon the extent of left-ventricular hypertrophy. This is true because diastolic filling is influenced not only the by compliance of the ventricular walls, but also by the rate of myocardial relaxation. This relaxation process is energy-requiring and involves the transport of calcium ions from the intracellular spaces of the myocytes back into the sarcoplasmic reticulum. This "inactivation process" may be impaired by aging, intermittent ischemia, chronic hypertrophy, or other myopathic processes.
>
> Diastolic heart failure is usually diagnosed either by prolongation of the time to peak filling, or peak filling rate by radionuclide ventriculography or reversal of the normal left-ventricular diastolic transmittal inflow pattern (i.e., a shift in the E/A ratio to less than one) by Doppler echocardiography (Figure 4).[114] This abnormal inflow pattern reflects increased resistance to early passive ventricular filling and augmented atrial contribution to the ventricular filling process. Ventricular filling indices (whether assessed by radioventriculography or echocardiography) are indirect measures of true diastolic function. Ventricular filling patterns are age-dependent and highly sensitive to changes in posture, sympathetic tone, heart rate, PR interval, and loading conditions.[114] Diastolic heart failure may exist despite "normal" noninvasively measured filling indices when marked elevation in left atrial pressure exists. More importantly, although pharmacological treatment using calcium-channel or beta-adrenergic blockers may favorably affect noninvasively measured indices of diastolic function, symptomatic improvement has never been shown to closely correlate with improvement in measured filling dynamics. Thus, serial measurements of diastolic function do not aid in guiding response to treatment.

The optimal treatment of diastolic dysfunction is not well-defined. For a full discussion, readers are referred to the recent review by Bonow and Udelson.[108] At this time, it appears that beta-blocking agents, calcium-channel blockers, and the judicious use of diuretics are the treatments of choice. Agents used to treat systolic dysfunction may be deleterious in patients with diastolic dysfunction.

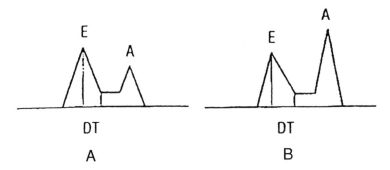

Figure 4. Patterns of Transmitral Flow in Health and Disease as Measured by Two-Dimensional Echocardiography

A. In a normal individual, the transmitral flow is biphasic, consisting of a tall initial E-wave followed by a shorter A-wave. The deceleration time (OT) is the interval between the peak early diastolic of low velocity and the onset of diastasis. This parameter measures how rapidly left-atrial and left-ventricular pressures equalize in early diastole and is related inversely to ventricular compliance.

B. In a patient with diastolic heart failure due to hypertensive heart disease, the mitral flow pattern shows reduction in early diastolic velocity (E-wave), increased late velocity following atrial contraction (A-wave), and prolongation of deceleration time (DT).

Adapted from Vasan R. et al. ArchIntern Med 1996;156:152.

Excessive diuresis can reduce stroke volume and cardiac output. Digitalis may further decrease left-ventricular compliance. The role of ACE inhibitors is not clear. Vasodilators may be detrimental in diastolic dysfunction although ACE inhibitors may have beneficial effects by directly improving ventricular relaxation and causing regression of hypertrophy.

Treatment
    No drug currently exists that has been shown to effectively improve isolated ventricular diastolic function. Recent American Heart Association/American College of Cardiology guidelines list only nitrates and diuretics as proven; effective therapy for controlling symptoms and neither alters diastolic function.[17] These agents improve congestive symptoms simply by reducing elevated preload. Although beta-adrenergic and calcium-channel blockers are theoretically appealing, neither has been shown to reliably improve symptoms or exercise capacity.[17,114] Further, no drug has been shown to improve the natural history of diastolic heart failure with the exception of agents that cause regression of left-ventricular hypertrophy.

Prognosis

Annual mortality for isolated diastolic heart failure has been reported to range widely from 1.3 percent to 17.5 percent.[107] The effects of age and underlying disease etiology undoubtedly influence these highly varied mortality rates. The impact of underlying ischemic heart disease on prognosis is controversial, with one study reporting no adverse impact and a second reporting a negative impact.[107,114] The largest studies of men aged 55–71 years have reported average mortality rates of 3–9 percent.[107,114] This estimate is considerably lower than that for patients with symptomatic left-ventricular systolic dysfunction where annual mortality often approaches 20 percent. Little information has yet been published on the causes of death in this population, or whether treatment strategies can improve survival.

Determination of Specific Etiologies for Left-Ventricular Systolic Dysfunction

Once left-ventricular dysfunction is confirmed, the results of the history and physical examination should be reviewed to search for clues to potentially treatable causes of heart failure. Additional information should be sought as appropriate. Clinicians should follow up any positive findings with appropriate laboratory testing. Routine use of myocardial biopsy is not warranted. (Strength of Evidence = C.)

The most common causes of left-ventricular systolic dysfunction are coronary artery disease, idiopathic dilated cardiomyopathy, hypertension and alcohol abuse. The most common potentially reversible cause of heart failure is myocardial ischemia. Therefore, patients should be carefully questioned concerning a history of chest pain or recurring episodes of sudden pulmonary edema suggestive of ischemia.

Exertional dyspnea is often an anginal equivalent. Painless myocardial ischemia is more common in diabetics and may manifest itself solely as dyspnea on exertion.

Evaluation of patients with angina is discussed subsequently in the section on revascularization. Alcoholism is important to detect and treat because alcohol may aggravate cardiac dysfunction.[116–118]

Alcoholic cardiomyopathy is increasing in prevalence in late adolescence and young adulthood. This form of cardiomyopathy requires at least 10 years of moderate alcohol consumption. As many young teens are consuming alcohol before entering high school, it is no longer uncommon to encounter alcoholic cardiomyopathy in patients in their early 20s. Recent data also suggest that women are more susceptible to the chronic effects of alcohol. Lower cumulative doses of alcohol appear to produce both cardiomyopathy and skeletal myopathy in women.[115]

Where appropriate, patients should also be asked about cocaine use, and a urine test for cocaine may be helpful in selected patients. Specific treatable etiologies (e.g., sarcoidosis) should be considered when the constellation of systemic findings suggests a diagnosis. Patients with a history of liver disease, unexplained hepatomegaly, diabetes or other endocrine dysfunction, or bronze discoloration of the skin should be evaluated for hemochromatosis with a serum iron level, total iron binding capacity, and ferritin level. An exhaustive search for the etiology of heart failure in a patient without specific findings on history and physical examination is of little value.

The role that myocarditis, an autoimmune inflammatory disease, plays in the development of acute or chronic dilated cardiomyopathy remains controversial. Myocarditis was initially felt to produce 20–40 percent of all cases of dilated cardiomyopathy. However, as more rigorous histologic criteria for its diagnosis were established (which now require the presence of both an inflammatory cell infiltrate and associated myocyte necrosis for an unequivocal diagnosis), the yield of endomyocardial biopsy has fallen to below 10 percent of cases. Detection of myocarditis remains most likely when heart failure symptoms have been present for less than 6 months. Further, the Multicenter Myocarditis Treatment Trial reported no beneficial effect of cyclosporine and prednisone immunosuppression on outcome in patients with documented myocarditis.[119] The low diagnostic yield coupled with the lack of an effective treatment for myocarditis has led most clinicians to limit the diagnostic use of endomyocardial biopsy. Biopsy may still be indicated for selected patients such as those with acute onset dilated cardiomyopathy and rapidly deteriorating function, or a systemic disease known to affect the myocardium such as sarcoidosis, eosinophilic myocarditis, lupus erythematosus, or less commonly, amyloidosis.

Patient and Family Education and Counseling

Commentary by Barry Rayburn, M.D.

General Counseling

Physicians are often asked to become more and more efficient in the way they practice medicine. For a primary care physician, this often means seeing as many patients as possible in the course of a day, and spending less time with each individual patient. The subject of this chapter, patient and family education and counseling, by its very nature requires a commitment of time on the part of the practitioner. While this is time which could potentially be relegated to other health professionals such as nurses and dieticians, it nonetheless requires the practitioner to initiate the process and to convey its importance to the patient. In prioritizing the use of time, it is critical to remember the nature of heart failure. This is a chronic disease and one which carries a high cost in terms of mortality, morbidity, and inherently, physician time. It is well argued that it is more efficient to spend time on patient and family education at a scheduled visit than it is to deal with the consequences of noncompliance or poor judgment in the emergency room or hospital.

(Continued)

(Continued from previous page)

The panel presents an excellent overview of the topic in this chapter. Our goal is to provide some practical ideas on implementing an education and counseling strategy based on our experience. Where newer data is available, we have also tried to update the information presented. As in many areas of medicine, there are few randomized controlled trials in the area of education and counseling. There are studies in other chronic illnesses such as asthma and diabetes which support the concept that patient education can reduce morbidity and be cost-effective.[120,121] Combined with available studies in heart failure and the expert opinions presented by the panel, we feel strongly that practitioners should incorporate a plan for education and counseling into their routine management of patients with heart failure. The exact nature of this plan will vary according the circumstances of the practitioner, but its content is outlined here.

After a diagnosis of heart failure is established, patients and their families or caregivers should be counseled regarding the nature of heart failure, drug regimens, dietary restrictions, symptoms of worsening heart failure, what to do if these symptoms occur, and prognosis. The impact of heart failure on a patient's life may be related as much to psychological adaptation to the disease as to impairment in physical functioning. Nursing interventions, family involvement, and support groups may all help patients cope with heart failure. All patients should be encouraged to complete advance directives regarding their health care preferences. Practitioners should emphasize the importance of not smoking or chewing tobacco. Practitioners should recommend that patients receive vaccination against influenza and pneumococcal disease. (Strength of Evidence = C.)

It is vital that patients understand their condition and be involved in developing the plan for their care. Patients and their families should be encouraged to ask questions about any aspect of the management of heart failure and about any aspect of a recommended intervention. Patient and family education regarding any intervention should be designed to help patients arrive at realistic expectations about the outcome of an intervention. Patient and family education material and systems can be very useful to help clarify information and enhance understanding of heart failure and its management. A list of suggested topics for discussion is presented in Table 5.

It is impossible for patients to absorb all necessary information in one session. For patients who have been hospitalized, it is important to discuss medications and diet before discharge from the hospital and to repeat this information in the out-

Table 5.   Suggested Topics for Patient, Family, and Caregiver Education
and Counseling

General Counseling
    Explanation of heart failure and the reason for symptoms
    Cause or probable cause of heart failure
    Expected symptoms
    Symptoms of worsening heart failure
    What to do if symptoms worsen
    Self-monitoring with daily weights
    Explanation of treatment/care plan
    Clarification of patient's responsibilities
    Importance of cessation of tobacco use
    Role of family members or other caregivers in the treatment/care plan
    Availability and value of qualified local support group
    Importance of obtaining vaccinations against influenza and pneumococcal disease

Prognosis
    Life expectancy
    Advance directives
    Advice for family members in the event of sudden death

Activity Recommendations
    Recreation, leisure, and work activity
    Exercise
    Sex, sexual difficulties, and coping strategies

Dietary Recommendations
    Sodium restriction
    Avoidance of excessive fluid intake
    Fluid restriction (if required)
    Alcohol restriction

Medications
    Effects of medications on quality of life and survival
    Dosing
    Likely side effects and what to do if they occur
    Coping mechanisms for complicated medical regimens
    Availability of lower cost medications or financial assistance

Importance of Compliance With the Treatment/Care Plan

---

patient setting. This will allow patients time to assimilate the information and to formulate more questions. Because of the large number and often specialized nature of topics that are important to discuss with heart failure patients, practitioners should seek the assistance of dieticians, nurse educators, clinical nurse specialists, pharmacists, and support groups as part of a team approach to providing patient education. Visiting or home health nurses can be especially useful.

Finally, providers should be sensitive to differences in language and culture that may impair patients' understanding and compliance. Concerted attempts should be made to mitigate the influence of these factors.

The typical symptoms of worsening heart failure (orthopnea, paroxysmal dyspnea, leg edema, or exercise intolerance) should be explained, and patients should be advised to contact their doctor or nurse if such symptoms develop. All patients should also be told to obtain a bathroom scale and to weigh themselves each morning (after urinating and before eating). They should contact their provider if their weight has changed by more than 3–5 pounds since their last clinical evaluation. If patients know the symptoms and signs of worsening heart failure, they may be able to seek care early and avoid hospitalization. In addition, in compliant patients a diuretic regimen that the patient adjusts on the basis of weights taken at home can be a useful method for preventing decompensation and hospitalization.

An explanation of what patients can expect to experience will help avoid anxiety over symptoms and prevent patients from becoming afraid to perform daily activities that might provoke shortness of breath. Patients should be advised to stay as active as possible, as described in the section on activity recommendations. However, patients should understand that they may feel tired the following day if they overexert themselves. Sexual difficulties are common in these patients, and part of this arises from fear that exertion is detrimental. Sexual practices might need to be modified to accommodate patients with limited exercise tolerance. The practitioner should not expect the patient to bring up these issues; when appropriate, these topics should be discussed directly and openly.

Patients with heart failure must understand the serious implications of this diagnosis. Patients must be provided with accurate information in order to make decisions and plans for the future (see subsequent section on discussion of prognosis). At the same time, it is important to maintain hope and morale. Psychological factors may be more important to patients' quality of life and social functioning than the degree of physiologic impairment.[122,123] Clinical nurse specialists, educators, family members, other caregivers, and qualified local support groups can all play an important role in optimizing patients' functioning and quality of life.

We approach the general education and counseling about heart failure in a staged manner. As mentioned above, patients are often unable to absorb all the necessary information at one time. Our first education discussion with the patient (and his or her family, if possible) occurs once the acute situation has stabilized. If the patient is referred as an outpatient, we try to incorporate this discussion into the initial visit. Our goal in this first stage is to convey in simple terms the basic pathophysiology of the patient's condition. We have found that a patient is often very apprehensive when he or she hears the term "heart failure" and feel it is important to explain that the heart is not about to stop completely. During this initial discussion, we talk to the patient about the importance of strictly following our instructions regarding medication and diet, and promise to explain in more detail why this is so important during a later discussion. Finally, we try to alert the patient and his or her family to the signs and symptoms they should be alert for that can signal increasing heart failure. At this initial point, we simply ask them to call us if they notice any of these symptoms.

On subsequent visits, each of these three areas—the nature of heart failure, medical therapy, and diet—is fleshed out in increasing detail. Additional counseling regarding exercise, prognosis, and issues of health maintenance is also covered during subsequent sessions. After discussing the nature of heart failure in terms appropriate to the education level of the patient, we have a conversation concerning the actions of the patient's medications. While the nuances of the medications may not be understood, it is extremely important that the patient understand the importance of taking his or her medications as directed. Understanding the role of each medication is often helpful to the patient in this regard. It is also important for the patient to understand that many over-the-counter medications (such as nonsteroidal anti-inflammatory agents) can be extremely harmful to patients with heart failure. Our second area of emphasis is on diet. Specific recommendations are discussed below, but the patient needs to understand that dietary changes are as essential to managing his or her illness as are medications. Finally, we discuss with the patient techniques to monitor the progression of their illness and to assist in its management. This conversation is customized depending on the education level and compliance of the patient and their family. The technique described by the panel involving the patient weighing themselves daily is an easy, inexpensive way for the patient to play a role in his or her own therapy. Ideally, after discharge from the hospital or their first clinic visit, the patient should use the scale at home and use that weight as a baseline. Assuming that increased diuresis is a goal, then the pa-

(Continued)

(Continued from previous page)

tient should be told to expect weight loss and be given a target weight. Once the practitioner identifies an ideal weight—that is a weight where the patient's congestive symptoms are well controlled without dehydration—the patient should be given instructions on how to defend that weight. For many patients this may involve the use of a sliding-scale diuretic regimen based on trends in their weight at home. If the patient is on maximal doses of loop diuretics, then supplemental doses of a thiazide (usually metolazone) are useful. Alternatively, the patient may be able to alternate between once-a-day and twice-a-day dosing of a loop diuretic to achieve the desired goal.

We have found that by making patients active participants in their disease, they are more likely to be compliant with their medications, are more likely to call early in the event of a problem, and are more likely to notice how dietary factors affect their heart failure.

Activity Recommendations

Regular exercise such as walking or cycling should be encouraged for all patients with stable NYHA Class I–III heart failure.[a] (Strength of Evidence = B.)

Since the publication of these guidelines, several additional studies have been published regarding the effects of exercise training in heart failure.[124–126] An excellent review on this topic was published by McKelvie et al. in the Journal of the American College of Cardiology.[126] In addition to providing background information on the topic, these authors point out that to date there continue to be no definitive studies showing improvements in ventricular function, hospital stay, or mortality. Nevertheless, improvements in exercise tolerance and quality of life have been demonstrated and certainly constitute reasonable goals in this severely debilitated population. We routinely recommend exercise to the majority of our heart failure patients except those in an acute decompensation, immediately postinfarction, or who are severely symptomatic at rest.

---

[a]The NYHA classification is a four-level scheme for grading the functional incapacity of patients with cardiac disease. NYHA levels can be described as follows: I—Cardiac disease without resulting limitations of physical activity; II—Slight limitation of physical activity—comfortable at rest, but ordinary physical activity results in fatigue, palpitation, dyspnea, or anginal pain; III—Marked limitation in physical activity—comfortable at rest, but less than ordinary physical activity causes fatigue, palpitation, dyspnea, or anginal pain; IV—Inability to carry on any physical activity without discomfort or symptoms at rest. Although criticized for a lack of reliability, this system is still widely used.

There is insufficient evidence at this time to recommend the routine use of supervised rehabilitation programs for patients with heart failure, although such programs may be of benefit to patients who are anxious; are dyspneic at a low work level; or have angina, a recent MI, or a recent CABG. (Strength of Evidence = C.)

Until the past few years, reduced activities and bed rest were considered a standard part of the care of patients with heart failure.[127] Although this practice may promote diuresis in the short term, it may also carry important risks and have a long-term detrimental effect on physical functioning.[128] Even short periods of bed rest result in reduced exercise tolerance and aerobic capacity[129–131] as well as muscular atrophy and weakness.[130,132] Recent studies show that patients with heart failure can exercise safely, and regular exercise may improve functional status and decrease symptoms.[133–137] Neurohormonal activation is also diminished by a regular home exercise program.[138] Moreover, there is no evidence that exercise negatively affects the natural history of heart failure, with the possible exception of patients with acute myocarditis or a recent MI, who may be harmed by exercise.[139,140]

The clinical improvement that occurs with exercise training programs probably results from effects on skeletal muscle rather than changes in myocardial function.[137,141–143] Lactate production at submaximal exercise levels is reduced after training. Bicycle ergometry and arm ergometry have both been used for training programs, and Coats et al. have shown improvements with an unsupervised home cycling program.[133] There is insufficient evidence to recommend a specific type of training program or the routine use of supervised rehabilitation programs. However, such programs may benefit patients who are anxious about exercising; are dyspneic at a low work level; or have stable angina, a recent MI, or a recent CABG. In addition, supervised rehabilitation programs can provide patient and family counseling, regular encouragement and interpersonal contact, and assistance with facilitating patient compliance with treatment recommendations.

Encouraging exercise in patients with heart failure can be very challenging. Patients may initially feel worse while exercising or immediately afterwards. Likewise, their families may actively encourage them to take it easy and not overexert. Even many practicing physicians will advise heart failure patients to avoid exercise, despite the data outlined in this section. These negative influences can be overcome by informing the patient of the goals of exercise and of realistic expectations as to progress. A major stumbling block for many patients is lack of access to an exercise facility or rehabilitation program. We do not routinely recommend formal rehabilitation programs for our heart failure patients, in part because of the difficulty in reimbursement of these services. Rather, we structure our program around

(Continued)

(Continued from previous page)

walking. Walking requires no special equipment, coordination, or facility and progress is easily monitored in time and distance. In the event of inclement weather, many shopping malls and local school gymnasia are excellent places to walk while in a controlled environment. We initially encourage patients to walk three to four times a week for a minimum of twenty minutes at a time and pace that allows them to finish their walk feeling just slightly winded. A good goal to set for patients who are on a stable medical regimen is to double the distance walked in a period of three to four weeks. It is important to emphasize that activities of daily living, while sometimes modestly strenuous, do not substitute for regular exercise. Such activities are often stop-and-start in nature, and are unlikely to provide the type of aerobic benefit that sustained exercise provides. We do encourage patients to avoid extremely strenuous exercise or exercise occurring in intense bouts such as weight-lifting. An exercise program can begin as soon as the practitioner decides that the patient is unlikely to have active ischemia and is on a good medical regimen.

Dietary Recommendations

Dietary sodium should be restricted to as close to 2 grams per day as possible. In no case should sodium intake exceed 3 grams daily. (Strength of Evidence = C.)

Alcohol use should be discouraged. Patients who drink alcohol should be advised to consume no more than one drink per day. (Strength of Evidence = C.)

Patients with heart failure should be advised to avoid excessive fluid intake. However, fluid restriction is not advisable unless patients develop hyponatremia. (Strength of Evidence = C.)

Although a reduced-sodium diet has been a mainstay in managing heart failure, no studies have evaluated a specific dietary sodium restriction.[145–152] Thus, it is not clear from the literature whether mild sodium restriction (3 grams per day) is adequate for most patients or whether moderate restriction (2 grams per day) is beneficial. A 2-gram sodium diet is unpalatable for most patients, and the cost of low-sodium foods can be a burden for some patients.[149] This may lead to noncompliance, which is a major factor precipitating hospital admission for heart failure (see below). However, if dietary salt intake is excessive, diuretic dosing may be complicated or excessive, and potassium wasting may be exacerbated.[153]

A 3-gram sodium diet may be a reasonable and realistic target for patients with mild-to-moderate heart failure. This level of sodium intake can be achieved fairly easily by not adding salt to foods and avoiding salty foods.[151] However, many elderly patients may find even a 3-gram sodium diet unpalatable. Counseling and flexibility may be needed to promote compliance and to ensure that patients do not become malnourished. Patients who require high doses of diuretics will need to reduce their daily sodium intake to 2 grams or less. Avoiding processed foods and milk products (e.g., cheese) can reduce daily sodium intake to as little as 1 gram.[145]

All heart failure patients should receive specific dietary guidelines. Referral to a dietician, clinical nurse specialist, or nurse practitioner for dietary education and counseling is recommended. Handouts and educational guides are often inadequate for patients with reading difficulties and patients from ethnic groups with different food preferences. In all cases, it is essential to involve the spouse and family in educational efforts concerning the importance of diet and salt restrictions. In some cases, family recipes and menus may need to be altered in order to facilitate compliance with salt restrictions.

Acute ingestion of alcohol depresses myocardial contractility in patients with known cardiac disease.[154,155] This may be clinically significant in patients with heart failure, although there are no studies that address this issue. Complete abstention from alcohol is crucial for patients with alcohol-induced cardiomyopathy.[116–118] For patients without a history of alcoholism, it is unclear whether abstinence makes a difference in functional status or mortality. In general, alcohol use should be discouraged. If patients want to continue to drink, they should be strongly advised to have no more than one drink per day. One drink equals a glass of beer or wine, or a mixed drink or cocktail containing no more than 1 ounce of alcohol.

Other dietary restrictions should be discouraged unless clearly indicated (e.g., a low-fat, low-cholesterol diet for severe hypercholesterolemia). Many patients with severe heart failure suffer from a syndrome of chronic wasting, referred to as "cardiac cachexia," that may be exacerbated by unnecessary dietary restrictions. Vitamin supplementation may be advisable because of water-soluble vitamin loss associated with diuresis and problems with gastrointestinal absorption of fat-soluble vitamins.

As noted, a simple and practical starting point in dietary management is the elimination of table salt from the patient's diet. While other dietary modifications may be prudent for some heart failure patients, few patients are able to stick to a dramatically altered diet. Elimination of added salt is an important first step. Once the patient is able to tolerate the lack of added salt, attempts at further reducing salt intake should be directed at the avoidance of canned or prepared foods. The need to increase the dose of diuretics required to maintain stability should prompt a review of the patient's sodium intake and, if necessary, further levels of restriction. Patients should be encouraged to try various alternative spices for seasoning, but to be cautious of salt substitutes. These are often based on potassium chloride and can create great difficulties in maintaining the patient's potassium homeostasis.

(Continued)

(Continued from previous page)

The importance of involving the patient's family in dietary discussions cannot be overemphasized. Regardless of the role the patient plays in the family, dietary alterations will likely affect all members. The support (and monitoring) of other family members is critical to success.

Finally, the panel mentions briefly that fluid restriction should be used only when patients become hyponatremic. We concur with this recommendation. However, it is equally important to inform patients not to increase their baseline fluid intake. It is a surprisingly common occurrence that patients grow to believe that by drinking more, their diuretic works better. One pharmacy in our area even labels furosemide prescriptions with a notation to "take with plenty of fluids." Explaining to patients why their condition makes them feel thirsty is helpful. When a fluid restriction is required, we find the following technique to be practical and useful. Ask the patient to get a 2 liter plastic softdrink bottle. Have him or her make a mark on the bottle appropriate for the desired level of fluid restriction. At the beginning of the day, the patient should fill the bottle with water to the mark and place it in the refrigerator. If the patient wants a drink of water, he or she should take it from the bottle. If the patient wants to drink something else, he or she should pour the same amount from the bottle. This technique, while not perfect, provides a simple visual guide throughout the day.

Discussion of Prognosis

Patient counseling with respect to prognosis should be guided by recent trials[12,21,22,156] and the Framingham experience,[157] which indicate that the average annual mortality rate for patients with heart failure is approximately 10 percent per year. For patient subgroups, the following estimates of mortality rates per year can be made: NYHA Class II, 5–10 percent; NYHA Class III, 10–20 percent; NYHA Class IV, 20–50 percent.

These studies may overestimate the mortality rates for the general population of patients with heart failure. In a recent study from the Mayo Clinic, it was found that the heart failure patients from a population-based cohort had a lower mortality rate than patients who were followed at the Mayo Clinic, suggesting a referral bias.[158] The population-based cohort with EFs less than 35 percent had a mortality rate of approximately 5 percent per year.

Within each NYHA class, the presence of more severe symptoms, progressive symptoms, or accompanying angina would push these estimates to the higher end of the range; conversely, milder symptoms, clinical stability, and absence of angina would shift the estimate to the lower end. As many as half of all cardiac deaths are sudden, and up to 25 percent of all deaths occur without significant worsening of heart failure.[12,21,158]

It is vital that patients receive accurate information concerning prognosis in order to make decisions and plans for the future. Practitioners should discuss

patients' desires regarding resuscitation, and all patients should be encouraged to complete a durable power of attorney for health care or another form of advance directive.

If a patient desires resuscitation, family members should consider the learning cardiopulmonary resuscitation. Such a course should be combined with psychosocial support for patients and family members because it may otherwise have negative psychological consequences. If a patient decides that resuscitation is not desired, it is crucial to discuss with family members or caretakers what to do in the event of sudden death. If paramedics are called, a chain of events is likely to take place that may be difficult to control and contrary to the patient's wishes. A call to 911 is often a reflex response to a loved one's death. Instead, when resuscitation is not desired, family members or other caregivers should be instructed to call a doctor, nurse, hospice worker, or other designated responsible individual.

Discussions of prognosis are perhaps the most difficult of all. Certainly, given the gravity of heart failure from systolic dysfunction, they are appropriate. We strongly feel that a patient's principal practitioner should hold this conversation as soon as is practical. The goal should be to present a realistic overview of potential outcomes of the patient's illness including progressive heart failure, sudden cardiac death, or stabilization for an indefinite period of time. We agree that discussions of advance directives are appropriate, though they should be presented in such a way as to not make the patient feel that mortality is imminent unless the practitioner believes that. Because sudden cardiac death is potentially survivable with a return to the patient's previous baseline, we do encourage family members to learn cardiopulmonary resuscitation.

The Problem of Noncompliance

Because noncompliance is a major cause of morbidity and unnecessary hospital admissions in heart failure, the use of educational programs or support groups should be a routine part of the care of patients with heart failure. Noncompliance may reduce life expectancy and is also a major cause of hospitalizations. Practitioners should be attuned to the problem of noncompliance and its causes and should discuss the importance of compliance at followup visits and assist patients in removing barriers to compliance (e.g., cost, side effects, or complexity of the medical treatment regimen). (Strength of Evidence = B.)

Noncompliance is an important problem with any chronic disease, and heart failure is no exception.[80,160] Noncompliance may reduce life expectancy (e.g., when patients fail to take beneficial medications) and may also be a major cause of hospitalizations. Ghali et al. found a 54 percent rate of noncompliance with diet or medications, and noncompliance was the most common factor precipitating readmission.[160] Vinson et al. found that 27 percent of 140 patients hospitalized for heart failure were rehospitalized within 90 days of discharge and 27 percent were rehospitalized at least once for recurrent heart failure.[80] Twenty-two separate admissions were subjectively judged to have resulted from medication or dietary noncompliance. Readmissions for heart failure could be substantially reduced if compliance were improved.

Although it is clear that noncompliance is a major problem in caring for patients with heart failure, it is less clear what should be done to improve this situation. Rosenberg evaluated the impact of a coordinated team approach to planning education, and supervision on dietary compliance and readmission rates.[82] Patient-directed group meetings were at the core of the program. Dietary compliance was improved, and hospital admissions were reduced from 46 to 12 percent compared with the previous year and from 31 to 17 percent compared with a control group of patients at another hospital. These results are very encouraging because group programs can provide a more cost-effective intervention than one-on-one teaching. The group process may have other therapeutic aspects besides its educational component. Meta-analyses of educational programs for other chronic diseases also support their value in improving compliance and outcomes.[161,162] Educational programs or qualified local support groups should be a routine part of the treatment and care of patients with heart failure. Physicians and other practitioners should be aware of the problem of noncompliance and its causes and should reinforce the importance of compliance at routine visits. In addition, although not tested in heart failure patients, effective interventions to promote compliance in hypertensives and patients with coronary artery disease have included family involvement in care and the use of patient contracts. Similar techniques may prove effective in the context of heart failure.

To incorporate all of the suggestions made in this chapter requires a serious commitment of time. While suggestions to include dieticians and clinical nurse specialists in the education and counseling process are certainly one way to reduce the time requirements on the individual practitioner, access to such resources is often limited. We feel that the intense education and counseling that should ideally be provided to heart failure patients may be an excellent indication for early referral to a heart failure center. Such referrals provide an excellent opportunity for practitioners to work cooperatively in providing care for this complex and ill population. In any case, we have found that time spent on patient education pays large dividends in patient satisfaction. This combined with the available data on improved morbidity and lower rates of hospital admission makes the effort worthwhile.

6

Pharmacological Management

Commentary by G. William Dec, Jr., M.D.

Initial Pharmacological Management

Diuretic Therapy

Patients with heart failure and signs of significant volume overload should be started immediately on a diuretic. Patients with mild volume overload can be managed adequately on thiazide diuretics, whereas those with more severe volume overload should be started on a loop diuretic. (Strength of Evidence = C.)

Physical examination and chest x-ray findings are quite useful in diagnosing acute heart failure but become less reliable when chronic heart failure exists. For instance, the enhanced lymphatic drainage associated with chronic elevation in left-sided filling pressures frequently results in the absence of pulmonary rales on physical examination and only mild pulmonary venous redistribution on chest film despite pulmonary capillary wedge pressures in excess of 20 mmHg. Likewise, a third heart sound is often absent despite severe impairment in systolic function during periods of clinical compensation. The finding of rales, a third heart sound, jugular venous distention, or interstitial pulmonary edema on chest film establishes the diagnosis when present, but their absence should not exclude consideration of heart failure as a potential diagnosis.

Symptoms of volume overload include orthopnea, paroxysmal nocturnal dyspnea, and dyspnea on exertion; signs include pulmonary rales, a third heart sound, jugular venous distention, hepatic engorgement, ascites, peripheral edema, and pulmonary vascular congestion or pulmonary edema on chest x-ray. There are few studies of optimal diuretic therapy for heart failure. Patients with mild heart failure can usually be managed adequately on thiazide diuretics.[163,164] Moreover, some patients prefer a thiazide diuretic over furosemide, probably because it causes less acute diuresis than furosemide.[163] If a patient has severe volume overload at the time of presentation, severe renal insufficiency (estimated creatinine clearance <30 mL/min), or persistent edema despite thiazide diuretics, a loop diuretic should be used instead of a thiazide. Treatment of mild heart failure with ACE inhibitors alone is discussed in the next section.

Diuretic dosing is summarized in Table 6. Proper dosing depends on the patient's size, age, renal function, compliance with dietary sodium restriction, and the amount of edema. Hydrochlorothiazide should generally be given in doses of 25–50 mg per day. Patients who have persistent volume overload on 50 mg of hydrochlorothiazide per day or the equivalent should be changed to a loop diuretic. Furosemide should be started at 20–40 mg once daily. Elderly patients may be started on 10 mg per day initially. In elderly patients with urinary incontinence or urgency, guidance should be provided concerning the timing of diuretic administration (especially loop diuretics) in relation to the patient's activities to minimize noncompliance and prevent patients from isolating themselves from society.

Patients with pulmonary edema or with marked volume overload (e.g., anasarca) should be given intravenous furosemide initially.

> During periods of decompensated right-sided heart failure, increased edema of the bowel wall frequently leads to inadequate oral absorption of diuretics. Such patients obtain almost immediate benefit from intravenous loop diuretics to break the vicious cycle of progressive volume overload and promote prompt diuresis.

Diuretics should then be titrated to achieve resolution or improvement of signs and symptoms of volume overload. There is no standard target dose. Occasionally, a patient with mild heart failure may require a diuretic on alternating days or as needed.

Note: Figure 5 shows the content and organization of this chapter.

For patients with asymptomatic left-ventricular dysfunction or very mild heart failure symptoms, diuretics should be avoided whenever possible. These agents frequently lead to electrolyte disturbances and may promote the development of ventricular arrhythmias. In addition, diuretics have been shown to further activate the renin-angiotensin-aldosterone axis and may ultimately produce detrimental effects on long-term survival. The optimum treatment strategy should utilize as little diuretic as possible to control congestive symptoms secondary to volume overload. Following a period of clinical stability and optimization of ACE inhibitor therapy, a subgroup of patients may be successfully withdrawn from diuretic therapy without clinical deterioration.[168]

It is generally better to give hydrochlorothiazide or furosemide as a single daily dose in the outpatient setting. If the initial oral dose is inadequate, more diuresis will usually be obtained by doubling the dose rather than by giving the same dose twice daily. At high doses, furosemide can be given twice daily, but it should usually not be given more frequently.

A flexible diuretic program is often useful in patients who require large doses of furosemide.[166] Administration of two or even three synergistic diuretics is often more effective then continued escalation of furosemide or bumetanide alone. Agents that act at the proximal or distal renal tubules are most effective in potentiating the effects of a loop diuretic.

Inpatients with severe volume overload may require more frequent intravenous doses to obtain the desired brisk diuresis. Doses of furosemide as high as 240 mg twice per day may be required in the most refractory patients, but doses over about 160 mg per day usually require additional efforts to improve diuresis (discussed subsequently). It is very important to avoid excessive diuresis before starting ACE inhibitors. Volume depletion may lead to hypotension or renal insufficiency when ACE inhibitors are started. The ACE inhibitor may facilitate diuresis in some patients. In general, the dose of diuretic may be increased in parallel with the ACE inhibitor, but it is important to avoid excessive diuresis that could prevent titrating the ACE inhibitor to full therapeutic levels.

Potassium depletion commonly occurs when patients are treated chronically with diuretics. However, ACE inhibitors decrease renal potassium losses and raise serum potassium levels, so many patients with heart failure who are treated with

Table 6.   Medications Commonly Used for Heart Failure

Drug	Initial Dose (mg)	Target Dose (mg)
Thiazide Diuretics		
Hydrochlorothiazide	25 QD	As needed
Chlorthalidone	25 QD	As needed
Loop Diuretics		
Furosemide	10–40 QD	As needed
Burnetanide	0.5–1.0 QD	As needed
Torsemide	5 QD	As needed
Ethacrynic acid	50 QD	As needed
Thiazide-Related Diuretic		
Metolazone	2.5a	As needed
Potassium-Sparing Diuretics		
Spironolactone	25 QD	As needed
Triamterene	50 QD	As needed
Arniloride	5 QD	As needed
ACE Inhibitors		
Enalapril	2.5 BID	10 BID
Captopril	6.25–12.5 TID	50 TID
Lisinopril	5 QD	20 QD
Quinapril	5 BID	20 BID
Digoxin	See text	See text
Hydralazine	10–25 TID	75 TID
Isosorbide Dinitrate	10 TID	40 TID

aGiven as a single test dose initially.

Recommended Maximal Dose (mg)	Major Adverse Reactions
50 QD 50 QD	Postural hypotension, hypokalemia, hyperglycemia, hyperuricemia, rash. Rare severe reaction includes pancreatitis, bone marrow suppression, and anaphylaxis.
240 BID 10 QD 20 QD 200 BID	Same as thiazide diuretics.
10 QD	Same as thiazide diuretics.
100 BID 100 BID 40 QD	Hyperkalemia, especially if administered with ACE inhibitor; rash; gynecomastia (spironolactone only).
20 BID 100 TID 40 QD 20 BID	Hypotension, hyperkalemia, renal insufficiency, cough, skin rash, angioedema, neutropenia.
See text 100 TID 80 TID	Cardiotoxicity, confusion, nausea, anorexia, visual disturbances. Headache, nausea, dizziness, tachycardia, lupus-like syndrome. Headache, hypotension, flushing.

Note: ACE = angiotensin-converting enzyme, BID = twice a day, QD = once a day, TID = three times a day.

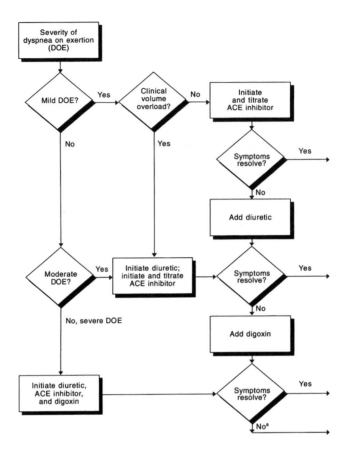

^a Obtain cardiology consult if not already done.
^b Beta blockers and calcium-channel blockers may also be effective but should be considered investigational.

Figure 5.   Pharmacological Management of Patients With Heart Failure

aObtain cardiology consult if not already done.

bBeta blockers and calcium-channel blockers may also be effective but should be considered investigational.

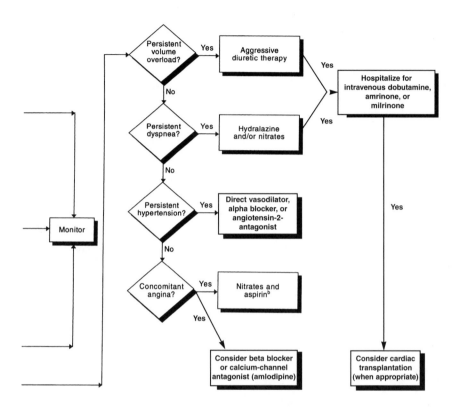

both agents may not develop potassium depletion. All patients should have their serum potassium levels checked frequently (e.g., every 3 days until stable) during initiation, titration, or modification of diuretic or ACE inhibitor therapy and every few months thereafter.

> The frequency with which serum electrolytes and renal function should be checked is dependent upon the strength of the diuretics prescribed, the amount of diuresis needed, the type of agents chosen, and existing renal function. Laboratory studies once or twice per week are usually sufficient in the majority of patients rather than every three days as suggested in the guideline.

Note, however, that serum potassium can be an unreliable indicator of total body potassium stores; patients with normal serum potassium levels can have low total body potassium stores.[165,167] Thus, patients who have a serum potassium less than 4.0 mEq/L should be given a potassium-sparing agent or oral potassium supplementation.

Potassium-sparing diuretics may be more effective than oral potassium supplements at maintaining total body potassium stores.[167] When an ACE inhibitor is used together with a potassium-sparing agent or potassium supplements, the serum potassium level must be followed closely (e.g., every 3 days until stable).

> A potassium-sparing diuretic (spirolactone or amiloride) is often useful in promoting diuresis as a second agent. This strategy is frequently more effective than further increasing the dose of loop diuretic and decreases the risk of further potassium wasting. The role of aldactone is currently being re-examined, since this agent may have beneficial effects beyond those related to diuresis and potassium sparing. Aldactone has been recently shown to improve myocardial remodeling in experimental heart failure models. The Randomized Aldactone Study (RALES) is currently examining the role of aldactone on long-term survival in patients with advanced heart failure.[168]

Diuretics can also cause magnesium depletion, which often accompanies potassium depletion. If high doses of diuretics are used, magnesium levels should be followed and oral supplementation given when necessary. Hypocalcemia may be a useful clue to possible significant hypomagnesemia.

ACE Inhibitors

Patients with heart failure due to left-ventricular systolic dysfunction should be given a trial of ACE inhibitors unless specific contraindications exist: (1) history of intolerance or adverse reactions to these agents, (2) serum potassium greater than 5.5 mEq/L that cannot be reduced, or (3) symptomatic hypotension (see below). Patients with systolic blood pressures less than 90 mmHg have a higher risk of complications and should be managed by a physician experienced in utilizing ACE inhibitors in such patients. (Strength of Evidence = A.) Caution and close monitoring are also required for patients who have a serum creatinine greater than 3.0 mg/dL or an estimated creatinine clearance of less than 30 mL/min; half the usual dose should be used in this setting. (Strength of Evidence = B.)

Although there are no studies on patterns of ACE inhibitor usage in medical practice, the panel concurs with Cody's conclusion that vasodilators are under used in heart failure because of clinicians' concerns regarding excessive blood pressure reduction.[169]

Although a variety of vasodilators is currently available including smooth muscle relaxants (e.g., hydralazine and isosorbide dinitrate), alpha-adrenergic blockers, angiotensin-2 receptor antagonists, and ACE inhibitors, data on the efficacy of ACE inhibitor therapy are quite convincing and indicate that this class of drug is the preferred treatment for symptomatic heart failure whenever possible. Despite their acknowledged benefits, studies indicate that only about 50 percent of all symptomatic heart failure patients are currently receiving ACE inhibitor therapy. Although this percentage has steadily increased during the past decade, a large segment of the heart failure population remains undertreated for their disease. Concern is often greatest about initiating ACE inhibitor therapy in the elderly. Yet, this is the population in whom heart failure is most prevalent and, therefore, includes the largest number of patients who may potentially benefit from such treatment. It is well recognized that the risk of orthostatic hypotension is increased in elderly patients, so ACE inhibitors need to be titrated upward slowly and blood pressure should be frequently assessed either at home or in the office setting.

ACE inhibitors may be considered as sole therapy in the subset of heart failure patients who present with fatigue or mild dyspnea on exertion and who do not have any other signs or symptoms of volume overload. Diuretics should be added if these symptoms persist. (Strength of Evidence = C.)

Most patients with heart failure have some degree of volume overload and therefore require a diuretic. However, some patients have no evidence of volume overload and present with fatigue or mild dyspnea on exertion. This population seems to fall in between the group with asymptomatic left-ventricular dysfunction (many of whom actually have poor exercise tolerance on careful questioning or exercise testing) and those patients with clinically evident heart failure. There are no data to guide appropriate care of these patients. Because ACE inhibitors should be used in all patients with left-ventricular dysfunction, regardless of symptoms, it is reasonable to start an ACE inhibitor in patients with very mild symptoms and determine whether the symptoms resolve. If symptoms do not totally resolve after the target dose of ACE inhibitor is reached, diuretics should be added.

The role of ACE inhibitor therapy in asymptomatic or minimally symptomatic heart failure patients will be briefly summarized. Two populations have been examined: patients in whom depressed left-ventricular function is detected during routine evaluation (such as the SOLVD Prevention Trial population) and asymptomatic post-MI trial populations. In the SOLVD Prevention Trial, 83 percent of the population had ischemic heart disease as the etiology for their chronic heart failure. In this study, enalapril reduced cardiovascular mortality by 12 percent ($p = 0.12$) and significantly lowered the number of hospitalizations for new-onset heart failure during a 36-month followup.[19] Chronic ACE inhibitor therapy in this population has also been shown to slow or reverse left-ventricular dilatation in asymptomatic left-ventricular dysfunction.[170] Post-MI trials (including SAVE, AIRE, SMILE, GISSI-3 and ISIS-4) have demonstrated a 10–27 percent reduction in all-cause mortality and a 20–50 percent reduction in the risk of developing symptomatic heart failure.[18,171,172] The goals of such post MI treatment include prevention of abnormal ventricular dilatation and remodeling, reduction in the development of symptomatic heart failure, lowering of heart failure hospitalizations, and improvement in long-term survival. Administration of intravenous ACE inhibitors such as enalapril during the early phases of acute MI offers no survival advantage and may be detrimental as shown by the CONSENSUS II Trial.[37] However, oral ACE inhibitor therapy appears both safe and beneficial when initiated within 24 hours of acute MI. Beneficial effects of post MI ACE inhibitor therapy are evident in patients who have received thrombolytic therapy, aspirin, or beta-blocker treatment.[173] The optimum duration of ACE inhibitor therapy following MI is uncertain. In the SMILE study, zofenopril administered for only 6 weeks reduced 12-month mortality by 29 percent suggesting that long-term therapy may not always be necessary.[172] Oral ACE inhibitors appear most beneficial in patients when left-ventricular EF is reduced below 40 percent.[173] There is no convincing evidence that one agent is superior to any other ACE inhibitor.

Benefits of ACE Inhibitors. The ACE inhibitor enalapril has been shown to reduce mortality in patients with moderate[21] and severe[12] heart failure; moreover, enalapril has been shown to reduce mortality more than the combination of isosorbide dinitrate and hydralazine.[22] In the CONSENSUS trial, which studied only patients with NYHA Class IV heart failure, 1-year mortality was reduced from 52 percent with placebo to 36 percent with enalapril.[12] The degree of benefit is more modest in the general heart failure population. The SOLVD treatment trial found that enalapril reduced overall 4-year mortality from 40 percent to 35 percent.[21] The survival curves indicate that median survival in patients receiving enalapril was increased by approximately 6 months. The effect of captopril on mortality in patients with clinically evident heart failure has not been studied.

> Captopril has also been shown to reduce long-term mortality in mild heart failure patients (the Munich Mild Heart Failure Trial).[174]

Enalapril and captopril enhance functional status in patients with heart failure, with 40–80 percent of patients showing an improvement in NYHA class.[12,21,175–183] Although some patients may improve more than one functional class, the average improvement is 0.5–1 functional class. Beneficial effects on physical functioning have also been reported with other ACE inhibitors.[184–187]

> Results of the Captopril-Digoxin Trial and other control trials indicate that beneficial effects of ACE inhibitor treatment are not immediate but require 6–12 weeks before symptomatic improvement and enhanced exercise capacity can be demonstrated. It is important to advise patients of this "lag time" so that they do not inappropriately discontinue treatment prematurely.

The SOLVD treatment trial also found that enalapril decreased the number of patients hospitalized over the study period from 74 to 69 percent and the number of patients hospitalized for cardiovascular reasons from 63 to 57 percent.[21] The total number of hospitalizations was also decreased by 15 percent. The beneficial effects of ACE inhibitors in the prevention of heart failure in patients with reduced left-ventricular performance have been discussed earlier in this document.

Side Effects of ACE Inhibitors and Contraindications. Side effects of ACE inhibitors, particularly decreases in blood pressure and increases in serum creatinine and potassium, have been emphasized in many studies.[188–198] These concerns may have made some physicians reluctant to use ACE inhibitors. However, the average changes in blood pressure and serum chemistries in the SOLVD trial were actually quite small, with systolic blood pressure decreasing an average of 5 mmHg, diastolic blood pressure decreasing 4 mmHg, creatine increasing 0.1 mg/dL, and potassium increasing 0.2 mEq/L.[21] Only 2.2 percent of those eligible had symptomatic hypotension when enalapril was initiated. Even in the CONSENSUS trial, which enrolled only patients with NYHA Class IV heart failure, only 5.5 percent of those treated with enalapril were withdrawn because of symptomatic hypotension, and there was only a 1.5 percent increase in withdrawals due to renal insufficiency compared with patients receiving placebo.[12]

Thus, relatively low blood pressure, moderate renal insufficiency, and mild hyperkalemia are not contraindications to ACE inhibitors. If serum creatine is 3.0 mg/dL or greater, ACE inhibitors should be used with caution and titrated upward slowly, as tolerated, to a maximum of half the usual maintenance dose.

> Patients with heart failure secondary to ischemic heart disease often have widespread atherosclerotic disease. Renal artery stenosis is not uncommon in this population. Many patients with difficult to manage hypertension and chronic renal dysfunction may benefit from further evaluation of renal perfusion. If renal artery stenosis is detected, angioplasty may not only improve renal function and lower blood pressure but may also permit cautious introduction of ACE inhibitor therapy.

The risks and benefits in these latter patients are not known because they were excluded from major trials. Patients with lesser degrees of renal insufficiency also require close followup and reduction in doses if the glomerular filtration rate is less than 30 mL/min. A serum potassium of 5.5 mEq/L or greater is considered by most panelists to be a contraindication to ACE inhibitor therapy unless the serum potassium can be reduced.

Potassium-sparing diuretics (e.g., spironolactone, amiloride, triamterene) should be stopped in all patients who are being started on ACE inhibitors, regardless of the serum potassium.

> This advice applies to outpatients initiating ACE inhibitor therapy. Hospitalized patients are often continued on potassium-sparing diuretics provided that the dose is either lowered or serum potassium frequently checked.

These agents may be restarted if the patient remains hypokalemic on full therapeutic doses of ACE inhibitors Potassium supplements should usually also be withheld unless the patient has a low serum potassium (<4.0 mEq/L). If potassium supplements are continued, serum potassium levels must be followed closely (i.e., every few days until stable).

Patients with low blood pressure must also be carefully monitored, but therapy should be continued. The panel agreed with Cody, who has argued that, in the absence of orthostatic hypotension, a systolic blood pressure of 90 mmHg is perfectly acceptable.[169]

Many patients with Class III or IV heart failure symptoms will tolerate systolic blood pressure values of greater than 80 mmHg rather than 90 mmHg as indicated in the text. Close attention is needed for orthostatic symptoms, evidence of renal hypoperfusion based upon worsening blood urea nitrogen or creatinine concentration, or worsening of fatigue. Use of a short-acting ACE inhibitor such as captopril may be especially useful in patients with marginal blood pressure (<95 mmHg) to prevent sustained hypotensive effects. Although less convenient, short-acting agents may produce less deterioration in renal function.[199]

Some patients with heart failure will feel best with a blood pressure below 90 mmHg. If a physician is uncomfortable starting therapy in the setting of low blood pressure, he or she should refer the patient to someone with expertise in treating heart failure rather than abandon attempts to use ACE inhibitors or other vasodilators.

Cough is common in patients taking ACE inhibitors, but it is also common in patients with heart failure. In the SOLVD treatment trial, 37 percent of patients receiving enalapril reported cough, compared with 31 percent of those receiving placebo.[21] Cohn et al. reported similar figures, but only 1 percent of patients receiving enalapril and 1 percent of those receiving isosorbide dinitrate and hydralazine stopped the study medication because of cough.[22] Thus, patients who report cough while taking ACE inhibitors should be evaluated to see whether this results from pulmonary congestion before considering discontinuing ACE inhibitors. For most patients, the cough is a nuisance that they are willing to tolerate in exchange for the benefits of the medication. Dizziness and angioedema also occur, but these symptoms are usually mild and do not require discontinuation of the drug. Angioedema of the oropharyngeal region is an absolute contraindication to further use of an ACE inhibitor.

The ACE inhibitor-induced cough can often be adequately suppressed with medications. Reasonable control of nocturnal cough is essential in patients with advanced heart failure symptoms since many also suffer from sleep disorders such as sleep apnea. Patients who experience paroxysmal coughing on one agent are just as likely to experience this side effect with any other ACE inhibitors since it results from drug activation within the pulmonary bed.

Initiating Therapy With ACE Inhibitors. In the opinion of the Heart Failure Guideline Panel, all ACE inhibitors are likely to be effective in treating heart failure; no particular agent is recommended over another. ACE inhibitors other than enalapril and captopril (e.g., lisinopril, quinipril) are available and have been shown to improve exercise tolerance.[184–187,200] However, there are no data available on whether these other agents reduce mortality or what dose might be required to do so. Note that enalapril is the only ACE inhibitor shown to affect mortality in patients with clinically evident heart failure.

Recent long-term data from the Munich Mild Heart Failure Trial demonstrates that captopril can also decrease mortality in chronic heart failure patients.[174] The extensive body of medical data suggests that the beneficial effects associated with chronic ACE inhibition are related to the class of drug rather than any particular agent.

After diuretic therapy is initiated in patients with clinical volume overload, and left-ventricular systolic dysfunction is confirmed as the cause of the patient's symptoms, an ACE inhibitor should be added. Patients should be assessed closely for volume depletion before therapy is initiated (orthostatic hypotension, prerenal azotemia, metabolic alkalosis), and if volume depletion is evident, diuretics should be withheld for a brief period (24–48 hours) until volume depletion resolves.

Patients who are at high risk for first-dose hypotension (severe left-ventricular systolic dysfunction, initial systolic blood pressure <100 mmHg, or serum sodium <135 mEq/L) should be given a small dose of a short-acting agent (e.g., captopril 6.25 mg) and monitored closely for 2 hours.[192] Patients over the age of 75 may also be at increased risk for hypotension and may be started on once-daily dosing initially.[195] If the test dose is tolerated, or if a test dose is unnecessary, captopril 12.5 mg TID or enalapril 2.5 mg BID can be started. Patients with hypertension can be started on captopril 25 mg TID or enalapril 5 mg BID.

Patients should be seen within 1 week of initiation of ACE inhibitor to monitor blood pressure, renal function, and serum potassium. It is appropriate to contact the patient by telephone 48 hours after an ACE inhibitor is initiated to ask about symptoms of hypotension, such as dizziness or weakness. Treatment should be modified if the patient develops (1) an increase in serum creatinine of 0.5 mg/dL or more, (2) a serum potassium of 5.5 mEq/L or higher, or (3) symptomatic hypotension. Patients who develop renal insufficiency or hypotension should have their volume status reassessed. In patients who become hypovolemic as a result of diuresis, the diuretic dose should be reduced and the ACE inhibitor tried again. Patients failing a second trial should be placed on hydralazine and isosorbide dinitrate (HYD/ISDN), as described subsequently, instead of an ACE inhibitor. If hyperkalemia develops, ACE inhibitors should not be retried, and therapy should be changed to HYD/ISDN.

Doses of ACE inhibitors should be titrated upward over 2–3 weeks with the goal of reaching the doses used in large-scale clinical trials: captopril 50 mg TID or enalapril 10 mg BID.

The optimum dosing of ACE inhibitors remains to be defined. The physiologic effects of ACE inhibition are not routinely measured nor is the dosage determined by the degree of inhibition of angiotensin-2 production. Most beneficial effects on symptoms and survival have been demonstrated at relatively high doses of these agents. Uncontrolled studies suggest fewer hospitalizations in patients receiving high- versus low-dose enalapril but no data exists on the optimum dose to enhance survival. Whether low-dose regimens (i.e., captopril 6.25 mg TID or enalapril 2.5 mg QD) are actually beneficial for those patients unable to tolerate higher doses due to hypotension or renal dysfunction remains uncertain. The ATLAS study is currently evaluating survival in patients randomized to receive long-term high- or low-dose lisinopril treatment and should help clarify this important question.

Volume status should be reassessed if hypotension or a rise in the serum creatinine of 0.5 mg/dL occurs as the dose is increased. If there is evidence of volume depletion, the dose of the ACE inhibitor should be reduced to the highest dose that was previously tolerated and the diuretic dose reduced. The dose of the ACE inhibitor should then be increased again. If higher doses are not tolerated despite euvolemia, then the lower dose should be continued or a trial of HYD/ISDN instituted.

In patients with creatinine clearances of 30 mL/min or less, ACE inhibitors should be used with caution and titrated upward slowly, as tolerated, to a maximum of half the usual maintenance dose. With judicious dosing and close followup, almost all patients can tolerate these agents. The full effect of ACE inhibitors on functional status may not be seen for several months. Patients who tolerate the preceding doses but who remain symptomatic may benefit from higher doses (e.g., enalapril 20 mg BID or captopril 100 mg TID). Maximal doses of these agents and the risks and benefits of higher doses have not been defined.

Digoxin

Digoxin can prevent clinical deterioration in patients with heart failure due to left-ventricular systolic dysfunction and improve patients' symptoms (Strength of Evidence = A). However, its effects on mortality are not clear. Digoxin should be used routinely in patients with severe heart failure and should be added to the medical regimen of patients with mild or moderate failure who remain symptomatic after optimal management with ACE inhibitors and diuretics. (Strength of Evidence = C.)

Cardiac glycosides have been used to treat heart failure for more than 200 years. Although they are clearly the drug of choice to treat heart failure patients with atrial fibrillation and a rapid ventricular response, their use in patients with sinus rhythm has been controversial. Although a number of cardiac glycosides are available, digoxin is commonly considered the preferred agent and is the only one discussed in this guideline. The recent RADIANCE trial has provided additional evidence that digoxin improves physical function and decreases symptoms in at least some (if not most) patients with heart failure (see subsequent discussion).[201] However, whether all patients with heart failure due to left-ventricular systolic dysfunction benefit from the addition of digoxin to a regimen of ACE inhibitors and diuretics is not clear. In addition, no RCT has yet been completed with sufficient numbers of patients to determine whether digoxin affects the mortality of patients with heart failure.

A large multicenter trial, sponsored by the National Institutes of Health, is currently underway to determine the effects of digoxin on mortality rate. At present, the effects of digoxin on mortality are unknown.

The Digoxin Investigation Group has yet to publish the results of their trial but a preliminary analysis has been orally presented.[202] There were 7,788 patients enrolled at 301 centers across the United States and Canada. No overall mortality benefit was seen in congestive heart failure patients on diuretics and ACE inhibitors receiving digoxin as compared to placebo. It appeared that digoxin treated patients had a statistically significant reduction in the risk of death due to heart failure. This benefit may have been offset by an increase in death probably due to myocardial infarction or arrhythmia. Digoxin treated patients, however, had a statistically significant reduction in mortality (overall or CHF) and CHF hospitalization compared with the placebo group. Further subgroup analysis is underway. It appears that digoxin at least does not increase mortality in patients with heart failure.

Many published trials of digoxin were performed in the era before the routine administration of vasolidators, and their relevance to current treatment strategies is questionable.

Studies that have examined digoxin's effect on functional status and nonmortality outcomes have shown conflicting results. This confusing picture has resulted in part from the large number of studies with major methodologic flaws.[203] Jaeschke et al. attempted to remedy this by analyzing only the seven randomized, placebo-controlled trials of digoxin that they found in the literature.[203] Their meta-analysis found that digoxin reduced the percentage of patients with clinical deterioration severe enough to require study withdrawal from 18 percent for those who received placebo ($N = 354$) to 6 percent for those who received digoxin ($N = 357$) (risk difference, 12 percent; 95 percent confidence interval of –20 to –3 percent). In addition, the Captopril-Digoxin Multicenter Research Group found a trend toward fewer emergency department visits or hospital admissions for heart failure in patients treated with digoxin compared with those who received placebo and a diuretic (16 versus 27 percent, $p = 0.08$).[204] The RADIANCE trial found that when digoxin was withdrawn from patients taking digoxin, diuretics, and an ACE inhibitor, patients were 6 times more likely to have clinical deterioration than patients who continued to take digoxin.[201] It is unclear, however, whether digoxin withdrawal studies are relevant to the question of when digoxin should be initiated in the first place.

Unfortunately, virtually all digoxin studies have withdrawn patients from active treatment and examined the subsequent likelihood of clinical deterioration as a measure of drug efficacy. This study design may select those patients who are more likely to respond to the drug since they have been receiving it chronically and presumably have been achieving some symptomatic benefit. An excellent study by Lee et al. using a double-blind crossover placebo-controlled design clearly demonstrated that the heart failure scores (a combination of signs and symptoms of heart failure) decreased significantly when digoxin was introduced and increased during the months that the same patients were crossed over to receive placebo.[205] This study suggests that the addition of digoxin can result in symptomatic improvement and not just prevent clinical deterioration.

Digoxin also appears to improve physical functioning and decrease symptoms in some patients with heart failure. Although the Captopril-Digoxin Multicenter Research Group[201] found no difference in exercise tolerance or NYHA classification in patients treated with digoxin, DiBianco et al.[206] found a 65-second (14 percent) increase in exercise time, and when digoxin was withdrawn from patients in the RADIANCE trial, exercise tolerance NYHA class, and quality-of-life scores deteriorated.[201]

Based on these findings, digoxin should be initiated with ACE inhibitors and diuretics in patients with severe heart failure and should be added in patients who remain symptomatic despite optimal management with ACE inhibitors and diuretics. However, because there is no evidence that digoxin decreases mortality, patients who are asymptomatic after treatment with ACE inhibitors and diuretics may not benefit from digoxin. Some panelists employ this agent routinely in all patients with left-ventricular systolic dysfunction, however.

> The administration of digoxin for asymptomatic left-ventricular dysfunction or even mild heart failure symptoms should not be encouraged until the results of the Digoxin Investigation Group mortality study demonstrate the effects of this agent on long-term survival. Multiple other agents with positive inotropic properties have been associated with an increased risk of sudden cardiac death. The risk to benefit ratio of positive inotropes does not currently favor their use in asymptomatic populations.

Loading doses of digoxin are not generally needed. In the presence of normal renal function, the typical dose of 0.25 mg daily may be instituted. Patients who have reduced renal function, have baseline conduction abnormality, or are small or elderly should be started on 0.125 mg daily or lower and titrated to an adequate serum digoxin level. Steady state will be reached in approximately 1 week in patients with normal renal function, although 2–3 weeks may be needed in patients with renal impairment. When steady state is achieved, the patient should be checked for symptoms of toxicity and an ECG, serum digoxin level, serum electrolytes, BUN, and creatinine obtained. The value of obtaining regular serum digoxin levels is uncertain, but it is probably reasonable to check levels once yearly after a steady state is achieved. In addition, levels should be checked if:

> The yearly assessment of a digoxin level is probably too infrequent for most chronic heart failure patients. Drug levels can fluctuate quite frequently as these patients often have changes in renal function. Digoxin levels should be checked every 3–6 months or more frequently if clinical deterioration occurs or if the patient has impairment in renal funtion.

- Heart failure status worsens.
- Renal function deteriorates.
- Additional medications are added that could affect the digoxin level (see below).
- Signs of toxicity develop (e.g., confusion, nausea, anorexia, visual disturbances).

In the absence of toxicity, serum digoxin levels as high as 2.5 ng/mL may be tolerated, although levels of 0.7–1.5 ng/mL are generally considered therapeutic. It is unclear whether the beneficial effects of digoxin are greater at higher serum levels.

> The optimum dosing of digoxin has not been established. Most studies have aimed to achieve a trough level of 1–1.5 ng/ml, a level that has been shown to produce favorable positive inotropic effects. However, data from experimental models of heart failure show that digoxin partially corrects the abnormal baroreceptor response associated with chronic heart failure. This neuroregulatory effect occurs at levels below 1.0 ng/ml.[207] Until additional information is available, digoxin should be dosed to achieve a trough level of 1–1.8 ng/ml as has been the clinical approach for the past several decades.

Digoxin should be discontinued (often with consideration of reinstitution at a lower dose after 2–3 days) if any of the following is noted:

- Elevated serum digoxin level.
- Substantial reduction in renal function.
- Symptoms of toxicity (as above).
- Significant conduction abnormality (e.g., symptomatic bradycardia due to second- or third-degree atrioventricular [AV] block or high-degree AV block in atrial fibrillation).
- Increase in ventricular arrhythmias.

Before a new medication is instituted, the prescriber should determine whether the medication interacts with digoxin. The most frequent medications that raise the digoxin level are quinidine, verapamil, and amiodarone. Additional pharmacological agents that may raise serum digoxin levels include (1) antibiotics, which may decrease gut flora and prevent bacterial inactivation of digoxin, and (2) anticholinergic agents, which decrease intestinal motility.[208] Serum digoxin levels should be checked approximately 1 week after any of these agents are added to the therapeutic regimen.

Hydralazine/Isosorbide Dinitrate

HYD/ISDN is an appropriate alternative in patients with contraindications or intolerance to ACE inhibitors. (Strength of Evidence = B.)

Patients who have contraindications to ACE inhibitors or who cannot tolerate ACE inhibitors should be given a trial of HYD/ISDN. No studies have specifically addressed the use of HYD/ISDN for patients who cannot take or tolerate ACE inhibitors. HYD/ISDN is not as beneficial as enalapril in reducing mortality during the first 2 years of treatment.[22] However, this combination has been shown to achieve an absolute reduction in mortality, compared with placebo, from 19 to 12 percent and from 47 to 36 percent, in patients with heart failure at 1 and 3 years, respectively.[20] The mortality difference between treated and untreated patients was not significant beyond 3 years, although this may have been due to a lack of statistical power of the study beyond 3 years.

The effect of HYD/ISDN on functional status is not clear, but these agents increased exercise capacity as much as enalapril.[22] Side effects are a significant problem, however; 18–33 percent of patients in these trials discontinued one or both of the medications. Headache, palpitations, and nasal congestion occur more frequently with these medications than with ACE inhibitors. On balance, the use of HYD/ISDN represents an important alternative to ACE inhibitors when patients do not tolerate the latter class of agents.

Anecdotal reports, the Hy-C Trial[209], and personal experience suggest that the combination of hydralazine and isosorbide dinitrate treatment is well tolerated by the majority of ACE-intolerant patients. Although smooth muscle vasodilators are less effective in prolonging survival than ACE inhibitors, they can unquestionably provide significant symptomatic benefit. Smooth muscle vasodilators, particularly hydralazine, are especially useful in improving forward cardiac output when functional mitral or tricuspid regurgitation exists. Nitrates are frequently added to ACE inhibitors in order to control angina pectoris and to reduce persistent congestive symptoms through sustained preload reduction.

Isosorbide dinitrate should generally be initiated at a dose of 10 mg TID and increased weekly to 40 mg TID as tolerated. Hydralazine should generally be initiated at a dose of 25 mg TID, and increased weekly to 75 mg TID. Patients with low blood pressure, severe heart failure, or advanced age can be started at 10 mg TID for both agents. In the Veterans Affairs Vasodilator-Heart Failure Trial (VHeFT) II, which compared enalapril with HYD/ISDN, the average daily doses of hydralazine and isosorbide dinitrate were 200 mg and 100 mg, respectively.[22]

Lower daily doses may not be effective. Clinical trials of HYD/ISDN have used QID dosing. Although there is no evidence that TID dosing is equally efficacious, concerns about nitrate tolerance and poor compliance with QID dosing regimens makes TID dosing with these agents a more reasonable approach than QID dosing.[210]

> An attempt should be made to utilize a QID dosing schedule for nitrates and hydralazine as validated in the two Veterans Administration Heart Failure Trials (VHeFT I and II). If compliance or side effects become problematic, a TID dosing schedule may be utilized. As pointed out in the guideline, there are no data supporting the efficacy of the less intensive dosing regimen.

Note that although the Food and Drug Administration (FDA) has not approved HYD/ISDN for use in patients with heart failure, these agents may nonetheless be used in this context as appropriate, in accordance with the preceding discussion.

> Recently, a new class of drugs, the angiotensin-2 receptor antagonists, has been developed for the treatment of hypertension. Several ongoing trials are examining their utility in heart failure populations. Losartan is commercially available for hypertension management and has favorable hemodynamic effects in chronic heart failure.[211] Losartan is being evaluated in both ACE-intolerant patients and as combination therapy for patients with persistent symptoms despite maximized ACE inhibitor treatment. Although the hemodynamic effects of angiotensin-2 receptor antagonists are similar to ACE inhibitors, the latter have additional benefits including inhibition of bradykinin. It remains to be proven whether angiotensin-2 antagonists will exert beneficial effects on mortality and post-MI left-ventricular remodeling. Such studies are either underway or being planned.

Anticoagulation

Routine anticoagulation is not recommended. Heart failure patients with a history of systemic or pulmonary embolism, recent atrial fibrillation, or mobile left-ventricular thrombi should be anticoagulated to a prothrombin time ratio of 1.2–1.8 times each individual laboratory control time (International Normalization Ratio of 2.0–3.0). (Strength of Evidence = C.)

Some authors have suggested that anticoagulation be considered for patients with heart failure, even in the absence of atrial fibrillation or history of embolism.[212,213] However, there has never been a controlled trial of anticoagulation for patients with dilated cardiomyopathy.[214] Some information is available on the risk of stroke from retrospective studies[215–218] and a prospective study of patients with heart failure.[21] The rate varied in these studies from 1.4 to 5.5 strokes per 100 patient-years. One study reported an incidence of 42 strokes per 100 patient-years.[212] Selection bias in such observational studies may result in a higher incidence of stroke than exists for typical patients with heart failure.

Data on fatal stroke are available from recent RCTs of ACE inhibitors, although the total number of strokes has not been reported. In the SOLVD trial, which included patients with NYHA Class II or III heart failure, the incidence of fatal stroke was only 0.24 per 100 patient-years.[21] The CONSENSUS trial included only patients with NYHA Class IV heart failure.[12] Half of those enrolled had atrial fibrillation, but only one-third of all patients were receiving anticoagulation at the start of the trial. Of 253 patients, 3 suffered a stroke over the average followup period of 6 months, for an incidence of 2.3 strokes per 100 patient-years. The number of patients who suffered a stroke and also had atrial fibrillation that was not treated with anticoagulation was not specified.

When compared with the stroke rate of approximately 5 per 100 patient-years reported for patients with nonrheumatic atrial fibrillation, the rate of stroke in patients with heart failure appears to be a somewhat lower, but clinically important, rate.[219–222] However, it is difficult to interpret the stroke incidence because many patients with heart failure have concomitant atrial fibrillation that predisposes them to stroke. The stroke rate may be higher in patients with worse functional status, although the incidence of bleeding complications could also be higher in this group.

The observed incidence of stroke in patients with heart failure must be compared with the reported incidence of major and minor bleeding complications resulting from anticoagulation. In recent randomized clinical trials, the risk of serious bleeding complications ranged from 0.8 to 2.5 percent per year in patients anticoagulated to prothrombin time ratios of 1.2–1.8.[219–222] However, the incidence of serious or fatal bleeding was not different from that observed in the controls. It is possible that patients with heart failure could have a higher incidence of complications due to intermittent hepatic congestion, which could impair warfarin metabolism.

Until there is evidence from RCTs, the dictum of *primum non nocere* ("first do no harm") suggests that patients with heart failure should not be anticoagulated unless they have atrial fibrillation or a history of systemic or pulmonary emboli. Patients with mobile left-ventricular thrombi on echocardiogram should be anticoagulated until the thrombus is no longer visible. Prothrombin times should be closely monitored, particularly during periods of exacerbations of heart failure when hepatic congestion may occur. Although patients with NYHA Class IV heart failure may benefit from anticoagulation even in the absence of the preceding indications, this practice cannot be advocated routinely until more data become available.

The issue of anticoagulation for patients with depressed left-ventricular function remains controversial. It has been hypothesized that patients with idiopathic dilated cardiomyopathy are at greater risk for embolization than patients with ischemic left-ventricular dysfunction because areas of hypokinesis are more likely to dislodge small mural thrombi than akinetic areas. Although no data exist to prove this point, the observation that patients with left-ventricular aneurysms are quite unlikely to embolize appears to lend support to this theory. Further, results from the two Veterans Administration controlled heart failure trials in which over 80 percent of patients had ischemic heart disease as the cause for their chronic heart failure reported an embolic complication rate below 2.5 percent per 100 patient-years.[223] This rate is substantially lower than that described in earlier uncontrolled series of patients with dilated cardiomyopathy.

It is often assumed that embolic risk is directly related to the extent of left-ventricular dysfunction. However, studies have not been performed evaluating the relationship between left-ventricular EF and embolic risk in patients who remain in normal sinus rhythm. While it is true that asymptomatic patients experience fewer embolic complications than patients with overt symptomatic heart failure, this observation has not been specifically linked to the degree of impairment in contractile function. Until controlled data are available, the indications for anticoagulation in chronic heart failure should remain quite limited, as described in this guideline.

Additional Pharmacological Management

Many patients with heart failure remain symptomatic despite the measures discussed earlier under Initial Pharmacological Management. Others have comorbid conditions, such as angina or hypertension, which can adversely affect heart failure if not properly managed. This section addresses the management of these patients. Few controlled trials are available to provide guidance in these complex situations, so most recommendations derive from clinical experience. Although hypertension and angina can often be managed by primary care physicians, the treatment of patients with resistant heart failure is more complex, and the risks of treatment are greater.

If patients remain symptomatic on a combination of a diuretic, an ACE inhibitor, and digoxin, a consultation should be obtained with a practitioner who has expertise in the management of heart failure, if this has not been done previously. (Strength of Evidence = C.)

Treatment of Persistent Heart Failure

Patients with persistent volume overload despite initial medical management may require more aggressive administration of the current diuretic (e.g., intravenous administration), more potent diuretics, or a combination of diuretics. (Strength of Evidence = C.)

In patients with persistent volume overload, furosemide can be increased to as much as 480 mg per day in divided doses, as discussed.

> Addition of a second or even a third diuretic that acts synergistically with a maintenance loop diuretic agent is generally preferable to escalating a single loop agent to quite high levels. This author prefers to add an agent that acts on either the proximal tubule (such as hydrochlorothiazide) or distal tubule (aldactone or amiloride) when the daily furosemide dose exceeds 120 mg BID. Metolazone is usually reserved for patients who fail to respond to a diuretic program and is often used as a booster to achieve a target weight. As discussed, close attention to rapidity of weight loss and electrolyte disturbances is essential when using combination diuretic therapy.

Salt restriction should be re-emphasized and compliance assessed and encouraged.

> A fluid restriction must also be instituted when refractory symptoms develop and escalating doses of diuretics are contemplated. Limiting fluid intake to 1.5 to 2 liters per day is quite helpful in managing chronic volume overload, even in the absence of hyponatremia. This aspect of heart failure management is very frequently overlooked and may often permit a gradual decrease in the overall daily diuretic requirement.

Patients with persistent volume overload despite appropriate initial medical management may require additional measures to achieve diuresis. Several alternatives are available if additional measures are required (see Table 6 for agents and doses):

- Administer one or more doses of diuretic intravenously in an attempt to reduce any intestinal edema that may be impairing the absorption of orally administered loop diuretics.

- Administer a single dose of 2.5 mg of metolazone orally. Metolazone is extremely potent, and even a single dose can cause marked volume losses, hypotension, and hypokalemia. Patients who are treated with this therapy should be monitored carefully in the outpatient setting or admitted to the hospital. The combination of a loop diuretic and metolazone is extremely kaluretic, and almost all patients on this combination of drugs will require supplemental potassium. After the initial response is assessed, it can be decided whether dosing should be every third day, every other day, or every day. If necessary, the dose can be increased to 5–10 mg daily, with careful monitoring. Once adequate diuresis is achieved, it may be possible to reduce the dose of (or to discontinue) metolazone. Patients should be examined and electrolytes measured every third day during the initiation and titration of metolazone. Metolazone should not be used in the outpatient setting unless patients can be closely monitored for volume status, blood pressure, and electrolytes.

- Add spironolactone to loop diuretics and ACE inhibitors in patients with normal renal function and serum potassium levels. The usual dose of spironolactone is 25–50 mg twice per day. Because spironolactone is a potassium-sparing agent, potassium supplementation should be discontinued at the start of therapy.

Discontinuation of potassium supplementation is not always necessary when a potassium-sparing agent such as spironolactone is first initiated. If the patient has normal renal function and requires large doses of potassium repletion to maintain a serum potassium level >3.5 meq/L, total discontinuation of potassium supplementation can be deleterious. This author generally decreases the potassium supplementation by 25–50 percent and monitors electrolytes frequently. Potassium supplementation should be held during initiation of potassium-sparing agents when renal insufficiency exists. Mild renal dysfunction (serum creatinine value less than 2.5 mg/dl) may still allow judicious use of a potassium-sparing agent under close monitoring.

Because the combination of spironolactone and an ACE inhibitor may induce hyperkalemia, use of this combination of agents should be undertaken cautiously and with close observation. Potassium levels should be checked about every 3 days (depending on initial potassium level) until stable.

- Hospitalize the patient and institute intravenous inotropic therapy such as intravenous dobutamine to increase renal blood flow and facilitate diuresis.

Initiation of inotropic therapy with agents such as dobutamine, milrinone, or amrinone requires hospitalization. Indications for such intravenous pharmacologic treatment include worsening renal function during attempted diuresis, refractory heart failure symptoms, or persistent hypotension with end-organ dysfunction. Careful hemodynamic monitoring using a pulmonary artery catheter is often necessary in order to determine the optimum dose of inotropic agent. Although most patients typically respond to dobutamine at doses of 4–8 μg/kg/min, careful hemodynamic assessment during pharmacologic intervention permits optimization of dosing based on filling pressures and cardiac index. Once the optimum dose has been established for an individual patient, treatment is often continued for several days until volume overload has been eliminated and end-organ function has been stabilized. During subsequent hospitalizations, the patient may not require invasive hemodynamic monitoring since the most effective inotropic dose has previously been established. Dobutamine (a beta-adrenergic agonist), amrinone, and milrinone (phosphodiesterase inhibitors) appear equally efficacious in improving cardiac function and promoting diuresis. Although dobutamine may occasionally produce long-term benefits in cardiac function, it usually simply aids in achieving diuresis, and its effects wane when the drug is tapered and discontinued.

Home dobutamine may offer palliation for a minority of patients with refractory symptoms. Such treatment requires frequent monitoring of electrolytes and the dose should be kept below 6–8 μg/kg/min to decrease the risk of proarrhythmic effects. The only controlled study of dobutamine demonstrated a significant improvement in quality of life and functional capacity when the drug was administered three times per week. However, the study was terminated prematurely because of a very high incidence of sudden cardiac death. The arrhythmic risk may be decreased by using lower doses of the drug, intermittent infusions of inotrope, close attention to electrolyte balance, and the empiric suppression of nonsustained ventricular tachycardia with amiodarone. It is only a rare situation in which the potential benefits of home treatment outweigh its arrhythmic risks. At present, this approach is not typically covered by Medicare, which is the most frequent payer source for those patients most likely to require this palliative form of treatment.

(Continued)

(Continued from previous page)

Patients who require intermittent hospitalizations for intravenous inotropic therapy have a very limited life expectancy and an exceedingly poor quality of life. Other treatment options including cardiac transplantation or participation in controlled trials of investigational heart failure therapies should be considered in appropriate, highly motivated patients. In the future, implementation of a portable, electrically driven, left-ventricular assist device may prove the most effective form of long-term treatment for patients with end-stage disease.

Once a certain level of diuresis is reached, patients often do well on an oral diuretic alone, sometimes at reduced doses. Adjustment of diuretic dosage requires regular monitoring of blood pressure, serum sodium and potassium, and renal function. In general, patients should be re-evaluated no later than 1 week after changing diuretics. Development of hyponatremia may require institution of fluid restriction. Potassium-sparing agents or supplemental potassium should be administered as needed to maintain serum potassium above approximately 4.0 mEq/L. If patients previously had their daily sodium intake restricted to 3 grams, the daily sodium intake should be decreased to 2 grams or less.

The use of a flexible diuretic program for patients with difficult to control volume overload should be encouraged. A target weight (the best weight based upon blood pressure, extent of peripheral edema, and renal function) should be established and a 1–3 drug maintenance diuretic program administered. Use of short pulses of a potent agent such as metolazone may be prescribed in order to maintain the target weight. Likewise, instructions should be carefully reviewed to decrease diuretics when weight falls below the target value to avoid excessive prerenal azotemia or frank dehydration.

A few other practical points should be considered for patients with severe heart failure. Total freedom from peripheral edema, while desirable, may not be possible in all patients without risking excessive prerenal azotemia. In addition, a moderate degree of prerenal azotemia (blood urea nitrogen values of 30–50 mg/dl; creatinine <2.0 mg/dl) may be required in order to minimize symptoms of volume overload in end-stage disease.

Patients with persistent dyspnea after optimal doses of diuretics, ACE inhibitors, and digoxin should be given a trial of hydralazine and/or nitrates. (Strength of Evidence = C.)

Hydralazine may be particularly useful in patients with persistent relative hypertension (i.e., diastolic blood pressure >110 mmHg) and in patients with evidence of severe mitral regurgitation. Alternatively, if a patient primarily has symptoms of pulmonary congestion or has a low systolic blood pressure nitrates are preferred (Table 6), such as isosorbide dinitrate, 40 mg TID. Topical nitroglycerin ointment may also be used, although its efficacy in heart failure has not been well documented Nitroglycerin patches are probably inadequate. Oral nitrates should not be used more often than three times a day because of the problem of tachyphylaxis.[210] A 12-hour period between the evening dose and the morning dose is recommended. Patients who complain primarily of paroxysmal nocturnal dyspnea may be started on nitroglycerin ointment, 1 inch at bedtime. In addition, nitroglycerin tablets or spray often will alleviate transient symptoms of pulmonary congestion.

The utility of nocturnal, topical nitroglycerin preparations in managing paroxysmal nocturnal dyspnea should not be underestimated. It is now well recognized that nitrates are not only useful in relieving angina pectoris but can be quite effective in chronically reducing preload and improving both rest and exertional dyspnea. Addition of a second vasodilator such as hydralazine or losartan for patients with persistent symptoms requires further study. While it is theoretically appealing, no controlled studies have yet been completed to validate this multidrug treatment approach for refractory symptoms.

Beta-adrenergic blockers may improve functional status and natural history in patients with heart failure, but this form of treatment should be considered experimental therapy at this time. (Strength of Evidence = B.)

Many studies have examined the effect of metoprolol in patients with heart failure.[224–234] In an RCT of 383 patients with heart failure from idiopathic dilated cardiomyopathy, metoprolol treatment was associated with a trend toward reduction in the combined endpoint of mortality and need for heart transplantation.[237] There was a significant improvement in exercise capacity at 12 months. Existing data are inadequate to identify the population of patients in whom beta blockers may be safe and effective. Moreover, the effect of beta blockers on mortality has not been established. Thus, beta blockers should be considered an experimental, albeit promising, therapy.

Beta-adrenergic blockers are felt to exert their cardioprotective effects through blockade of the adverse effects of excessive sympathetic tone that occur in chronic heart failure. Beta-receptor density is increased and myocardial contractility enhanced following a period of chronic beta-blocker treatment. Over a decade of studies have shown that these agents (principally metoprolol) can improve symptoms and increase EF by up to 6–8 EF units. Despite earlier concerns, exacerbation of chronic heart failure sufficient to require drug cessation occurs in fewer than 5 percent of patients. Unfortunately, the two largest controlled trials—Metoprolol in Dilated Cardiomyopathy (MDC) and Cardiac Insufficiency Bisoprilol Study (CIBIS)—failed to demonstrate a survival benefit when metoprolol or bisoprilol were added to conventional therapy including digoxin, diuretics, and ACE inhibitors. Thus, no beta blocker has FDA approval for heart failure treatment at this time. Recently, a new class of beta blockers that also have vasodilatory properties has been studied. Carvedilol, a nonselective beta blocker with vasodilator and antioxidant effects, has been shown to improve symptoms and decrease mortality by 67 percent in a combined series of over 1,000 treated patients.[235] Carvedilol produced beneficial effects for patients with mild to severe heart failure symptoms and was equally effective for ischemic and cardiomyopathic left-ventricular dysfunction.

Selection of patients for beta-blocker therapy remains difficult. Certainly, beta blockade should be considered in patients with active angina pectoris or atrial fibrillation that remains poorly controlled despite a therapeutic digoxin level. Some investigators believe that those patients with the highest levels of sympathetic stimulation (as manifested by a resting tachycardia) are most likely to demonstrate benefit. Others have not found tachycardia to be a predictor of treatment success. When initiated, these drugs must be started at quite low dosages (e.g., metoprolol 5 mg po BID) and slowly titrated up as tolerated over 4–8 weeks. Although many patients will show transient worsening in symptoms and require an increase in diuretic therapy during the first 2–3 weeks of treatment, symptomatic benefits usually appear within one month. It is anticipated that carvedilol will probably be approved by the FDA for heart failure treatment; its widespread availability may alter future recommendations of treatment to include the earlier use of beta-adrenergic blockade.

Angina and Heart Failure

Patients with heart failure and angina who will not or cannot undergo revascularization (see next section) should be treated with nitrates and aspirin. (Strength of Evidence = A.)

Because of their negative inotropic effect, calcium-channel blockers and beta blockers should be employed only by practitioners experienced in the use of these agents in patients with heart failure. (Strength of Evidence = C.)

Patients with heart failure and persistent angina who are not surgical candidates should be treated with long-acting nitrates, such as isosorbide dinitrate, in addition to aspirin. ACE inhibitors are not effective in reducing angina in patients with stable, exertional angina,[236] although they may decrease the incidence of recurrent MI or unstable angina.[18]

Although ACE inhibitors are ineffective as antianginal drugs, their benefit in decreasing the risk of recurrent MI or unstable angina in post-MI populations has been convincingly demonstrated by the SAVE trial results.[237] It is increasingly recognized that ACE inhibition has direct vasculoprotective effect that is independent of its hemodynamic properties. Documented and hypothesized benefits of ACE inhibition have recently been concisely reviewed.[238]

Beta blockers must be used with caution because of their negative inotropic effect. Calcium-channel blockers must be used with caution because of their negative inotropic effect and tendency to activate the renin-angiotensin and adrenergic nervous systems. Different calcium-channel blockers may differ in the magnitude of these effects. Patients with heart failure and persistent angina despite nitrate therapy should consult with or be followed by a cardiologist.

Beta-adrenergic blockers remain a mainstay in the management of patients with symptomatic angina pectoris even in the presence of significant left ventricular EF. Although such agents must be carefully introduced, the vast majority of heart failure patients will tolerate and benefit from beta-adrenergic blockade when angina pectoris coexists. The future availability of third generation agents such as bucindolol, bisoprolol, and carvedilol, which possess potent vasodilatory effects that partially offset their negative inotropic properties, may further minimize the detrimental effects of beta-adrenergic blockade.

(Continued)

(Continued from previous page)

Results of the Diltiazem Post-Infarction Trial indicate that calcium-channel blockers may exacerbate symptoms and increase mortality in patients with overt heart failure. This fact must be balanced against their benefits in controlling anginal symptoms. When active angina pectoris requires treatment, a beta blocker should generally be chosen before a calcium-channel blocker. Amlodipine has recently been shown to improve both angina and heart failure symptoms in patients with underlying ischemic heart disease enrolled in the PRAISE trial.[239] However, a survival benefit was observed only for those patients with nonischemic left-ventricular dysfunction. Encouragingly, amlodipine, unlike earlier calcium-channel blockers, did not increase mortality in ischemic heart disease patients and may be a useful agent for patients with ongoing anginal symptoms despite treatment with nitrates and beta blockers.

Persistent Hypertension Despite ACE Inhibitors and Diuretics

Persistent hypertension should be treated with a direct vasodilator, an alpha$_1$-adrenergic blocker, or a centrally acting alpha blocker. Because of their negative inotropic effect, calcium-channel blockers and beta blockers should be given only under the care of practitioners experienced in the use of these agents. (Strength of Evidence = C.)

Reduction of high blood pressure may in itself have a beneficial effect on the signs and symptoms of heart failure. Hypertension is a relative concept in patients with heart failure. Although a blood pressure of 135/85 mmHg may be acceptable for a patient with a normal EF, that same blood pressure may be harmful for a patient with severe left-ventricular systolic dysfunction. Some patients with heart failure will feel better when their blood pressure is low because their cardiac output is generally higher. Most patients will have some reduction in blood pressure with ACE inhibitors and diuretics, but some will remain hypertensive or have high-normal blood pressure. Additional diuresis may achieve some blood pressure reduction, and consideration should be given to increasing the dose of ACE inhibitors.

If additional antihypertensive treatment is necessary, direct vasodilators, alpha$_1$-adrenergic blockers, centrally acting alpha blockers, should be used (Table 7). Nitrates have only a small antihypertensive effect when blood pressure is elevated, although they frequently decrease blood pressure substantially in patients who are already marginally hypotensive All calcium-channel blockers and beta blockers have a negative inotropic effect. As discussed previously, there is some evidence that patients with heart failure can tolerate beta blockers and have improved symptoms or functional status (see section on beta blockers), so these

96   *Heart Failure*

Table 7. Medications to Treat Hypertension or High-Normal Blood Pressure in Patients With Heart Failure

Drug	Initial Dose (mg)	Maximum Dose (mg)	Major Adverse Reactions
Direct Vasodilators			
Hydralazine	10 TID	75 TID	Headache, nausea, dizziness, tachycardia, lupus-like syndrome.
Minoxidil	2.5 QD	80 QD	Fluid retention, hair growth, thrombocytopenia, leukopenia.
Alpha$_1$-Adrenergic Blockers			
Doxazosin	1 QD	16 QD	Postural hypotension, dizziness, syncope, headache.
Terazosin	1 QD	20 QD	
Prazosin	1 TID	10 TID	
Centrally Acting Alpha Blockers			
Clonidine tablets	0.1 BID	0.6 BID	Sedation, dry mouth, blurry vision, headache, bradycardia.
Clonidine patch	0.1 weekly	0.3 weekly	Same as clonidine; contact dermatitis.
Guanabenz	4 BID	64 BID	Similar to clonidine.
Iosartan	25 mg	100 mg	Postural hypotension

Note: QD = once a day, BID = twide a day, TID = three times a day.

agents are not absolutely contraindicated. However, they must be used with extreme caution as antihypertensive agents, and they should only be used by practitioners with experience in the use of these agents for heart failure. See preceding discussion (Angina and Heart Failure) regarding calcium-channel blockers.

Antiarrhythmic Therapy

Sudden cardiac death remains a major cause of mortality in heart failure populations and accounts for 20–40 percent of all deaths. Patients with symptomatic ventricular tachycardia or fibrillation require antiarrhythmic treatment. The choice of pharmacologic treatment is often guided by electrophysiologic findings in this high-risk population. It should be noted that antiarrhythmic drug efficacy declines in proportion to left-ventricular EF and proarrhythmic effects increase dramatically when LVEF falls below 35 percent. Amiodarone is generally the most effective pharmacologic agent for recurrent VT/VF but it is not uniformly protective and many patients may require implantation of an automatic cardioverter defibrillator (AICD).

(Continued)

(Continued from previous page)

While this device dramatically decreases the risk of sudden cardiac death, a significant portion of patients die within 5 years of progressive heart failure syptoms.

Optimum management of patients with asymptomatic nonsustained ventricular tachycardia (NSVT) remains to be defined. Two large-scale controlled clinical trials (GESICA and CHF STAT) have evaluated this issue with conflicting results.[59,240] All-cause mortality was decreased by 26 percent at two years in patients receiving low-dose amiodarone in the GESICA trial.[240] There was also a trend towards lower sudden cardiac death in this study in which the majority of patients had nonischemic left-ventricular dysfunction. In contrast, the CHF STAT Trial study population was predominantly composed of patients with ischemic heart disease and no benefit was detected for amiodarone in lowering sudden cardiac death or improving long-term survival. A nonsignificant trend toward improved survival in the small cohort of patients with nonischemic heart failure was observed.[59] At present, clinicians should not attempt antiarrhythmic suppression of asymptomatic NSVT and no effective strategy for lowering sudden cardiac death in this population has been validated.

The Role of Revascularization

Commentary by Barry Rayburn, M.D.

Heart Failure and Coronary Artery Disease

The AHCPR panel should be applauded for their efforts to include information about this important topic in this clinical guideline. Perhaps more than any other area of this guideline, the role of revascularization in the treatment of heart failure is undergoing rapid evolution. It was not many years ago that there was an almost universal sentiment that patients with clinical heart failure, severe left-ventricular dysfunction, and coronary artery disease were deemed unsuitable for revascularization. Many of the studies cited here are truly pioneering in this area. Consequently, virtually all of the topics in this section are given a strength of evidence grade of C—expert opinion. The reader is encouraged not to dismiss this topic as less important or less relevant because of the lack of randomized clinical trials. Such trials, at least on a small scale, are likely to be done in the near future, and may alter the recommendations accordingly. The expert opinion provided by the AHCPR panel is based both on the results of the trials that have been published and we suspect, on the observation by many experts in the care of heart failure patients that some patients benefit greatly from revascularization. Originally motivated by the grave lack of available donor hearts, revascularization may evolve as a preferred, alternate treatment in carefully selected individuals. Our goal in this chapter is to provide some practical commentary on the guidelines, and to update the available information where possible.

Coronary artery disease was the second most common identifiable risk factor for heart failure (after hypertension) in the Framingham study[157] but may now well be the most common etiology. The risk of developing heart failure is increased 2–3 times in patients with angina and 4–6 times for patients with a previous MI.[241] In the SOLVD trial, 38 percent of patients had current angina, and 66 percent had suffered a previous MI.[21] Most patients with angina and some patients with a previous MI have areas of myocardial ischemia that contribute to the degree of left-ventricular systolic dysfunction. This suggests that there may be a large number of patients with heart failure and potentially reversible ischemia.

Unfortunately, there are few published data on the prevalence of clinically significant ischemia in patients with heart failure. To provide guidance to clinicians, the panel defined three-subgroups of heart failure patients who are likely to have very different probabilities of significant ischemia: patients with (1) angina, (2) a history of MI but no current angina, and (3) neither angina nor a past history of MI. Although patients with heart failure and normal epicardial coronary arteries can have exertional chest pain,[158,242,243] the majority of patients with this combination of symptoms will have some degree of myocardial ischemia due to epicardial coronary artery disease. Patients who have suffered previous MIs may have areas of viable myocardium in the region of the infarction or ischemic regions supplied by other coronary arteries.

Kotler and Diamond have summarized studies of the detection of multivessel disease following MI.[244] In these reports, 31–56 percent (weighted average: 44 percent) of patients who suffered an MI had significant ischemia in the distribution of another coronary artery. It is unclear how many of these patients had significant angina or heart failure. This finding suggests that a substantial number of patients with heart failure and a previous MI may have other significant areas of ischemia. Whether detection and correction of this "silent" ischemia would improve prognosis is not known. This issue is discussed subsequently in more detail.

Even less is known about the prevalence of significant ischemia in patients with heart failure and no angina or prior MI. The likelihood of ischemia in a given patient is highly dependent on the presence of other risk factors for heart failure (e.g., alcoholism, severe hypertension) and risk factors for coronary artery disease (e.g., age, sex, diabetes mellitus, smoking, family history, hypertension, hypercholesterolemia). Patients with multiple risk factors for coronary artery disease and no other obvious etiology for heart failure have a much higher likelihood of having reversible ischemia as a causative or contributing factor to their heart failure. Thus, it is probably worthwhile to pursue an evaluation for ischemia in such patients. Patients with another obvious etiology for heart failure and a low risk for coronary disease are much less likely to benefit from testing.

Note: Figure 6 shows the content and organization of this chapter.

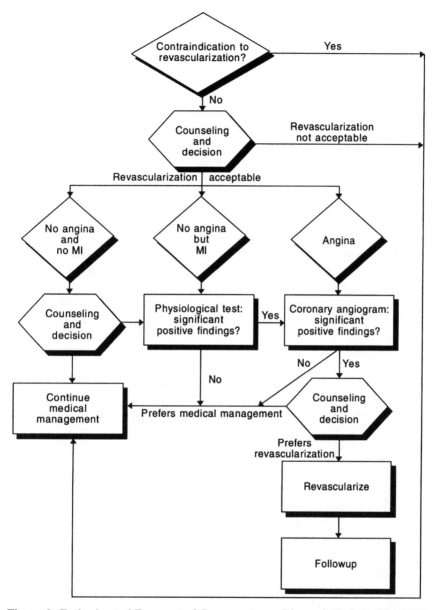

Figure 6. Evaluation and Treatment of Coronary Artery Disease in Patients With Heart Failure

While the authors agree that not every patient presenting with heart failure needs a cardiac catheterization or even an evaluation for ischemia, our practice has been to evaluate the majority of such patients in some way. The traditional risk factors for coronary disease are based on epidemiologic evidence from population studies, and not from a group of patients presenting with heart failure. Therefore, assuming that a heart failure patient is unlikely to have coronary artery disease because of the absence of traditional risk factors may be flawed. In the author's experience, many patients with heart failure present at some point in their course with chest pain. As mentioned by the panel, this can occur even in patients with no epicardial coronary disease. While the origin of this pain is uncertain, prior documentation of the presence or absence of ischemia on noninvasive testing, or coronary artery disease on cardiac catheterization can be extremely useful in the management of such patients. Finally, unexpectedly finding reversible ischemia in a patient with heart failure can offer a therapeutic option that may improve the patient's long-term prognosis. This may not be available at a later date if the patient goes on to have irreversible damage in that area of myocardium.

We generally screen patients with recognized risk factors, or a history of MI or angina with coronary angiography combined with some functional assessment for ischemia and viability. The majority of other patients receive noninvasive testing for the presence of ischemia. The only patients we routinely do not screen for ischemia are (1) the very young, (2) patients with another clear-cut etiology for their ventricular dysfunction (e.g., biopsy-proven adriamycin toxicity) and (3) patients in whom we would not consider any type of revascularization because of comorbidities or patient wishes.

Benefits of CABG

For patients with ischemic cardiomyopathy, the goal of myocardial revascularization is to prevent further ischemic injury to remaining functional myocardium or to restore function to so-called hibernating myocardium (i.e., nonfunctional myocardial wall segments that are underperfused but still viable). Although it has not been proven that achievement of these goals increases survival in patients with compromised left-ventricular function, some survival benefit seems likely. Conversely, patients without remaining ischemic functional or hibernating myocardium are unlikely to benefit from revascularization.

No RCTs have evaluated the outcomes of revascularization in heart failure patients. The three RCTs of CABG versus medical management all excluded patients with heart failure or severe left-ventricular dysfunction (EF <35 percent),[245–247] so these studies cannot answer the question of whether CABG is beneficial for patients with heart failure. However, most cohort studies that have evaluated the effect of CABG on survival in patients with both heart failure or severe left-ventricular dysfunction and severe or limiting angina (Table 8) have shown positive results.[11,247–255] For example, Bounous[11] et al. found that adjusted 3-year mortality was reduced from 32 percent for the medical cohort to 14 percent for the surgical cohort. This differential benefit may persist for many years.[256] However, interpretation and generalization of these findings are limited because operative mortality was not reported and most patients who underwent CABG were without heart failure symptoms at the time of surgery.

CABG has not been shown to improve survival in patients with heart failure who do not have angina. Although individual case reports suggest that some heart failure patients with large areas of reversible ischemia and no history of angina are improved with CABG,[258,259] several case series and cohort studies show no evidence that patients without angina benefit from surgery.[247,253,260,261] Alderman et al.[247] analyzed the Coronary Artery Surgery Study registry from 1975 to 1979 and found that patients with dyspnea on exertion or fatigue as their predominant complaint had the same 3-year mortality and symptom-free survival with CABG as with medical management (both 45.2 percent). The perioperative mortality rate was 7 percent. It is not clear whether more modern surgical techniques produce fewer perioperative deaths and better outcomes from surgery than reported in these studies.

In patients without angina, revascularization is most likely to be beneficial in the subset of patients with demonstrable myocardial ischemia or large areas of residual viable but jeopardized or hibernating myocardium. It is reasonable to assume that CABG in these patients would result in somewhat less reduction in mortality than that observed for patients with angina, although patients with large areas of ischemia might obtain a degree of improvement comparable to that seen in patients with angina. Also, patients whose heart failure symptoms are felt to represent ischemia (i.e., angina equivalent), such as those with episodic, severe heart failure or exertional dyspnea out of proportion to the degree of resting left-ventricular dysfunction, may benefit from revascularization as much as patients with angina. Patients who have only small amounts of ischemia would probably receive little or no benefit. However, there are no controlled studies to support any particular viewpoint on this subject.

Table 8. Cohort Studies of CABG Versus Medical Management for Patients

Author, Date	Study Years	Inclusion Criteria	Group	N	Average Age (years)[a]
Yatteau et al., 1974[253]	1968–72	EF <25%	Medical	42	55
			Surgical	24	51
Manley et al., 1976[249]	1968–71	Depressed left-ventricular function	Medical	155	55
			Surgical	246	54
Faulkner et al., 1977[248]	1969–75	EF <30%	Medical	70	56
			Surgical	46	56
Vliestra et al., 1977[251]	1966–72	EF <25%	Medical	21	
			Surgical	10	(52)
Pigott et al., 1982[250]	1970–77	EF <35%	Medical	115	54
			Surgical	77	54
Alderman et al., 1983[247]	1975–79	EF <35%	Medical	420	54
			Surgical	231	56
Hammermeister et al., 1982[252]	1969–74	Clinical heart failure	Medical	44	(53)
			Surgical	83	(54)
Bounous et al., 1988[11]	1976–83	EF <40%	Medical	409	54
			Surgical	301	55
		Ischemic	Medical	72	56
Luciani et al., 1993	1985–1990	Cardiomyopathy	CABG	20	56
		EF ≤30%	OHT	51	53

[a]Number in parentheses indicate values for a larger group of patients in the study or for the combination of medical and surgical patients. Data on subsets of patients were not given.

[b]Medical mortality minus surgical mortality.

[c]Hazard ratio for death in patients with clinical heart failure treated with surgery compared with medical management.

[d]Adjusted for baseline prognostic factor.

With Heart Failure or Reduced EF and Coronary Artery Disease

Percentage With Clinical Heart Failure[a]	Percentage With Limiting Angina[a]	Mean Ejection Fraction[a]	Operative Mortality (percent)	Followup (years)	Total Mortality (percent)	Absolute Mortality Difference[b] (percent)
(50)	(76)	(19%)	NA		31	
			33	1.0	50	19
60	100	29%	NA		68	
56	100	24%	14	6.0	43	25
66	74	20%	NA		53	
43	98	21%	4	2.0	23	30
		NR	NA		67	
NR	100	NR	NR	2.0	60	7
26	37	25%	NA		66	
21	65	27%	1.3	5.0	37	29
19	51	26%	NA		33	
11	72	27%	7	3.0	23	10
100	(82)	NR	NA		Hazard ratio 0.85c	
100	(96)	NR	NR	6.0		NA
NR	NR	29%	NA		32 d	
NR	NR	33%	NR	3.0	14 d	18
55	43	21%	NA		72	
46	70	22%	20	5	20	52
80	35	23%	13.7		18	

Note: CABG = coronary artery bypass graft surgery, EF = ejection fraction, NA = not applicable, NR = not reported.

Note: OHT = orthotopic heart transplant.

The results from the studies reviewed in Table 8, especially the earlier ones, must be interpreted cautiously. Many of the initial studies cited were done prior to the era of modern CABG techniques, and therefore do not represent current practice. Also notable in the earlier studies was the fact that angina was chiefly the limiting complaint and not heart failure. It was in these studies, predominantly of patients with angina as the limiting complaint, where a mortality benefit was demonstrated with CABG. The role for CABG in patients with ischemic cardiomyopathy and heart failure who do not have angina is less clear, as pointed out by the panel. Earlier cohort studies of patients without angina failed to show a mortality benefit from surgery.

A more recent study by Luciani et al. (appended in Table 8) evaluated 143 patients with ischemic cardiomyopathy referred between 1985 and 1990.[257] Patients were nonrandomly selected to receive medical therapy, or undergo CABG or heart transplantation. In this population, where the predominant symptoms were mixed between heart failure and angina, there was a marked mortality benefit with CABG over medical therapy. Five-year survival was comparable between CABG and transplantation, though functional status was better in the transplant group. The patients in the revascularization group did have a higher incidence of angina than the other groups, but 30 percent had only heart failure.

Newer studies have shown improvements in mortality and symptom class in an ever-expanding population of patients with ischemic cardiomyopathy undergoing CABG. Based on the results of viability assessment, Dreyfus et al. prospectively used CABG or orthotopic heart transplantation among 50 patients referred for transplant evaluation between 1990 and 1992.[262] Forty-six of the 50 were found to have viability by means of thallium scintigraphy and/or PET scanning and subsequently underwent CABG. The unique feature about this cohort was that heart failure was present in all of the patients, with dyspnea being the main symptom in 80 percent. Operative mortality in this group was quite low at 2.2 percent, however, patients were excluded if their cardiac index was less than 1.5 L/min/m^2 or the mean pulmonary pressure was greater than 40 mmHg. Preoperatively, 41 patients (89 percent) were in NYHA Class III, 5 in Class IV, and all had received medical ther-

(Continued)

(Continued from previous page)
apy for heart failure, including diuretics and ACE inhibitors. Over a mean followup of 18 months, there were 5 late deaths. Of the survivors, all were in NYHA Class II or better and an improvement in mean EF was seen from 23 to 39 percent. Several studies have demonstrated symptomatic heart failure improvement along with a fairly dramatic improvement in the mean EF in patients undergoing CABG, although there is marked variability in the data.[262-267] For example, in the series reported by Lansman in 1993, of 42 patients with EFs of less than 20 percent who underwent CABG, there was an improvement in EF from 15.7 percent to 22.6 percent (p <0.0002) and an improved NYHA Class from 3.4 to 1.8 (p <0.0001).[265]

Risks of CABG

As recently as 1982, EF was considered the most important predictor of perioperative mortality for CABG. In 1986, improved perioperative and surgical techniques had reduced EF to the fourth most important predictor, behind repeat CABG, emergent CABG, and age.[263] However, patients with depressed left-ventricular function are still at increased mortality risk.[263,264,266] It is difficult to predict the actual perioperative mortality risk in patients with heart failure. Compared with patients with EFs of 40 percent or greater, patients whose EFs were below 20 percent or between 20 and 39 percent had 3.4 and 1.5 times the chance of dying in the perioperative period, respectively.[264] Christakis et al. reported a perioperative mortality rate of 11.7 percent in a series of 264 patients with EFs below 20 percent who underwent CABG at the University of Toronto between 1982 and 1986.[263]

Mortality rates increase substantially when the EF is below 20 percent or the heart failure is severe (NYHA Class IV).[263,264,266] Important additional determinants of mortality risk with CABG include age (risk increases approximately 0.5 percent per year above age 60); sex (higher in women, although part of this difference is explained by a higher mortality rate in small individuals); comorbid conditions (e.g., diabetes, significant renal dysfunction, significant COPD, or clinical cerebrovascular disease); prior cardiothoracic surgery (substantially increases risk); need for emergent CABG (e.g., failed PTCA or acute ischemic syndrome), or concomitant valve surgery.[261,264,266]

Perioperative mortality rates for CABG can vary significantly, but generally range from 5 to 30 percent depending on various underlying factors and comorbidity.[268] Certainly, operative mortality in the population of patients with severe ischemic cardiomyopathy has improved during recent years with advancements in operative techniques as well as experience in centers performing these procedures.

Kron et al. reported an operative mortality rate of 2.6 percent in a series of 39 patients who underwent CABG with EFs below 20 percent from 1983 to 1988.[269] The mean followup was 21 months (range 3 to 60 months) with 8 late deaths. Therefore, the total mortality rate during the followup was 21 percent. Seven deaths were due to arrhythmias. Only 3 patients continued to have severe heart failure, one of whom underwent successful cardiac transplantation. A study by Langenburg also done at the University of Virginia (and including the above cohort) between 1983 and 1993 reported a survival to hospital discharge rate of 92 percent in 96 patients.[270] This study is important in that there was no difference in EF among survivors and nonsurvivors. Also noted was that the lack of angina did not necessarily predict a poor result contrary to many earlier series. In this study, age was shown to be significantly, higher (68.8 vs. 62.6) in nonsurvivors. Perhaps the most interesting finding was that poor vessel quality as judged by a blinded observer of preoperative catheterization films had a 100 percent predictive value for perioperative death ($p < 0.05$).

Lansman et al. reported a 30-day mortality of 4.8 percent in 42 patients with EFs of 20 percent or less who underwent CABG from 1986 to 1990.[265] This high-risk group had very acceptable short-term results with improvement in symptoms as well as mean EF.

It is very important to note that in some of the more recent studies, the EF of operative survivors did not significantly differ from nonsurvivors. Therefore, within the cohort of patients with low EFs, the exact value of the EF is not particularly helpful in predicting outcome. This observation is similar to that seen in the care of heart failure patients in general. While in a large population, the lower the EF the higher the mortality, among patients with very low EFs, the exact value of the EF plays little role in predicting outcome. More important is their clinical status on medical therapy and the presence of comorbidities. This strongly argues that heart failure patients considered for revascularization should be optimally managed before moving forward with surgery.

These studies indicate that for patients with clinical heart failure due to left-ventricular systolic dysfunction, perioperative mortality rates in excellent centers will range from about 5 percent in patients under age 60 with mild heart failure without any comorbid conditions to more than 30 percent in patients over age 70 with severe heart failure and several comorbid conditions. In addition to mortality risk, the risk of surgical morbidity and complications must also be considered. In the New York State Cardiac Surgery Reporting System, the risk of perioperative MI was 1.5 percent, the risk of stroke was 1.6 percent, and the risk of all major nonfatal complications was 9.2 percent.[264] Centers and surgeons vary considerably in their experience with patients with severe left-ventricular dysfunction. Perioperative mortality rates for CABG also vary significantly.[271] Patients should be informed of the mortality and complication rates of the surgeon performing the operation and of the facility where the surgery will be done. The patient's primary provider should be aware of variations in operative outcomes and consider referral to a center with substantial experience with heart failure patients and demonstrated good outcomes.

Benefits and Risks of PTCA

As with CABG, the benefits of PTCA in patients with heart failure are unclear. No studies have addressed survival after PTCA compared with CABG or standard medical management. However, several case reports and case series indicate that PTCA can relieve angina and improve ventricular function or wall motion.[272–277]

Less is known about the risks of PTCA for patients with heart failure. Serota et al. reported a series of 73 patients with EF of 40 percent or less who underwent PTCA, 45 percent of whom had a history of heart failure.[276] Five patients (7 percent) had serious procedure-related complications; of the three patients with MIs, two were fatal; and two had acute coronary closure with one patient death related to acute closure. The total in-hospital mortality was 5.5 percent. Hartzler et al. reported a "procedural mortality" of 2.7 percent for a series of 664 patients with EFs of 40 percent or less who underwent PTCA.[273] The rates of nonfatal MI and emergent CABG were 0.7 and 2.0 percent, respectively. The patient populations and reporting techniques in these series are different from those reported in studies of CABG, so a direct comparison is not possible. Thus, it is not known whether PTCA has a higher, lower, or equivalent complication rate for patients with heart failure, compared with CABG.

Because PTCA has not been shown to improve survival, CABG is usually considered the procedure of choice for patients with heart failure and angina. However, numerous considerations enter into the decision regarding recommendation of PTCA versus CABG, including multiple technical factors, underlying risk of surgery, the greater morbidity associated with CABG, and patient preferences. A discussion of these factors is beyond the scope of this guideline.

Patient Counseling and Decisionmaking

Patients without contraindication to revascularization should be advised of the possibility of revascularization, including its potential benefits and harms. Before embarking on an evaluation for ischemia, practitioners should determine whether patients are willing to consider revascularization or have contraindications to revascularization. (Strength of Evidence = C.)

Patients with heart failure and angina should be advised to undergo coronary artery angiography if they are surgical candidates. (Strength of Evidence = C.)

There are no absolute contraindications to revascularization except if the patient refuses surgery or is unable to give informed consent. However, a number of factors may preclude intervention or raise the risk above any expected benefit:

- Unwillingness to consider surgery.
- Severe comorbid diseases, especially renal failure, pulmonary disease, or cerebrovascular disease (e.g., severe stroke).
- Very low EF (<20 percent).
- Illnesses that imply a limited life-expectancy less than or equal to 1 year, including advanced cancer, severe lung or liver disease, chronic renal disease, advanced diabetes mellitus, and advanced collagen vascular disease.
- Technical factors, including previous myocardial revascularization or other cardiac procedure, inadequate vascular conduit, history of chest irradiation, and diffuse distal obstructive coronary artery atherosclerosis.

> As more studies are conducted in patients with severe ischemic cardiomyopathy, it has become increasingly apparent that a very low EF alone does not necessarily predict a poor outcome. Therefore, while these patients should understand that revascularization for them carries a higher risk than in patients without heart failure, it is not clear that this risk is inherently higher in a patient with an EF of 15 percent as compared to a patient with an EF of 25 percent.

It is important to balance the expected benefits and harms associated with revascularization. Patients may consider the relatively high perioperative mortality rate more acceptable when their life expectancy is not limited by other diseases or advanced age (i.e., when there is a good chance for long-term survival if they survive surgery). However, patients with diseases that, although not terminal, might be expected to reduce life expectancy may not consider the initial risk of perioperative mortality acceptable.

Patients, family members, and caregivers should be involved in decisionmaking at all steps of the treatment and care of heart failure, but this is particularly important when revascularization is being considered. The primary practitioner should provide patients with the information necessary to begin the decisionmaking process. Later, specialists should interact directly with the patient. Patients should be advised about the relative likelihood that they have clinically significant ischemia, about the risks of angiography, and about the likely benefits and harms of revascularization if ischemia is found. Some individuals may not want to undergo evaluation if there is a low likelihood that ischemia will be found. For others, the risks of surgery will be unacceptable regardless of the possible benefits. Patients should be encouraged to ascertain the perioperative mortality rate experienced by the providers in their area (or those covered by their insurance plan).

An individual's likelihood of having ischemia and his or her chance of surviving surgery can be estimated by the history, physical examination, and EF. These factors should be discussed with the patient before any diagnostic testing for ischemia. Some patients, in consultation with their primary practitioner, may decide at this point that no studies should be done. For other patients, this decision requires a balancing between expected benefits and risks. The amount of ischemic myocardium is the best predictor of the benefit of revascularization, and testing for the presence and amount of ischemia may be necessary before a patient can reasonably decide whether the risks of revascularization are acceptable.

As previously noted, in the patient subgroup we are discussing, the threshold for screening for coronary artery disease may be different than that used in the general population. The risk of coronary artery disease may be substantial even in the absence of traditional coronary artery risk factors. While indiscriminate use of coronary angiography is not warranted, every case should be closely examined on an individual basis. Given recent evidence suggesting that revascularization may improve mortality and symptom class in well-selected patients and at an acceptable level of risk, it appears that a fairly aggressive approach to evaluate these patients may be appropriate.

If a patient wishes to pursue an evaluation for ischemia, the provider must decide what test is most appropriate.

Heart failure patients without contraindications to revascularization and who have exercise-limiting angina, angina that occurs frequently at rest, or recurrent episodes of acute pulmonary edema should be advised to undergo coronary artery angiography as the initial test for operable coronary lesions. (Strength of Evidence = B.)

Some patients will need subsequent physiologic testing to determine the amount of ischemic myocardium or whether myocardium is viable, but it is not necessary to perform such tests routinely before angiography in this subgroup of patients.

Patients without significant angina but with a history of MI should be advised to undergo a physiologic test for ischemia, followed by coronary angiography if ischemic regions are detected. (Strength of Evidence = C.)

This strategy will miss a small number of patients with false-negative physiologic tests. However, in view of the lack of evidence that these patients benefit from surgery, together with a consideration of the morbidity, mortality, and cost of catheterizing all patients in this group, this drawback is considered relatively minor.

It is unclear whether patients without a history of MI or significant angina should be routinely evaluated for ischemia. Patients should be counseled concerning the expected benefits and risks of evaluation for ischemia, including the fact that there is no evidence from controlled trials to show that revascularization benefits heart failure patients in the absence of angina. The decision about whether to perform physiologic tests for ischemia or coronary angiography should be based on a consideration of patients' risk factors for coronary artery disease and the likelihood of alternative etiologies (e.g., alcoholic cardiomyopathy). If the decision is made to proceed with an evaluation, noninvasive testing for ischemia (e.g., thallium scanning) should be performed as the initial test; coronary angiography should be performed only if noninvasive testing demonstrates ischemia. (Strength of Evidence = C.)

Little scientific evidence is available to guide the evaluation and care of heart failure patients who have no history of angina or MI. Some of these individuals will have silent coronary artery disease as the cause of their heart failure, although this clearly depends on the patients' risk factors for coronary artery disease and the probability that there is another etiology for the heart failure. Patients without risk factors for coronary artery disease and patients with another probable cause of heart failure (e.g., alcoholic cardiomyopathy) are unlikely to benefit from angiography or testing for ischemia.

The panel was about evenly divided between advocating no further testing and advocating a physiologic test for ischemia in patients with no angina and no history of MI. Coronary angiography was considered advisable by some panelists in the uncommon presentation of unexplained heart failure in young patients with no history of angina or prior MI, with the rationale that these patients may benefit more from early revascularization for occult coronary artery disease than from later cardiac transplantation.

Based on the results of physiologic testing and/or coronary angiography, the physician should give the patient a refined estimate of the risks and benefits of revascularization. The patient can then decide whether he or she desires revascularization. (Strength of Evidence = C.)

No data are available that address the question of how much ischemia should be present to justify the risk of revascularization for the chance of an improvement in survival. In general, patients with severely depressed EFs (<20 percent) should undergo revascularization only if large areas of ischemia are detected. Patients with less severely depressed EFs may be willing to risk surgery for more modest-sized ischemic areas. The lack of data in this area makes it difficult to justify revascularization for small ischemic areas, except when severe angina is present.

Physiologic Testing for Ischemia

Although there are a number of acceptable physiologic tests for ischemia, the most widely available and accepted procedure for determining the presence of ischemic myocardium is myocardial perfusion scintigraphy, such as thallium scanning, with post-stress, redistribution, and rest reinjection imaging. (Strength of Evidence = C.)

As will be discussed below, recent data suggest that dobutamine echocardiography may be a more optimal and cost-effective initial noninvasive means for assessment of viable myocardium in patients with cardiomyopathy.[278]

Several studies have assessed the reversibility of perfusion defects or improvement in wall motion or EF after revascularization, but it is unclear whether these changes predict improvement in symptoms, exercise tolerance, or survival. Definitive outcome studies comparing the alternative tests have not been performed.

Thus, the clinician must choose from a range of acceptable alternatives. These include:

- Exercise or pharmacological stress myocardial perfusion scintigraphy (e.g., thallium scanning).
- Exercise or pharmacological stress echocardiography.
- Stress radionuclide angiocardiography.
- Positron emission tomography (PET).

If thallium is used, reinjection imaging should be performed at rest if an abnormality is identified during the stress portion of the study. This strategy improves the accuracy for identifying the presence and extent of viable myocardium.[279] PET may be a more sensitive test than perfusion scintigraphy for detecting viable myocardium,[280] but whether increased sensitivity translates into better patient outcomes is yet to be determined. In addition, PET is not widely available and is more costly than most alternative tests. Clinicians must be familiar with the availability, quality, and cost of the different physiologic tests for ischemia at their institution and should use this information in deciding what test to order. Myocardial perfusion scintigraphy is most useful for screening patients without a history of angina to determine whether coronary angiography is necessary. If this test is normal, angiography can reasonably be forgone. Because scintigraphy relies on differences in the distribution of myocardial perfusion to determine ischemia, an occasional patient with very balanced ischemia may have a "normal" study. Increased uptake of the isotope in the lungs may be a clue to this type of false-negative test.

Since the AHCPR guidelines were authored, additional approaches for physiologic testing for ischemia have been proposed. Recent literature suggests that the most optimal and cost-effective assessment is to proceed initially with pharmacological stress echocardiography (in this case using dobutamine).[278] If a patient did not show evidence of ischemic but viable myocardium, he or she underwent PET imaging. This combined strategy correctly identified all patients who subsequently demonstrated postoperative improvement in regional wall motion. Myocardial perfusion scintigraphy is still a reasonable alternative, especially for those patients where technical limitations prohibit echocardiographic interpretation. Dobutamine echocardiography has shown very good sensitivity and specificity when performed correctly for assessing viability (i.e., initial low dose incremental infusion).[281] It has also been shown to be comparable to delayed thallium-201 scintigraphy.[282] PET scanning, while perhaps slightly more sensitive, is also less readily available and considerably more expensive in most centers. It is clear that the approaches for demonstrating the presence of ischemic but viable myocardium are evolving. It is vital that clinicians caring for patients with heart failure understand the availability, expertise, and expense of the particular techniques available at their institution when considering the evaluation of such patients.

Evaluation for Heart Transplantation

Consideration should be given to cardiac transplantation in patients with severe limitation or repeated hospitalizations because of heart failure despite aggressive medical therapy in whom revascularization is unlikely to be beneficial. This guideline does not address the evaluation of patients for transplantation. (Strength of Evidence = C.)

In addition to heart transplantation, studies are underway to determine the benefits and harms of innovative treatments, including new drugs and mechanical ventricular assist devices. If appropriate, patients should be informed of the possibility of taking part in such studies.

For more information on heart transplantation, the reader is referred to the American College of Cardiology/American Heart Association report on this topic.[283]

Establishing guidelines for a field where the data are changing quickly is always a challenging task. The AHCPR panel provides an outstanding insight into this potentially very important mode of therapy for certain heart failure patients. It is by necessity, however, a snapshot in time. We hope that our comments have updated the snapshot and provided some insight into how we pursue the question of revascularization in our center. One final note seems appropriate. Revascularization in patients with severe heart failure and systolic dysfunction is challenging. One could easily surmise that numerous technical factors would potentially affect the outcome, such as the speed of the surgeon, the technique employed in weaning the patient from bypass, or the style of postoperative care. Given these variables, clinicians wishing to consider revascularization as a strategy in this patient population should seriously consider the experience of the surgeon and the center in caring for such patients.

8

Assessment of Outcomes and Patient Followup

Commentary by Edward K. Kasper, M.D.

Careful history and physical examination should be the main guide to determining outcomes and directing therapy. A thorough history should include questions regarding physical functioning, mental health, sleep disturbance, sexual function, cognitive function, and ability to perform usual work and social activities. (Strength of Evidence = B.)

The panel recommends against the routine use of invasive or noninvasive tests, such as echocardiography or maximal exercise testing, for monitoring patients with heart failure. (Strength of Evidence = B.)

Patients should be encouraged to keep a record of their daily weights and to bring the record with them when visiting their practitioner. Patients should be instructed to call if they experience an unexplained weight gain greater than 3–5 pounds since their last clinical evaluation. (Strength of Evidence = C.)

The criteria for assessing the response to therapy are similar to those by which heart failure is diagnosed—namely, the symptoms and physical findings discussed previously. On followup visits, patients should be asked about the presence of orthopnea, paroxysmal nocturnal dyspnea, edema, and dyspnea on exertion. As discussed previously, the presence and degree of orthopnea in particular can serve as a useful monitoring criterion.

Providers should determine and document the most strenuous activity that patients can perform without significant symptoms (i.e., their maximal asymptomatic activity), the type of activity that regularly produces symptoms, and the maximal activity that patients can perform (maximal tolerated activity). These activities can be defined in terms of walking (with attention to distance, pace, and grade), stair-climbing, or activities of daily living (e.g., bathing, dressing). Having defined these activities for individual patients, providers can then monitor patients' progress from visit to visit using a series of open-ended questions regarding these specific activities.

The physician should keep in mind that not all patients will have a similar subjective response to comparable degrees of impairment.[31] Some patients with minimal impairment in objective measurement may be severely compromised. Other patients will tolerate a much greater degree of impairment with few subjective symptoms. Younger patients in particular tend to tolerate a degree of left-ventricular dysfunction that would be intolerable to an older patient with a stiffer vasculature. Comorbidities may cloud the picture, with depression playing a major role as in any chronic illness.

It is important to remember that patients may experience worsening symptoms before there is evidence of a deteriorating condition by physical examination. Family members or other caregivers can often contribute important additional information about patients' status and compliance when asked similar questions. Family members or other caregivers should be interviewed separately from the patients when feasible to obtain the most candid information possible and to specifically address family members' or other caregivers' concerns.

Family members can often be helpful in obtaining candid information about the patient's condition. Anorexia is often denied by the patient, but can be of great concern to the caregiver.

In addition to questions about symptoms and activities, providers should ask about other aspects of the patient's health-related quality of life (HRQOL), including sleep; sexual function; mental health (or outlook on life); and the patient's ability to perform his or her usual social, recreational, and work activities. Cognitive function—such as alertness, memory, and concentration—should also be explored.

This is a great deal of information to obtain at each visit. While undeniably important, I would favor exploring these issues every 6 to 12 months or if the patient raises a concern.

Several HRQOL questionnaires have been developed specifically for patients with heart failure.[284–287] Formal use of these specific questionnaires is not essential, but questions adapted from these instruments could improve and standardize history taking. The reliability of patient histories is improved when patients are asked several questions about each of the major dimensions of HRQOL (i.e., symptoms, physical functioning, and mental health), rather than single questions in each area. Moreover, the rather large number of important topics listed above suggests that use of a formal questionnaire could facilitate history taking in patients with heart failure.

> HRQOL questionnaires are not usually part of the followup of most patients with heart failure. Of the various questionnaires available, the Minnesota Living With Heart Failure Questionnaire[288] is probably the most well accepted.

The information obtained from assessing HRQOL should be used to modify treatment and to guide additional patient and family teaching and counseling. Practitioners can enhance the patient's and family's ability to adapt to heart failure and its treatments by suggesting alterations in sleep, rest, or activity patterns, counseling about sexual difficulties, teaching new coping behaviors, and intervening when depression or other emotional disturbances develop.

> These suggestions are well-intended, but unlikely to be undertaken by the single practitioner. There are few cardiologists or internists with expertise in sleep disorders, sexual difficulties, coping behaviors, and depression. This argues for a team approach with input from multiple experts.

Careful physical examination for neck vein distention, a third heart sound, rales, hepatojugular reflux, and edema is also important. The low interrater reliability of physical findings such as rales and a third heart sound.[45,46] emphasizes the need for careful examination. However, the poor predictive value of physical findings reported in the literature should be interpreted cautiously because these studies evaluated patients at a single point in time. Although the presence or absence of a third heart sound does not make or exclude the diagnosis of heart failure, if a patient with heart failure develops a new third heart sound or rales, it is likely that this patient's heart failure has worsened. Thus, physical examination may be more helpful in following patients with heart failure than in making a diagnosis.

> The absence of rales in a patient with increasing dyspnea, orthopnea, or new paroxysms of nocturnal dyspnea is consistent with an increase in fluid retention and deserves treatment with an increase in the diuretic dose. It is rare for rales to develop in patients with chronic heart failure until the pulmonary capillary wedge pressure is quite high.

The panel recommends against the routine use of other tests (e.g., echocardiography, maximum exercise testing) for monitoring the response of heart failure patients to treatment. Although baseline EF[216,289–291] and maximum oxygen consumption[292] correlate with prognosis, changes in these parameters do not necessarily indicate that the prognosis has changed. Analysis of the two VHeFT trials found that a change in EF of more than 5 percent predicted subsequent survival even after adjustment for the baseline EF.[293] However, Franciosa et al. reported that minoxidil increased mean EF from 30 to 43 percent, but exercise tolerance was not improved and total clinical events (death, worsening heart failure, increased need for diuretics, angina, and arrhythmias) were increased in the group treated with minoxidil.[294] Milrinone also increases EF,[295,296] but it has not been shown to improve survival.[159]

Even if the VHeFT results prove to be valid for groups of patients, there is too much spontaneous variability in EF for serial measurement to be useful for individuals. Narahara et al. reported a variation in left-ventricular EF of 5.6 ± 5.5 percent over a 12-week period.[297] A change in EF of more than 13 percent would be required to exclude spontaneous variations as the cause of the change. Wackers et al. reported smaller spontaneous variability (2.3 ± 2.5 percent), but there were only 5 days between the two measurements.[298] Finally, detecting patients with a declining EF is of limited value because there is no evidence that intensifying treatment will alter their prognosis.

In view of the preceding, repeated assessment of EF or exercise tolerance is generally not indicated. However, repeat testing may be useful in patients with a new murmur, new MI, sudden deterioration despite compliance with medications and diet, or progressive symptoms that suggest the need to refer the patient for consideration of heart transplantation.

Repeated assessment of left-ventricular function is usually unwarranted. Similarly, repeat catheterization is also unwarranted unless the suspicion for ischemic dysfunction is high and the patient is a candidate for revascularization. Measurements of left-ventricular function and cardiac catheterization are not needed with each readmission for heart failure either. Cardiopulmonary stress testing with respiratory gas analysis is probably useful in timing cardiac transplantation.[299] Patients demonstrating a major improvement in peak oxygen consumption or left-ventricular EF while on a cardiac transplant waiting list may have a better prognosis with medical therapy than with transplantation.

References

Note that the bullet point (■) indicates material referenced by the editor—ed.

■ 1. Ellerbeck EF, Jencks SF, Radford MJ, et al. Quality of care for medicare patients with acute myocardial infarction: a four-state pilot study from the cooperative Cardiovascular Project. JAMA 1995;273:1509–1514.

■ 2. Tumulty PA. The effective clinician. Philadelphia: WB Saunders; 1973:4. *This should be required reading for all physicians.*

3. Thom T. (National Heart, Lung, and Blood Institute). Letter to: David C. Hadorn. Written communication: 1993 Apr 12.

4. Levit KR, Lazenby HC, Cowan CA, et al. National health expenditures, 1990. Health Care Fin Rev 1991;13:29–54.

5. National Center for Health Statistics. Detailed diagnoses and procedures, National Hospital Discharge Survey, 1990. Vital and health statistics, Series 13, No. 113. Hyattsville (MD): The Center; 1992. DHHS publication No. 92-1774.

6. National Center for Health Statistics. National Ambulatory Medical Care Survey, 1989 summary. Vital and health statistics, Series 13, No. 110. Hyattsville (MD): The Center; 1992. DHHS publication No. 92-1771.

7. National Center for Health Statistics. Discharges from nursing homes: 1985 National Nursing Home Survey. Vital and health statistics, Series 13, No. 103. Hyattsville (MD): The Center; 1990. DHHS publication No. (PHS) 90–1764.

8. Daley J, Jencks S, Draper D, et al. Predicting hospital-associated mortality for Medicare patients. A method for patients with stroke, pneumonia, acute myocardial infarction, and congestive heart failure. JAMA 1988 Dec 23–30;260:3617–24.

9. Iezzoni LI, Ash AS, Coffman G, et al. Admission and mid-stay MedisGroups scores as predictors of death within 30 days of hospital admission. Am J Public Health 1991;81:74–8.

10. Keeler EB, Kahn KL, Draper D, et al. Changes in sickness at admission following the introduction of the prospective payment system. JAMA 1990 Oct 17;264: 1962–8.

11. Bounous EP, Mark DB, Pollock BG, et al. Surgical survival benefits for coronary disease patients with left-ventricular dysfunction. Circulation 1988 Sep;78(3 Pt 2):I-151 to I-157.

12. CONSENSUS Trial Study Group. Effects of enalapril on mortality in severe congestive heart failure. N Engl J Med 1987;316:1429–35.

13. Kahn KL, Rogers WH, Rubenstein LV, et al. Measuring quality of care with explicit process criteria before and after implementation of the DRG-based prospective payment system. JAMA 1990;264;1969–73.

14. Kosecoff J, Kahn KL, Rogers WH, et al. Prospective payment system and the impairment at discharge: the "quicker and sicker" story revisited. JAMA 1990 Oct 17;264:1980–3.

15. Retchin SM, Brown B. Elderly patients with congestive heart failure under prepaid care. Am J Med 1991;90:236–42.

16. Fleg JL, Hinton PC, Lakatta EG, et al. Physician utilization of laboratory procedures to monitor outpatients with congestive heart failure. Arch Intern Med 1989;149:393–6.

■ 17. Guidelines for the evaluation and management of heart failure: Report of the American College of Cardiology/American Heart Association Task Force on Practice Guidelines (Committee on Evaluation and Management of Heart Failure). J Am Coll Cardiol 1995;26:1379–1398.
This publication takes a more patient management objective approach to the diagnosis and treatment of heart failure. The overall recommendations are similar, but no algorithms are provided. Acute heart failure and diastolic dysfunction are also covered.

18. Pfeffer MA, Braunwald E, Moy LA, et al. Effect of captopril on mortality and morbidity in patients with left-ventricular dysfunction after myocardial infarction: results of the survival and ventricular enlargement trial. N Engl J Med 1992;327:669–77.
The SAVE study randomized patients with asymptomatic left-ventricular dysfunction (LVEF <35 percent) following MI to captopril or placebo. Captopril reduced all-cause mortality by 19 percent, risk of development of overt heart failure by 37 percent, and recurrent infarction by 25 percent. Beneficial effects were observed regardless of whether thrombolytic therapy or beta blockers were administered.

19. SOLVD Investigators. Effect of enalapril on mortality and the development of heart failure in asymptomatic patients with reduced left-ventricular ejection fractions. N Engl J Med 1992;327:685–91.
Enalapril was found to substantially reduce the incidence of overt heart failure and decrease hospitalizations when administered to over 2000 patients with asymptomatic left-ventricular dysfunction (LVEF <35 percent). A nonsignificant trend toward fewer cardiovascular deaths at 48 months was also noted in patients randomized to ACE inhibitor therapy.

20. Cohn JN, Archibald DG, Ziesche S, et al. Effect of vasodilator therapy on mortal-

ity in chronic congestive heart failure: results of a Veterans Administration Cooperative Study. N Engl J Med 1986;314:1547–52.

21. SOLVD Investigators. Effect of enalapril on survival in patients with reduced left-ventricular ejection fractions and congestive heart failure. N Engl J Med 1991 Aug 1;325:293–302.

22. Cohn JN, Johnson G, Ziesche S, et al. A comparison of enalapril with hydralazine-isosorbide dinitrate in the treatment of chronic congestive heart failure. N Engl J Med 1991 Aug;325:303–10.

■ 23. Kasper EK, Agema WRP, Hutchins GM, et al. The causes of dilated cardiomyopathy: a clinicopathologic review of 673 consecutive patients. J Am Coll Cardiol 1994;23:586–590.
The causes of dilated cardiomyopathy in a referral population at a tertiary care center are presented. The most common causes were idiopathic origin (47 percent), idiopathic myocarditis (12 percent), and coronary disease (11 percent).

24. Chalmers I. Evaluating the effects of care during pregnancy and childbirth. In: Chalmers I, Enkin M, Keirse MJ, editors. Effective care in pregnancy and childbirth. Oxford: Oxford University Press; 1989. Chapter 1.

25. Chalmers TC, Smith H Jr, Blackburn B, et al. A method for assessing the quality of a randomized control trial. Controlled Clin Trials 1981;2:31–49.

26. Detsky AS, Naylor CD, O'Pourke K, et al. Incorporating variations in the quality of individual randomized trials into meta-analysis. J Clin Epidemiol 1992;45: 255–65.

27. Feinstein AR. Epidemiologic analyses of causation: the unlearned scientific lessons of randomized trials. J Clin Epidemiol 1989;42:481–502.

28. Liberati A, Himel HN, Chalmers TC. A quality assessment of randomized control trials of primary treatment of breast cancer. J Clin Oncol 1986;4:942–51.

■ 29. Stevenson WG, Stevenson LW, Middlekauff HR, et al. Improving survival for patients with advanced heart failure: a study of 737 consecutive patients. J Am Coll Cardiol 1995;26:1417–1423.
The one-year mortality of patients with severe heart failure referred to a tertiary care institution with an interest in heart failure and transplantation decreased from 33 percent before 1989 to 16 percent after 1990. The largest impact was on sudden death. The reason for this decrease in mortality was felt to be the application of therapeutic advances demonstrated to be efficacious in clinical trials to this patient population.

■ 30. Rich MW, Beckham V, Wittenberg C, et al. A multidisciplinary intervention to prevent the readmission of elderly patients with congestive heart failure. N Engl J Med 1995;333:1190–1195.
The intervention in this study consisted of largely patient education, diet, social service consultation, and appropriate discharge planning. They were able to decrease the 90-day hospital readmission rate for heart failure by 56.2 percent.

■ 31. Nease RF, Kneeland T, O'Connor GT, et al. Variation in patient utilities for outcomes of the management of chronic stable angina: implications for Practice Guidelines. JAMA 1995;273:1185–1190.
The authors suggest that guidelines for the management of chronic stable angina

should be based on patient preferences rather than on symptoms alone. There is no reason to suspect that patients with heart failure are any different.

■ 32. Gibson TC, White KL, Klainer LM. The prevalence of congestive heart failure in two rural communities. J Chron Dis 1966;19:141–152.

■ 33. McKee PA, Castelli WP, McNamara PM, Kannel WB. The natural history of congestive heart failure: The Framingham study. New Engl J Med 1971;285: 1441–1446.

■ 34. Schocken DD, Arrieta MI, Leaverton PE, Ross EA. Prevalence and mortality rate of congestive heart failure in the United States. J Am Coll Cardiol 1992;20: 301–306.
This is the largest study of the epidemiology of symptomatic congestive heart failure and has the advantage of representing a diverse sample of the United States population. It is limited in that it does not incorporate objective assessment of ventricular function.

■ 35. Rodeheffer RJ, Jacobsen SJ, Gersh BJ, et al. The incidence and prevalence of congestive heart failure in Rochester, Minnesota. Mayo Clin Proc 1993;68: 1143–1150.

■ 36. McDonagh TA, Morrison CE, McMurray JJ, et al. Global left ventricular systolic function in North Glasgow. J Am Coll Cardiol 1996;27:106A–107A..
This is a preliminary report of the first study to employ echocardiography to measure ventricular function in a population-based sample. A limitation to its generalizability is the fact that it was conducted in North Glasgow, an area which was determined in the MONICA Study to have an extraordinarily high prevalence of coronary artery disease. These observations, nevertheless, demonstrate that a substantial proportion of persons with treatable left-ventricular systolic dysfunction have few or no symptoms to bring them to medical attention.

37. Swedberg K, Held P, Kjekshus J, et al. Effects of the early administration of enalapril on mortality in patients with acute myocardial infarction: results of the Cooperative New Scandinavian Enalapril Survival Study II (CONSENSUS II). N Engl J Med 1992;327:678–84.
The CONSENSUS II trial examined the role of very early administration (within 24 hours) of intravenous enalapril during acute MI. Unlike other studies which utilized oral ACE inhibitors within several days and demonstrated beneficial effects, this approach produced a high incidence of early hypotension and did not improve 6-month survival.

38. Marantz PR, Tobin JN, Wassertheil-Smoller S, et al. The relationship between left-ventricular systolic function and congestive heart failure diagnosed by clinical criteria. Circulation 1988;77:607–12.

39. Mattleman SJ, Hakki A, Iskandrian AS, et al. Reliability of bedside evaluation in determining left-ventricular function: correlation with left-ventricular ejection fraction determined by radionuclide ventriculography. J Am Coll Cardiol 1983;1:417–20.

40. Harlan WR, Oberman A, Grimm R, et al. Chronic congestive heart failure in coronary artery disease: clinical criteria. Ann Intern Med 1977;86:133–8.

41. Echeverria HH, Bilsker MS, Myerburg RJ, et al. Congestive heart failure: echocardiographic insights. Am J Med 1983;75:750–5.

42. Dougherty AH, Naccarelli GV, Gray EL, et al. Congestive heart failure with normal systolic function. Am J Cardiol 1984;778–82.

43. Stevenson LW, Perloff JK. The limited reliability of physical signs for estimating hemodynamics in chronic heart failure. JAMA 1989 Feb 10;261:884–8.

44. Chakko CS, Woska D, Martinez H, et al. Clinical, radiographic, and hemodynamic correlations in chronic congestive heart failure: conflicting results may lead to inappropriate care. Am J Med 1991 Mar;90:353–9.

45. Gadsbøll N, Høilund-Carlsen PF, Nielsen GG, et al. Symptoms and signs of heart failure in patients with myocardial infarction: reproducibility and relationship to chest x-ray, radionuclide ventriculography and right heart catheterization. Eur Heart J 1989;10:1017–28.

46. Ishmail AA, Wing S, Ferguson J, et al. Interobserver agreement by auscultation in the presence of a third heart sound in patients with congestive heart failure. Chest 1987;91:870–3.

47. Stapleton JF, Segal JP, Harvey WP. The electrocardiogram of myocardiopathy. Prog Cardiovasc Dis 1970 Nov;13:217–39.

■ 48. Kass S, MacRae C, Graber HL, et al. A gene defect that causes conduction system disease and dilated cardiomyopathy and maps to chromosome 1p1-1q1. Nature Genetics 1994;7:546–551.

■ 49. Olson TM, Keating MT. Mapping a cardiomyopathy locus to chromosome 3p22-p25. J Clin Invest 1996;97:528–532.

50. Arnsdorf MF, Bump TE. Management of arrhythmias in heart failure. Cardiol Clin 1989 Feb;7:145–69.

51. Francis GS. Development of arrhythmias in the patient with congestive heart failure: pathophysiology, prevalence, and prognosis. Am J Cardiol 1986;57:3–7.

52. Fletcher D, Archibald D, Orndorff J, et al. Dysrhythmias on short term Holter as an independent predictor of mortality in congestive heart failure [abstract]. J Am Coll Cardiol 1986 Feb;7:143A.

53. Olshausen KV, Stienen U, Schwarz F, et al. Long-term prognostic significance of ventricular arrhythmias in idiopathic dilated cardiomyopathy. Am J Cardiol 1988;61:146–51.

54. Cleland JG, Dargie HJ, Wilson JT. Clinical, haemodynamic, and antiarrhythmic effects of long term treatment with amiodarone of patients with heart failure. Br Heart J 1987;57:436–45.

55. Neri R, Mestroni L, Salvi A, et al. Ventricular arrhythmias in dilated cardiomyopathy: efficacy of amiodarone. Am Heart J 1987 Mar;113:707–15.

56. Nicklas JM, Mickelson JK, Das SK, et al. Prospective, randomized, double-blind, placebo-controlled trial of low dose amiodarone in patients with severe heart failure and frequent ventricular ectopy [abstract]. Circulation 1988;78(4 Pt 2):II-27.

57. Nicklas JM, McKenna WJ, Stewart RA, et al. Prospective, double-blind, placebo-controlled trial of low-dose amiodarone in patients with severe heart failure and asymptomatic frequent ventricular ectopy. Am Heart J 1991 Oct;122:1016–21.

58. Simonton CA, Daly PA, Kereiakes D, et al. Survival in severe left-ventricular failure treated with the new nonglycosidic, nonsympathomimetic oral inotropic agents. Chest 1987;92:118–23.

■ 59. Singh SN, Fletcher RD, Gross Fisher S, et al. Amiodarone in patients with congestive heart failure and asymptomatic ventricular arrhythmia. New Engl J Med 1995;333:77–82.

This is an important study which has helped to establish the limitations of amiodarone for the prevention of sudden death in heart failure patients. It has also provided data to suggest that amiodarone may have hemodynamic benefit in patients with nonischemic left-ventricular systolic dysfunction.

60. Bigger JT Jr. Why patients with congestive heart failure die: arrhythmias and sudden cardiac death. Circulation 1987;75(5 Pt 2):IV-28 to IV-35.

61. Chakko CS, Gheorghiade M. Ventricular arrhythmias in severe heart failure: incidence, significance, and effectiveness of antiarrhythmic therapy. Am Heart J 1985 Mar;109:497–504.

62. Franciosa JA. Why patients with heart failure die: hemodynamic and functional determinants of survival. Circulation 1987;75(5 Pt 2):IV-20 to IV-27.

63. Francis GS. Sudden death and heart failure. Curr Opin Cardiol 1990;5:291–4.

64. Ikegawa T, Chino M, Hasegawa H, et al. Prognostic significance of 24-hour ambulatory electrocardiographic monitoring in patients with dilative cardiomyopathy: a prospective study. Clin Cardiol 1987 Feb;10:78–82.

65. Suyama A, Anan T, Araki H, et al. Prevalence of ventricular tachycardia in patients with different underlying heart diseases: a study by Holter ECG monitoring. Am Heart J 1986 Jul;112:44–51.

66. Wilson JR, Schwartz JS, Sutton MS, et al. Prognosis in severe heart failure: relation to hemodynamic measurements and ventricular ectopic activity. J Am Coll Cardiol 1983 Sep;2:403–10.

67. Podrid PJ. Can antiarrhythmic drugs cause arrhythmias? J Clin Pharmacol 1984;24:313–9.

68. Podrid PJ. Aggravation of ventricular arrhythmia. A drug-induced complication. Drugs 1985;29(Suppl 4):33–44.

69. Poser R, Lombardi F, Podrid P, et al. Aggravation of induced arrhythmias with antiarrhythmic drugs during electrophysiological testing [abstract]. J Am Coll Cardiol 1983;1:709.

70. Ruskin JN, McGovern B, Garan H, et al. Antiarrhythmic drugs: a possible cause of out-of-hospital cardiac arrest. N Engl J Med 1983;309:1302–6.

71. Torres V, Flowers D, Somberg JC. The arrhythmogenicity of antiarrhythmic agents. Am Heart J 1985;109:1090–7.

72. Velebit V, Podrid P, Lown B, et al. Aggravation and provocation of ventricular arrhythmias by antiarrhythmic drugs. Circulation 1982;65:886–94.

73. Morganroth J, Horowitz LN. Flecainide: it's proarrhythmic effect and expected changes on the surface electrocardiogram. Am J Cardiol 1984;53:89B–94B.

74. Oetgen WJ, Tibbits PA, Abt MEO, et al. Clinical electrophysiologic assessment of oral flecainide acetate for recurrent ventricular tachycardia: evidence for exacerbation of electrical instability. Am J Cardiol 1983;52:746–50.

75. Winkle RA, Mason JW, Griffin JC, et al. Malignant ventricular tachyarrhythmias associated with the use of encainide. Am Heart J 1981;102:857–64.

76. The Cardiac Arrhythmia Suppression Trial II Investigators. Effect of the antiarrhythmic agent moricizine on survival after myocardial infarction. N Engl J Med 1992;327:227–33.

77. The Cardiac Arrhythmia Suppression Trial (CAST) Investigators. Preliminary report: effect of encainide and flecainide on mortality in a randomized trial of arrhythmia suppression after myocardial infarction. N Engl J Med 1989;321: 406–12.

■ 78. Grogan M, Smith HC, Gersh BJ, Wood DL. Left ventricular dysfunction due to atrial fibrillation in patients initially thought to have idiopathic dilated cardiomyopathy. Am J Cardiol 1992;69:1570–1573.

79. Rich MW, Freedland KE. Effect of DRGs on three-month readmission rate of geriatric patients with congestive heart failure. Am J Public Health 1988;78: 680–2.

80. Vinson JM, Rich MW, Sperry JC, et al. Early readmission of elderly patients with congestive heart failure. J Am Geriatr Soc 1990;38:1290–5.

81. Gooding J, Jette AM. Hospital readmissions among the elderly. J Am Geriatr Soc 1985 Sep;33:595–601.

82. Rosenberg S. Patient education leads to better care for heart patients. HSMHA Health Rep 1971;86:793–802.

83. Perlman LV, Isenberg EL, Donovan I, et al. Public health nurses and the prevention of recurrences of congestive heart failure. Geriatrics 1969 Sep;24:82–9.

■ 84. Butman SM, Ewy GA, Standen JR, et al. Bedside cardiovascular examination in patients with severe chronic heart failure: importance of rest or inducible jugular venous distention. J Am Coll Cardiol 1993;22:968–74.
   The ability of the cardiovascular physical examination and chest x-ray to accurately predict hemodynamic abnormalities was prospectively evaluated in 52 patients with chronic advanced heart failure. The presence of jugular venous distention had the best combination of sensitivity (81 percent), specificity (80 percent), and predicted accuracy (81 percent) for detecting elevation of left-sided filling pressures.

85. Acquatella H, Rodriguez-Salas LA, Gomez-Mancebo JR. Doppler echocardiography in dilated and restrictive cardiomyopathies. Cardiol Clin 1990 May;8: 349–67.

86. Aguirre FV, Pearson AC, Lewen MK, et al. Usefulness of Doppler echocardiography in the diagnosis of congestive heart failure. Am J Cardiol 1989 May 1;63:1098–102.

87. Aronow WS, Ahn C, Kronzon I. Prognosis of congestive heart failure in elderly patients with normal versus abnormal left-ventricular systolic function associated with coronary artery disease. Am J Cardiol 1990 Nov 15;66:1257–9.

88. Eagle KA, Quertermous T, Singer DE, et al. Left-ventricular ejection fraction: physician estimates compared with gated blood pool scan measurements. Arch Intern Med 1988 Apr;148:882–5.

89. Gadsbøll N, Høilund-Carlsen PF, Nielsen GG, et al. Interobserver agrement and accuracy of bedside estimation of right and left-ventricular ejection fraction in acute myocardial infarction. Am J Cardiol 1989;63:1301–7.

90. Soufer R, Wohlgelernter D, Vita NA, et al. Intact systolic left-ventricular function in clinical congestive heart failure. Am J Cardiol 1985;55:1032–6.

91. Strauss RH, Stevenson LW, Dadourian BA, et al. Predictability of mitral regurgitation detected by Doppler echocardiography in patients referred for cardiac transplantation. Am J Cardiol 1987 Apr;59:892–4.

92. Wong WF, Gold S, Fukuyama O, et al. Diastolic dysfunction in elderly patients with congestive heart failure. Am J Cardiol 1989 June 15;63:1526–8.

93. Folland ED, Parisi AF, Moynihan PF, et al. Assessment of left-ventricular ejection fraction and volumes by real-time, two-dimensional echocardiography. A comparison of cineangiographic and radionuclide techniques. Circulation 1979 Oct;60:760–6.

94. Stamm RB, Carabello BA, Mayers DL, et al. Two-dimensional echocardiographic measurement of left-ventricular ejection fraction: prospective analysis of what constitutes an adequate determination. Am Heart J 1982 Jul;104:136–44.

95. Albin G, Rahko PS. Comparison of echocardiographic quantitation of left-ventricular ejection fraction to radionuclide angiography in patients with regional wall motion abnormalities. Am J Cardiol 1990 Apr 15;65:1031–2.

96. Chen Y, Sherrid MV, Dwyer EM Jr. Value of two-dimensional echocardiography in evaluating coronary artery disease: a randomized blinded analysis. J Am Coll Cardiol 1985 Apr;5:911–7.

97. Diaz RA, Nihoyannopoulos P, Athanassopoulos G, et al. Usefulness of echocardiography to differentiate dilated cardiomyopathy from coronary-induced congestive heart failure. Am J Cardiol 1991 Nov 1;68:1224–7.

98. Ghali JK, Kadakia S, Cooper RS, et al. Bedside diagnosis of preserved versus impaired left-ventricular systolic function in heart failure. Am J Cardiol 1991 May 1;67:1002–6.

■ 99. Steimle AE, Stevenson LW, Fonarow GG, et al. Prediction of improvement in recent onset cardiomyopathy after referral for heart transplantation. J Am Coll Cardiol 1994;23:553–9.
This retrospective series compared the outcome of patients with acute and chronic dilated cardiomyopathy. Clinical and ventriculographic improvement occurred in 27 percent of patients with acute dilated cardiomyopathy. Predictors of spontaneous improvement included shorter duration of symptoms, lower atrial filling pressures, and higher initial serum sodium. Patients with acute dilated cardiomyopathy experience a greater likelihood of either spontaneous improvement or rapid progression than those with chronic cardiomyopathy and require frequent reassessment of medical therapy and need for transplant listing.

100. Medina R, Panidis IP, Morganroth J, et al. The value of echocardiographic regional wall motion abnormalities in detecting coronary artery disease in patients with or without a dilated left ventricle. Am Heart J 1985;109:799–803.

101. Wallis DE, O'Connell JB, Henkin RE, et al. Segmental wall motion abnormalities in dilated cardiomyopathy: a common finding and good prognostic sign. J Am Coll Cardiol 1984 Oct;4:674–9.

■ 102. Glamann DB, Lange RA, Corbett JR, Hillis LD. Utility of various radionuclide techniques for distinguishing ischemic from nonischemic dilated cardiomyopathy. Arch Intern Med 1992;152:769–772.
Radionuclide venticulography and exercise testing with thallium imaging were unable to differentiate ischemic from nonischemic causes of dilated cardiomyopathy. Segmental wall motion abnormalities were present in 48 percent and thallium perfusion abnormalities in 94 percent of patients with dilated cardiomyopathy.

■ 103.   Bach DS, Beanlands RB, Schwaiger M, Armstrong WF. Heterogeneity of ventricular function and myocardial oxidative metabolism in nonischemic dilated cardiomyopathy. J Am Coll Cardiol 1995;25:1258–62.

Relative preservation of systolic contractility in dilated cardiomyopathy was associated with higher regional oxidative metabolism, suggesting that regional variability in this disorder may be due to mechanisms other than abnormal local wall stress.

104.   Greenberg JM, Murphy JH, Okada RD, et al. Value and limitations of radionuclide angiography in determining the cause of reduced left-ventricular ejection fraction: comparison of idiopathic dilated cardiomyopathy and coronary artery disease. Am J Cardiol 1985 Feb;55:541–4.

■ 105.   Dec GW, Fuster V. Idiopathic dilated cardiomyopathy. N Eng J Med 1994;331: 1564–75.

Comprehensive review of clinical features, natural history, potential pathogenesis, diagnostic evaluation, and current treatment of idiopathic dilated cardiomyopathy.

■ 106.   DiSalvo TG, Mathier M, McNamara D, et al. Preserved right ventricular ejection fraction predicts exercise capacity and survival in advanced heart failure. J Am Coll Cardiol 1995;25:1143–53.

Right-ventricular EF >0.35 was found to be a powerful predictor of exercise capacity and long-term survival in patients with advanced heart failure referred for transplant evaluation.

■ 107.   Vasan RS, Benjamin EJ, Levy D. Prevalence, clinical features and prognosis of diastolic heart failure: an epidemiologic perspective. J Am Coll Cardiol 1995;26: 1565–74.

A comprehensive overview of published reports on the prevalence, clinical features, and prognosis of diastolic heart failure. Symptomatic diastolic heart failure prevalence varies widely from 13 percent to 74 percent of reported series and reported annual mortality ranges from 1.3 percent to 17.5 percent. The need for prospective, community-based studies to better characterize the natural history of the disease is emphasized.

108.   Bonow RO, Udelson JE. Left ventricular diastolic dysfunction as a cause of congestive heart failure: mechanisms and management. Ann Intern Med 1992; 117:502–10.

109.   Cuocolo A, Sax FL, Brush JE, et al. Left ventricular hypertrophy and impaired diastolic filling in essential hypertension. Diastolic mechanisms for systolic dysfunction during exercise. Circulation 1990;81:978–86.

110.   Fouad F, Slominiski M, Tarazi RC. Left ventricular diastolic function in hypertension: relation to left ventricular mass and systolic function. J Am Coll Cardiol 1984;3:1500–6.

111.   Fouad FM, Tarazi RC, Gallagher JH, et al. Abnormal left ventricular relaxation in hypertensive patients. Clin Sci 1980;59(Suppl 6):4114–45.

112.   Inouye I, Massie B, Loge D, et al. Abnormal left ventricular filling: an early finding in mild to moderate systemic hypertension. Am J Cardiol 1985;53:120–6.

113.   Cuocolo A, Sax FL, Brush JE, et al. Impaired diastolic function in hypertensive patients without left ventricular hypertrophy [abstract]. J Nucl Med 1989;30:780.

■ 114.   Vasan R, Benjamin EJ, Levy D. Congestive heart failure with normal left ventricular systolic function. Arch Intern Med 1996;156:146–57.
         An up-to-date review of differential diagnosis of diastolic heart failure and a brief discussion of current approaches to treatment.

■ 115.   Urbano-Marquez A, Estuch R, Fernandez-Sola J, et al. The greater risk of alcoholic cardiomyopathy and myopathy in women compared with men. J Am Med Assoc 1995;274:149–54.
         This study confirms that alcoholic cardiomyopathy is as common in women as in men, despite the fact that the mean total alcohol dose among females was 60 percent that of their male counterparts. As alcohol consumption continues to increase among women, this enhanced susceptibility to cardiac damage suggests that the incidence of alcoholic cardiomyopathy may increase in women.

  116.   Demakis JG, Proskey A, Rahimtoola SH, et al. The natural course of alcoholic cardiomyopathy. Ann Intern Med 1974 Mar;80:293–7.

  117.   Mølgaard H, Kristensen BO, Baandrup U. Importance of abstention from alcohol in alcoholic heart disease. Int J Cardiol 1990;26:373–5.

  118.   Regan TJ. Alcohol and the cardiovascular system. JAMA 1990 Jul 18;264:377–81.

■ 119.   Mason JM, O'Connell JB, Herskowitz A, et al. for the Multicenter Myocarditis Treatment Trial Investigators. A clinical trial of immunosuppressive therapy for myocarditis. N Engl J Med 1995;333:269–75.
         The effect of prednisone and cyclosporine immunosuppression was evaluated in 111 patients with histologically-verified myocarditis. EF at 28 weeks rose from 24 percent to 34 percent in both the control and immunosuppressed groups. Overall mortality was not influenced by treatment. Cyclosporine-based immunosuppression is ineffective therapy for dilated cardiomyopathy due to myocarditis.

■ 120.   Bolton MB, Tilley BC, Kuder J, et al. The cost and effectiveness of an education program for adults who have asthma. J Gen Intern Med 1991;6:401–407.

■ 121.   Glasgow RE, Osteen VL. Evaluating diabetes education. Are we measuring the most important outcomes? Diabetes Care 1992;15:1423–1432.

  122.   Dracup K, Walden JA, Stevenson LW, et al. Quality of life in patients with advanced heart failure. J Heart Lung Transplant 1992;2:273–9.

  123.   Rideout E, Montemuro M. Hope, morale and adaptation in patients with chronic heart failure. J Adv Nurs 1986;11:429–38.

■ 124.   Belardinelli R, Georgiou D, Scocco V, Barstow TJ, Purcaro A: Low intensity exercise training in patients with chronic heart failure. J Am Coll Cardiol 1995;26:975–982.

■ 125.   Hambrecht R, Niebauer J, Fiehn E, et al: Physical training in patients with stable chronic heart failure: effects on cardiorespiratory fitness and ultrastructural abnormalities of leg muscles. J Am Coll Cardiol 1995;25:1239–1249.

■ 126.   McKelvie RS, Teo KK, McCartney N, et al. Effects of exercise training in patients with congestive heart failure: a critical review. J Am Coll Cardiol 1995; 25:789–796.

  127.   Julian D. Cardiology. London: Bailliere Tindall; 1988.

  128.   On bedresting in heart failure [editorial]. Lancet 1990;336(8721):975–6.

  129.   Convertino VA, Goldwater DJ, Sandler H. Bedrest-induced peak VO_2 reduction

associated with age, gender, and aerobic capacity. Aviat Space Environ Med 1986 Jan;57:17–22.

130. Convertino VA, Doerr DF, Mathes KL, et al. Changes in volume, muscle compartment, and compliance of the lower extremities in man following 30 days of exposure to simulated microgravity. Aviat Space Environ Med 1989 Jul;60:653–8.

131. Saltin B, Blomqvist G, Mitchell JH, et al. Response to exercise after bed rest and after training. Circulation 1968;38(5 Suppl):VII-1 to VII-78.

132. Dudley GA, Duvoisin MR, Convertino VA, et al. Alterations of the in vivo torque-velocity relationship of human skeletal muscle following 30 days exposure to simulated microgravity. Aviat Space Environ Med 1989;60:659–63.

133. Coats AJ, Adamopoulos S, Meyer TE, et al. Effects of physical training in chronic heart failure. Lancet 1990;335(8681):63–6.

134. Kellermann JJ, Shemesh J, Fisman EZ, et al. Arm exercise training in the rehabilitation of patients with impaired ventricular function and heart failure. Cardiology 1990;77:130–8.

135. Maskin CS, Reddy HK, Gulanick M, et al. Exercise training in chronic heart failure: improvement in cardiac performance and maximum oxygen uptake [abstract]. Circulation 1986 Oct;74(4 Pt 2):II-310.

136. Meyer TE, Casadei B, Coats AJ, et al. Angiotensin-converting enzyme inhibition and physical training in heart failure. J Intern Med 1991;230:407–13.

137. Sullivan MJ, Higginbotham MB, Cobb FR. Exercise training in patients with chronic heart failure delays ventilatory anaerobic threshold and improves submaximal exercise performance. Circulation 1989;79:324–9.

138. Coats AJ, Adamopoulos S, Radaelli A, et al. Controlled trial of physical training in chronic heart failure. Exercise performance, hemodynamics, ventilation, and autonomic function. Circulation 1992;85:2119–31.

139. Arvan S. Exercise performance of the high risk acute myocardial infarction patient after cardiac rehabilitation. Am J Cardiol 1988 Aug 1;62:197–201.

140. Jugdutt BI, Michorowski BL, Kappagoda CT. Exercise training after anterior Q wave myocardial infarction: importance of regional left-ventricular function and topography. J Am Coll Cardiol 1988 Aug;12:362–72.

141. Dubach P, Froelicher VF. Cardiac rehabilitation for heart failure patients. Cardiology 1989;76:368–73.

142. Sullivan MJ, Higginbotham MB, Cobb FR. Exercise training in patients with severe left-ventricular dysfunction: hemodynamic and metabolic effects. Circulation 1988;78:506–15.

143. Sullivan MJ, Cobb FR. The anaerobic threshold in chronic heart failure. Relation to blood lactate, ventilatory basis, reproducibility, and response to exercise training. Circulation 1990 Jan;81(1 Suppl):II-47 to II-58.

144. AMA Council on Foods and Nutrition. Sodium-restricted diets: the rationale, complications, and practical aspects of their use. JAMA 1954 Nov 13;156: 1081–3.

145. Dahl L. Salt and hypertension. Am J Clin Nutr 1972;25:231–44.

146. Dyckner T, Wester P. Salt and water balance in congestive heart failure. Acta Med Scand 1986;707(Suppl):27–31.

147. Healy MA, Aslam M. Dietary sodium and cardiac oedema. Nurs Times 1984 Oct;80:41–5.

148. Hopkins BE, Taylor RR. Sodium restriction in cardiac failure: a survey of physicians' attitudes and practice. Med J Aust 1972 Feb;1:370–1.

149. Kris-Etherton PM, Kisloff L, Kassouf RA, et al. Teaching principles and cost of sodium-restricted diets. J Am Diet Assoc 1982;80:50–4.

150. Snively WD Jr, Beshear DR, Roberts KT. Sodium-restricted diet: review and current status. Nurs Forum 1974;13:59–66.

151. Snively WD Jr, Roberts KT, Beshear DR. The sodium-restricted diet revisited. J Indiana State Med Assoc 1974;67:1067–76.

152. Tobin JR. The treatment of congestive heart failure: digitalis glycosides are still the primary mode of therapy. Arch Intern Med 1978 Mar;138:453–4.

153. Tucker RM, Van Den Berg CJ, Knox FG. Diuretics: role of sodium balance. Mayo Clin Proc 1980;55:261–6.

154. Conway N. Hemodynamic effects of ethyl alcohol in coronary heart disease. Am Heart J 1968 Oct;76:581–2.

155. Gould L, Zahir M, DeMartino A, et al. Cardiac effects of a cocktail. JAMA 1971 Dec 20;218:1799–802.

156. Packer M, Carver JR, Rodeheffer RJ, et al. Effect of oral milrinone on mortality in severe chronic heart failure. N Engl J Med 1991 Nov;325:1468–75.

157. Kannel WB. Epidemiological aspects of heart failure. Cardiol Clin 1989;7:1–9.

158. Sugrue DD, Rodeheffer RJ, Codd MB, et al. The clinical course of idiopathic dilated cardiomyopathy: a population-based study. Ann Intern Med 1992;117:117–23.

159. Dracup K, Guzy PM, Taylor SE, et al. Cardiopulmonary resuscitation (CPR) training: for family members of high-risk cardiac patients. Arch Intern Med 1986;146:1757–61.

160. Ghali JK, Kadakia S, Cooper R, et al. Precipitating factors leading to decompensation of heart failure. Traits among urban blacks. Arch Intern Med 1988 Sep;148:2013–6.

161. Mullen PD, Green LW, Persinger GS. Clinical trials of patient education for chronic conditions: a comparative meta-analysis of intervention types. Prev Med 1985;14:753–81.

162. Mullen PD, Mains DA, Velez R. A meta-analysis of controlled trials of cardiac patient education. Patient Educ Couns 1992;19:143–62.

163. Küpper AJ, Fintelman H, Huige MC, et al. Cross-over comparison of the fixed combination of hydrochlorothiazide and triamterene and the free combination of furosemide and triamterene in the maintenance treatment of congestive heart failure. Eur J Clin Pharmacol 1986;30:341–3.

164. Whight C, Morgan T, Carney S, et al. Diuretics, cardiac failure and potassium depletion: a rational approach. Med J Aust 1974 Dec 7;2:831–3.

■ 165. Gristead WC, Francis MJ, Marks GF, et al. Discontinuation of chronic diuretic therapy in stable congestive heart failure secondary to coronary artery disease or to idiopathic dilated cardiomyopathy. Am J Cardiol 1994;73:881–886.
Addition of an ACE inhibitor may obviate the need for diuretic therapy in patients with chronic stable heart failure and LVEF >25 percent who require less than 40 mg of furosemide daily. The study does not indicate whether diuretic withdrawal is likely to succeed in patients who are already receiving ACE inhibitor therapy.

■ 166. Stevenson LW. Tailored therapy before transplantation for treatment of advanced heart failure effective use of vasodilator and diuretics. J Heart Lung Transplant 1991;10:468–76.

A detailed discussion of hemodynamically guided therapy for patients with advanced heart failure. Common misunderstandings concerning management of difficult patients are summarized.

167. Edmonds CJ, Jasani B. Total-body potassium in hypertensive patients during prolonged diuretic therapy. Lancet 1972 Jul 1;2(766):8–12.

■ 168. Dahlstrom U, Karlsson E. Captopril and spironolactone therapy for refractory congestive heart failure. Am J Cardiol 1993;71:29A–33A.

Potential benefits of aldosterone inhibition on ventricular fibrosis and remodeling are discussed. Similar to other heart failure agents, the actions of diuretics are often multifactorial.

169. Cody RJ. Management of refractory congestive heart failure. Am J Cardiol 1992 Jun 4;69:141G–149G.

■ 170. Konstam MA, Kronenberg MW, Rousseau MF, et al. for the SOLVD Investigators. Effects of the angiotensin converting enzyme inhibitor enalapril on the long-term progression of left ventricular dilatation in patients with asymptomatic systolic dysfunction. Circulation 1993;88(part 1):2277–83.

Compared to placebo, enalapril treatment slowed the rate of left-ventricular dilatation as measured by radionuclide ventriculography and by pressure-volume loop analysis in patients with asymptomatic left-ventricular dysfunction (LVEF <35 percent). Asymptomatic patients demonstrated a slower rate of spontaneous LV dilatation and less reduction in LV volumes by ACE inhibition than that previously noted in patients with symptomatic heart failure.

■ 171. The Acute Ramipril Efficacy Study Investigators. Effect of ramipril on mortality and morbidity of survivors of acute myocardial infarction with clinical evidence of heart failure. Lancet 1993:342:821–28.

The AIRE study randomized 2,006 patients to treatment with ramipril or placebo following acute MI. Ramipril reduced all-cause mortality by 27 percent and also decreased severe heart failure, MI, and stroke. These results extend those of the SAVE trial by demonstrating that ACE inhibitor treatment need not be confined only to post-MI patients with an LVEF <35 percent.

■ 172. Ambrosioni E, Borghi C, Magnani B, et al. The effect of the angiotensin-converting enzyme inhibitor zofenopril on mortality and morbidity after anterior myocardial infarction. N Engl J Med 1995;332:80–5.

The SMILE trial examined the utility of short-term (6 weeks) treatment with zofenopril or placebo following acute anterior MI on early and late outcomes. Brief ACE inhibitor treatment decreased the risk of death or severe heart failure by 34 percent at 6 weeks and also lowered 12 month mortality by 29 percent. This study raises but does not answer the important question: what is the optimal duration of ACE inhibitor treatment for asymptomatic post-MI patients?

■ 173. LeJemetel TH, Hochman JS, Sonnenblick EH. Indications for immediate angiotensin-converting enzyme inhibition in patients with acute myocardial infarction. J Am Coll Cardiol 1995;25(Suppl):47S–51S.

A comprehensive and concise review of all recent large randomized studies of

ACE inhibitor treatment in patients with acute MI. Recommendations for their administration are also provided.

■ 174.   Kleber FT, Niemoller L, Duering W. Impact of converting enzyme inhibition on progression of chronic heart failure: results of the Munich Mild Heart Failure Trial. Br Heart J 1992;67:289–296.
This trail examined the utility of ACE inhibitor treatment on prognosis in mild heart failure. Early captopril therapy resulted in a marked reduction in progression of disease to severe symptoms (NYHA Class IV) and significantly reduced mortality due to progressive heart failure. Sudden death risk was not reduced in this population.

175.   Bussmann WD, Storger H, Hadler D, et al. Long-term treatment of severe chronic heart failure with captopril: a double-blind, randomized, placebo-controlled, long-term study. J Cardiovasc Pharmacol 1987;9(Suppl 2):S50–60.

176.   The Captopril-Digoxin Multicenter Research Group. A placebo-controlled trial of captopril in refractory chronic congestive heart failure. J Am Coll Cardiol 1983;2:755–63.

177.   Franciosa JA, Wilen MM, Jordan RA. Effects of enalapril, a new angiotensin-converting enzyme inhibitor, in a controlled trial in heart failure. J Am Coll Cardiol 1985 Jan;5:101–7.

178.   Jennings G, Kiat H, Nelson L, et al. Enalapril for severe congestive heart failure: a double-blind study. Med J Aust 1984 Nov 24;141:723–6.

179.   Kleber FX, Niemoüller L, Fischer M, et al. Influence of severity of heart failure on the efficacy of angiotensin-converting enzyme inhibition. Am J Cardiol 1991;68:121D–126D.

180.   Magnani B, Magelli C. Captopril in mild heart failure: preliminary observations of a long-term, double-blind, placebo-controlled multicentre trial. Postgrad Med J 1986;62(Suppl 1):153–8.

181.   McGrath BP, Arnolda L, Matthews PG, et al. Controlled trial of enalapril in congestive cardiac failure. Br Heart J 1985;54:405–14.

182.   Remes J, Nikander P, Rehnberg S, et al. Enalapril in chronic heart failure, a double-blind placebo-controlled study. Ann Clin Res 1986;18:124–8.

183.   Sharpe DN, Murphy J, Coxon R, et al. Enalapril in patients with chronic heart failure: a placebo-controlled, randomized, double-blind study. Circulation 1984; 70:271–8.

184.   Chalmers JP, West MJ, Cyran J, et al. Placebo-controlled study of lisinopril in congestive heart failure: a multicentre study. J Cardiovasc Pharmacol 1987;9(Suppl 3):S89–97.

185.   Lewis GR. Comparison of lisinopril versus placebo for congestive heart failure. Am J Cardiol 1989 Feb 21;63:12D–16D.

186.   Riegger GA. The effects of ACE inhibitors on exercise capacity in the treatment of congestive heart failure. J Cardiovasc Pharmacol 1990;15(Suppl 2):S41–6.

187.   Riegger GA. Effects of quinapril on exercise tolerance in patients with mild to moderate heart failure. Eur Heart J 1991;12:705–11.

188.   Brogden RN, Todd PA, Sorkin EM. Captopril: an update of its pharmacodynamic and pharmacokinetic properties, and therapeutic use in hypertension and congestive heart failure. Drugs 1988 Nov;36:540–600.

189. Cleland JG, Dargie HJ. Heart failure, renal function, and angiotensin converting enzyme inhibitors. Kidney Int 1987;31(Suppl 20):S220–8.

190. Cleland JG, Gillen G, Dargie HJ. The effects of furosemide and angiotensin-converting enzyme inhibitors and their combination on cardiac and renal hemodynamics in heart failure. Eur Heart J 1988;9:132–41.

191. Crantock L, Prentice R, Powell L. Cholestatic jaundice associated with captopril therapy. J Gastroenterol Hepatol 1991;6:528–30.

192. Frank GJ. The safety of ACE inhibitors for the treatment of hypertension and congestive heart failure. Cardiology 1989;76(Suppl 2):56–67.

193. Hasford J, Bussmann WD, Delius W, et al. First dose hypotension with enalapril and prazosin in congestive heart failure. Int J Cardiol 1991;31:287–94.

194. Kjekshus J, Swedberg K. Tolerability of enalapril in congestive heart failure. Am J Cardiol 1988;62:67A–72A.

195. O'Neill CJ, Bowes SG, Sullens CM, et al. Evaluation of the safety of enalapril in the treatment of heart failure in the very old. Eur J Clin Pharmacol 1988; 35:143–50.

196. Packer M. Identification of risk factors predisposing to the development of functional renal insufficiency during treatment with converting-enzyme inhibitors in chronic heart failure. Cardiology 1989;76(Suppl 2):50–5.

197. Suki WN. Renal hemodynamic consequences of angiotensin-converting enzyme inhibition in congestive heart failure. Arch Intern Med 1989 Mar;149:669–73.

198. Warner NJ, Rush JE, Keegan ME. Tolerability of enalapril in congestive heart failure. Am J Cardiol 1989 Feb;63:33D–37D.

■ 199. Packer M, Lee WH, Yushak M, Medina R. Comparison of captopril and enalapril in patients with severe chronic heart failure. N Engl J Med 1986;315:847–853.

This randomized trial directly compared the short-term and long-term hemodynamic and clinical effects of captopril and enalapril in severe heart failure patients. The longer acting agent, enalapril, produced more symptomatic hypotension and renal dysfunction. These findings suggest that ACE inhibitor treatment should be initiated with a short-acting agent when severe heart failure exists. These results should not be extrapolated to patients with less severe disease in whom a once per day treatment has many potential advantages.

200. Giles TD, Katz R, Sullivan JM, et al. Short- and long-acting angiotensin-converting enzyme inhibitors: a randomized trial of lisinopril versus captopril in the treatment of congestive heart failure. J Am Coll Cardiol 1989 May;13: 1240–7.

201. Packer M, Gheorghiade M, Young D, et al. Withdrawal of digoxin from patients with chronic heart failure treated with angiotensin-converting-enzyme inhibitors. N Engl J Med 1993;329:1–7.

202. Presented at the 45th Annual Scientific Session of the American College of Cardiology, Orlando, Florida, March 24–27, 1996.

203. Jaeschke R, Oxman AD, Guyatt GH. To what extent do congestive heart failure patients in sinus rhythm benefit from digoxin therapy? A systematic overview and meta-analysis. Am J Med 1990;88:279–86.

204. The Captopril-Digoxin Multicenter Research Group. Comparative effects of ther-

apy with captopril and digoxin in patients with mild to moderate heart failure. JAMA 1988 Jan 22/29;259:539–44.

■ 205.   Lee DCS, Johnson RA, Bingham JB, et al. Heart failure in outpatients. A randomized trial of digoxin versus placebo. N Eng J Med 1982;306:699–705.

Digoxin's effects on heart failure signs and symptoms were examined in 25 patients in normal sinus rhythm using a randomized, double-blind, crossover protocol. Digoxin improved heart failure in 56 percent of patients; it was most likely to produce benefit in patients with advanced heart failure, lower EF, and a chronic third heart sound.

206.   DiBianco R, Shabetai R, Kostuk W, et al. A comparison of oral milrinone, digoxin, and their combination in the treatment of patients with chronic heart failure. N Engl J Med 1989;320:677–83.

■ 207.   Gheorghiade M, Ferguson D. Digoxin—a neurohormonal modulator in heart failure? Circulation 1991;84:2186.

This review briefly summarizes the experimental and clinical evidence supporting digoxin's effects on baroreceptor function in chronic heart failure and speculates that the agent's beneficial effects may result from its neurohormonal rather than positive inotropic properties.

208.   Marcus FI. Pharmacokinetic interactions between digoxin and other drugs. J Am Coll Cardiol 1985;5(Suppl A):82A–90A.

■ 209.   Fonarow GC, Chelmsky-Fallick C, Stevenson LW, et al. Effect of direct vasodilation with hydralazine versus angiotensin-converting enzyme inhibition with captopril on mortality in advanced heart failure: The Hy-C Trial. J Am Coll Cardiol 1992;19:842–850.

This single institution study directly compared the effects of an ACE inhibitor and smooth muscle vasodilators in 117 patients with severe heart failure. Although both regimens were titrated to achieve comparable hemodynamic effects, captopril resulted in substantially better 12 month survival (81 percent vs. 51 percent). However, crossover from captopril to hydralazine-isosorbide dinitrate therapy occurred in 40 percent of patients due to intolerable side effects or an inadequate hemodynamic response. Hydralazine-isosorbide dinitrate remains a second line treatment option for ACE intolerant patients.

210.   Elkayam U. Tolerance to organic nitrates: evidence, mechanisms, clinical relevance, and strategies for prevention. Ann Intern Med 1991;114:667–77.

■ 211.   Crozier I, Ikram H, Awan N, et al. Losartan in heart failure. Hemodynamic effects and tolerability. Circulation 1995;91:691–97.

Oral losartan, an angiotensin-2 receptor blocker, produced favorable hemodynamic effects at doses of 25 mg and 50 mg in patients with chronic heart failure during short-term administration. Additional hemodynamic benefits were observed after 12 weeks of therapy in patients who were also receiving digoxin, diuretics, and an ACE inhibitor.

212.   Kyrle PA, Korninger C, Gössinger H, et al. Prevention of arterial and pulmonary embolism by oral anticoagulants in patients with dilated cardiomyopathy. Thromb Haemost 1985;54:521–3.

213.   Sherman DG, Dyken ML, Fisher M, et al. Antithrombotic therapy for cerebrovascular disorders. Chest 1989 Feb;95(Suppl 2):1405–555.

214. Falk RH. A plea for a clinical trial of anticoagulation in dilated cardiomyopathy [editorial]. Am J Cardiol 1990 Apr 1;65:14–5.
215. Ciaccheri M, Castelli G, Cecchi F, et al. Lack of correlation between intracavitary thrombosis detected by cross sectional echocardiography and systemic emboli in patients with dilated cardiomyopathy. Br Heart J 1989 Jul;62:26–9.
216. Fuster V, Gersh BJ, Giuliani ER, et al. The natural history of idiopathic dilated cardiomyopathy. Am J Cardiol 1981 Mar;47:525–31.
217. Gottdiener JS, Gay JA, Van Voorhees L, et al. Frequency and embolic potential of left-ventricular thrombus in dilated cardiomyopathy: assessment by 2-dimensional echocardiography. Am J Cardiol 1983;52:1281–5.
218. Roberts WC, Siegel RJ, McManus BM. Idiopathic dilated cardiomyopathy: analysis of 152 necropsy patients. Am J Cardiol 1987;60:1340–55.
219. The Boston Area Anticoagulation Trial for Atrial Fibrillation Investigators. The effect of low-dose warfarin on the risk of stroke in patients with nonrheumatic atrial fibrillation. N Engl J Med 1990;323:1505–11.
220. Petersen P, Boysen G, Godtfredsen J, et al. Placebo-controlled, randomised trial of warfarin and aspirin for prevention of thromboembolic complications in chronic atrial fibrillation. The Copenhagen AFASAK study. Lancet 1989 Jan 28; 1(8631):175–9.
221. The Stroke Prevention in Atrial Fibrillation Investigators. Stroke prevention in atrial fibrillation study. Final results. Circulation 1991;84:527–39.
222. The Stroke Prevention in Atrial Fibrillation Investigators. Predictors of thromboembolism in atrial fibrillation: I. Clinical features of patients at risk. Ann Intern Med 1992 Jan 1;116:1–12.
■ 223. Baker DW, Wright RF. Management of heart failure IV. Anticoagulation for patients with heart failure due to left ventricular systolic dysfunction. JAMA 1994;272:1614–8.
   A critical review of the incidence of arterial thromboembolic complications in chronic heart failure patients who are in sinus rhythm and not receiving anticoagulation. The absence of controlled trials assessing the efficacy or risk of anticoagulation in heart failure populations is highlighted.
224. Anderson JL, Lutz JR, Gilbert EM, et al. A randomized trial of low-dose beta-blockade therapy for idiopathic dilated cardiomyopathy. Am J Cardiol 1985; 55:471–5.
225. Cucchini F, Compostella L, Papalia D, et al. Chronic treatment of dilated cardiomyopathy by beta-blocking drugs. Long term clinical and hemodynamic evaluation. G Ital Cardiol 1988 Oct;18:835–42.
226. Currie PJ, Kelly MJ, McKenzie A, et al. Oral beta-adrenergic blockade with metoprolol in chronic severe dilated cardiomyopathy. J Am Coll Cardiol 1984 Jan;3:203–9.
227. Fisher ML, Gottlieb SS, Hamilton B, et al. Beneficial effects of metoprolol in CHF associated with coronary artery disease [abstract]. Circulation 1991;84(4) (Suppl II):II–312.
228. Ikram H, Fitzpatrick MA. Beta blockade for dilated cardiomyopathy: the evidence against therapeutic benefit. Eur Heart J 1983;4(Suppl A):179–80.
229. Swedberg K, Hjalmarson A, Waagstein F, et al. Adverse effects of beta-blockade

withdrawal in patients with congestive cardiomyopathy. Br Heart J 1980; 44:134–42.

230. Verdin A, Wikstrand J, Wilhelmsson C, et al. Left-ventricular function and beta-blockade in chronic ischaemic heart failure. Double-blind, cross-over study of propranolol and penbutolol using non-invasive techniques. Br Heart J 1980; 44:101–7.

231. Waagstein F, Bristow MR, Swedberg K, et al. Beneficial effects of metoprolol in idiopathic dilated cardiomyopathy. Lancet 1993 Dec 11:342(8885):1441–6.

232. Weber KT, Likoff MJ, McCarthy D. Low-dose beta blockade in the treatment of chronic cardiac failure. Am Heart J 1982;104:877–9.

233. Yokota Y, Nomura H, Kawai H, et al. Effects of long-term beta-blockade (metoprolol) therapy in patients with dilated cardiomyopathy. Jpn Circ J 1991 Apr;55: 343–55.

234. Engelmeier RS, O'Connell JB, Walsh R, et al. Improvement in symptoms and exercise tolerance by metoprolol in patients with dilated cardiomyopathy: a double-blind, randomized, placebo-controlled trial. Circulation 1985 Sep;72:536–46.

■ 235. Packer M, Bristow MR, Cohn JN, et al. for the US Carvedilol heart failure study group. Effect of carvedilol on morbidity and mortality in chronic heart failure. N Eng J Med 1996 May 23; 334(21):1349–55.
    The effect of carvedilol on mortality was analyzed by pooling the results of four large controlled clinical trials. Carvedilol reduced all-cause mortality by 67 percent. The magnitude of the benefit was similar regardless of heart failure etiology or the severity of symptoms.

236. Cleland JG, Henderson E, McLenachan J, et al. Effect of captopril, an angiotensin-converting enzyme inhibitor, in patients with angina pectoris and heart failure. J Am Coll Cardiol 1991 Mar 1;17:733–9.

■ 237. Rutherford JD, Pfeffer MA, Moye LA, et al. Effects of captopril on ischemic events after myocardial infarction. Results of the survival and ventricular enlargement trial. Circulation 1994;90:1731–38.
    Among the 2,231 patients randomized in the SAVE trial, captopril therapy reduced the risk of recurrent MI by 25 percent and the risk of death from recurrent MI by 32 percent. The need for coronary revascularization was also reduced by captopril. Potential mechanisms are discussed.

■ 238. Lonn EM, Jha P, Montague TJ, et al. Emerging role of angiotensin-converting enzyme inhibitors in cardiac and vascular protection. Circulation 1994;90: 2056–67.
    The antiatherogenic and antiproliferative effects of ACE inhibitors are reviewed; results of completed ACE inhibitor trials in heart failure and post-MI populations summarized, and designs of ongoing ACE inhibitor trials are discussed.

■ 239. O'Connor CM, Belkin RN, Carson PE, et al. Effect of amlodipine on mode of death in severe chronic heart failure: the PRAISE trial. Circulation 1995; 92:I–143A.
    Amlodipine reduced sudden deaths by 38 percent and progressive heart failure deaths by 45 percent in patients with severe heart failure due to nonischemic cardiomyopathy. Unfortunately, no mortality reduction was observed for patients with ischemic heart disease.

■ 240. Doval HC, Nul DR, Grancelli HO, et al. Randomised trial of low-dose amiodarone in severe congestive heart failure. Lancet 1994;344:493–8.

Amiodarone (300 mg daily) reduced all cause mortality by 28 percent and also decreased hospitalizations in this randomized study of 562 patients with advanced heart failure and asymptomatic ventricular ectopy. Its beneficial effects were independent of the presence of complex ventricular arrhythmias.

241. Kannel WB, Cupples A. Epidemiology and risk profile of cardiac failure. Cardiovasc Drugs Ther 1988 Nov;2:387–95.

242. Bulkley BH. The cardiomyopathies. Hosp Pract 1984;19:59–73.

243. Pasternac A, Bourassa MG. Pathogenesis of chest pain in patients with cardiomyopathies and normal coronary arteries. Int J Cardiol 1983 Jun;3:273–80.

244. Kotler TS, Diamond GA. Exercise thallium-201 scintigraphy in the diagnosis and prognosis of coronary artery disease. Ann Intern Med 1990;113:684–702.

245. Murphy ML, Hultgren HN, Detre K, et al. Treatment of chronic stable angina: a preliminary report of the randomized Veterans Administration Cooperative Study. N Engl J Med 1977;297;621–7.

246. Varnauskas E. Twelve-year followup of survival in the randomized European Coronary Surgery Study. N Engl J Med 1988;319:332–7.

247. Alderman EL, Fisher LD, Litwin P, et al. Results of coronary artery surgery in patients with poor left ventricular function (CASS). Circulation 1983 Oct;68:785–95.

248. Faulkner SL, Stoney WS, Alford WC, et al. Ischemic cardiomyopathy: medical versus surgical treatment. J Thorac Cardiovasc Surg 1977 Jul;74:77–82.

249. Manley JC, King JF, Zeft HJ, et al. The "bad" left ventricle: results of coronary surgery and effect on late survival. J Thorac Cardiovasc Surg 1976 Dec;72:841–8.

250. Pigott JD, Kouchoukos NT, Oberman A, et al. Late results of medical and surgical therapy for patients with coronary artery disease and depressed ejection fraction [abstract]. Circulation 1982;66(Suppl 2):II–220.

251. Vliestra RE, Assad-Morell JL, Frye RL, et al. Survival predictors in coronary artery disease. Medical and surgical comparisons. Mayo Clin Proc 1977;52:85–90.

252. Hammermeister KE, DeRouen TA, Dodge HT. Comparison of survival of medically and surgically treated coronary disease patients in Seattle Heart Watch: a nonrandomized study. Circulation 1982;65(7 Pt 2):53–9.

253. Yatteau RF, Peter RH, Behar VS, et al. Ischemic cardiomyopathy: the myopathy of coronary artery disease. Am J Cardiol 1974;34:520–5.

254. Califf RM, Harrell FE Jr, Lee KL, et al. The evolution of medical and surgical therapy for coronary artery disease. A 15-year perspective. JAMA 1989 Apr 14;261:2077–86.

255. Coronary Artery Surgery Study (CASS) Principal Investigators and Their Associates. Coronary Artery Surgery Study (CASS): a randomized trial of coronary artery bypass surgery. Survival data. Circulation 1983;68:939–50.

256. Muhlbaier LH, Pryor DB, Rankin JS, et al. Observational comparison of event-free survival with medical and surgical therapy in patients with coronary artery disease. 20 years of follow-up. Circulation 1992;86(5 Suppl):II-198 to II-204.

■ 257. Luciani GB, Faggian G, Razzolini R, et al. Severe ischemic left ventricular failure: coronary operation or heart transplantation? Ann Thorac Surg 1993; 55: 719–723.

258.   Akins CW, Pohost GM, DeSanctis RW, et al. Selection of angina-free patients with severe left-ventricular dysfunction for myocardial revascularization. Am J Cardiol 1980 Oct;46:695–700.

259.   Luu M, Stevenson LW, Brunken RC, et al. Delayed recovery of revascularized myocardium after referral for cardiac transplantation. Am Heart J 1990 Mar; 119:668–70.

260.   Naunheim KS, Dean PA, Fiore DA, et al. Cardiac surgery in the octogenarian. Eur J Cardiothorac Surg 1990;4:130–5.

261.   Spencer FC, Green GE, Tice DA, et al. Coronary artery bypass grafts for congestive heart failure: a report of experiences with 40 patients. J Thorac Cardiovasc Surg 1971;62:529–42.

■ 262.   Dreyfus GD, Duboc D, Blasco A, et al. Myocardial viability assessment in ischemic cardiomyopathy: benefits of coronary revascularization. Ann Thorac Surg 1994;57:1402–7; discussion 1407–8.

263.   Christakis GT, Ivanov J, Weisel R, et al. The changing pattern of coronary artery bypass surgery. Circulation 1989 Sep;80(3 Pt 1):I151–61.

264.   Hannan EL, Kilburn H Jr, O'Donnell JF, et al. Adult open heart surgery in New York State. An analysis of risk factors and hospital mortality rates. JAMA 1990 Dec 5;264:2768–74.

■ 265.   Lansman SL, Cohen M, Galla JD, et al. Coronary bypass with ejection fraction of 0.20 or less using centigrade cardioplegia long-term follow-up. Ann Thorac Surg 1993;56:480–5; discussion 485–6.

266.   Higgins TL, Estafanous FG, Loop FD, et al. Stratification of morbidity and mortality outcome by preoperative risk factors in coronary artery bypass patients: a clinical severity score. JAMA 1992 May 6;267:2344–8.

■ 267.   Dreyfus G, Duboc D, Blasco A, et al. Coronary surgery can be an alternative to heart transplantation in selected patients with end-stage ischemic heart disease. Eur J Cardiothorac Surg 1993;7:482–7; discussion 488.

■ 268.   Baker DW, Jones R, Hodges J, et al. Management of heart failure. III. The role of revascularization in the treatment of patients with moderate or severe left ventricular systolic dysfunction. JAMA 1994;272:1528–1534.

■ 269.   Kron IL, Flanagan TL, Blackbourne LH, et al. Coronary revascularization rather than cardiac transplantation for chronic ischemic cardiomyopathy. Ann Surg 1989;210:348–52; discussion 352–4.

■ 270.   Langenburg SE, Buchanan SA, Blackbourne LH, et al. Predicting survival after coronary revascularization for ischemic cardiomyopathy. Ann Thorac Surg 1995;60:1193–6; discussion 1196–7.

271.   Williams SV, Nash DB, Goldfarb N. Differences in mortality from coronary artery bypass graft surgery at five teaching hospitals. JAMA 1991 Aug 14;226: 10–15.

272.   Cohen M, Charney R, Hershman R, et al. Reversal of chronic ischemic myocardial dysfunction after transluminal coronary angioplasty. J Am Coll Cardiol 1988 Nov;12:1193–8.

273. Hartzler GO, Rutherford BD, McConahay DR, et al. "High-risk" percutaneous transluminal coronary angioplasty. Am J Cardiol 1988 May;61:33G–37G.

274. Klein HH, Neuhaus KL. Delayed improvement of myocardial function after recanalization of a chronic coronary occlusion in a patient with intractable heart failure. Eur Heart J 1990;11:280–6.

275. Reinfeld HB, Samet P, Hildner FJ. Resolution of congestive failure, mitral regurgitation, and angina after percutaneous transluminal coronary angioplasty of triple vessel disease. Cathet Cardiovasc Diagn 1985;11:273–7.

276. Serota H, Deligonul U, Lee W, et al. Predictors of cardiac survival after percutaneous transluminal coronary angioplasty in patients with severe left-ventricular dysfunction. Am J Cardiol 1991 Feb 15;67:367–72.

277. Taylor GJ, Rabinovich E, Mikell FL, et al. Percutaneous transluminal coronary angioplasty as palliation for patients considered poor surgical candidates. Am Heart J 1986 May;111:840–4.

■ 278. Gerber B, Vanoverschelde JL, Bol A, et al. Sequential use of dobutamine echo and PET to identify viable myocardium. Circulation 1995;92:I-479(Abstract)

279. Kiat H. Berman DS, Maddahi J, et al. Late reversibility of tomographic myocardial thallium-201 defects: an accurate marker of myocardial viability. J Am Coll Cardiol 1988 Dec;12:1456–63.

280. Brunken R, Schwaiger M, Grover-McKay M, et al. Positron emission tomography detects tissue metabolic activity in myocardial segments with persistent thallium perfusion defects. J Am Coll Cardiol 1987;10:557–67.

■ 281. Cigarroa CG, deFilippi CR, Brickner ME, et al. Dobutamine stress echocardiography identifies hibernating myocardium and predicts recovery of left ventricular function after coronary revascularization. Circulation 1993;88:430–436.

■ 282. Marzullo P, Parodi O, Reisenhofer B, et al. Value of rest thallium-201/technetium-99m sestamibi scans and dobutamine echocardiography for detecting myocardial viability. Am J Cardiol 1993;71:166–172.

283. Mudge GH, Goldstein S, Addonizio LJ, et al. 24th Bethesda conference: Cardiac transplantation. Task Force 3: Recipient guidelines/prioritization. J Am Coll Cardiol 1993 Jul;22:21–31.

284. Goldman L, Hashimoto D, Cook EF, et al. Comparative reproducibility and validity of systems for assessing cardiovascular functional class: advantages of a new specific activity scale. Circulation 1981;64:1227–34.

285. Guyatt GH, Nogradi S, Halcrow S, et al. Development and testing of a new measure of health status for clinical trials in heart failure. J Gen Intern Med 1989;4:101–7.

286. Rector TS. Outcome assessment: functional status measures as therapeutic endpoints for heart failure. Top Hosp Pharm Manage 1990;10:37–43.

287. Tandon PK, Stander H, Schwarz RP Jr. Analysis of quality of life data from a randomized, placebo-controlled heart-failure trial. J Clin Epidemiol 1989;42: 955–62.

■ 288. Rector TS, Kubo SH, Cohn JN. Patients' self-assessment of their congestive heart failure: II. Content, reliability, and validity of a new measure—the Minnesota Living With Heart Failure Questionnaire. Heart Failure 1987;3:198–209.

This questionnaire consists of 21 items focused on the patient's perception of the impact of heart failure on his or her physical, psychological and socioeconomic life. To date, this instrument has been used in several multicenter randomized trials.

289.   Creager MA, Faxon DP, Halperin JL, et al. Determinants of clinical response and survival in patients with congestive heart failure treated with captopril. Am Heart J 1982 Nov;104:1147–54.

290.   Nelson GR, Cohn PF, Gorlin R. Prognosis in medically-treated coronary artery disease: influence of ejection fraction compared to other parameters. Circulation 1975 Sep;52:408–12.

291.   Schwarz F, Mall G, Zebe H, et al. Determinants of survival in patients with congestive cardiomyopathy: quantitative morphologic findings and left-ventricular hemodynamics. Circulation 1984;70:923–8.

292.   Cohn JN, Johnson GR, Shabetai R, et al. Ejection fraction, peak exercise oxygen consumption, cardiothoracic ratio, ventricular arrhythmias, and plasma norepinephrine as determinants of prognosis in heart failure. Circulation 1993;87(Suppl VI):VI-5 to VI-16.

293.   Cintron G, Johnson G, Francis G, et al. Prognostic significance of serial changes in left ventricular ejection fraction in patients with congestive heart failure. Circulation 1993;87(Suppl VI):VI-17 to VI-23.

294.   Franciosa JA, Jordan RA, Wilen MM, et al. Minoxidil in patients with chronic left heart failure: contrasting hemodynamic and clinical effects in a controlled trial. Circulation 1984 Jul;70:63–8.

295.   Baim D, McDowell A, Cherniles J, et al. Evaluation of a new bipyridine inotropic agent—milrinone—in patients with severe congestive heart failure. N Engl J Med 1983;309:748–56.

296.   Simonton CA, Chatterjee K, Cody RJ, et al. Milrinone in congestive heart failure: acute and chronic hemodynamic and clinical evaluation. J Am Coll Cardiol 1985;6:453–9.

297.   Narahara KA, The Western Enoximone Study Group and the REFLECT Investigators. Spontaneous variability of ventricular function in patients with chronic heart failure. Am J Med 1993;95:513–8.

298.   Wackers FJT, Berger HJ, Johnstone DE, et al. Multiple gated cardiac blood pool imaging for left ventricular ejection fraction: validation of the technique and assessment of variability. Am J Cardiol 1979 Jun;43:1159–66.

■ 299.   Mancini DM, Eisen H, Kussmaul M, et al. Value of peak exercise oxygen consumption for optimal timing of cardiac transplantation in ambulatory patients with heart failure. Circulation 1991;83:778–786.
There is no magic number to look for in evaluating patients for cardiac transplantation. Peak oxygen consumption is a continuous value, and the lower the peak oxygen consumption the greater the likelihood of significant problems with continued medical therapy.

Glossary

Ascites: Presence of free fluid within the peritoneal cavity.

Atrial Fibrillation: An irregular heart rhythm produced by lack of coordinated action of the atrial pacemaker.

Atrioventricular Block: Dissociation of the electrical impulses between the atrium and ventricle. Atrioventricular block generally results in a reduction in heart rate.

Beta-Adrenergic Blockers: Pharmacological agents whose principal action is to reduce the effect of beta-adrenergic agonist agents (e.g., epinephrine) on the body's tissues.

Bradyarrhythmias: Disturbances in cardiac rhythm that result in an abnormally slow heart rate.

Cardiomegaly: Enlargement of the heart.

Cardiomyopathy: Abnormality of the cardiac muscle.

Cineangiography: Motion pictures of blood vessels obtained using radiographic imaging of an injected contrast medium.

Coronary Angiography: A test in which a contrast medium is injected into the coronary arteries in order to determine coronary artery anatomy, including the presence, severity, and location of any obstruction.

Dyspnea: The sensation of shortness of breath or difficulty breathing.

Echocardiogram: A test that uses reflected sound waves to produce images of the heart to provide anatomical and functional information.

(Left-Ventricular) Ejection Fraction: The proportion of blood present in the left ventricle at the end of ventricular diastole that is pumped through the aortic valve during systole.

Heart Failure: A clinical syndrome or condition characterized by (1) signs and symptoms of intravascular and interstitial volume overload, including short-ness of breath, rales, and edema, or (2) manifestations of inadequate tissue perfusion, such as fatigue or poor exercise tolerance.

Left-Ventricular Diastolic Dysfunction: Inability of the left ventricle to fill nor-mally during diastole, often due to decreased compliance of the ventricle walls. Ejection fraction is generally normal, but the elevated pressures re-quired for ventricular filling can result in symptoms of pulmonary congestion. In addition, the reduced left-ventricular filling volume leads to lowered stroke volumes and symptoms of poor cardiac output.

Left-Ventricular Systolic Dysfunction: Reduction in the pumping power of the left ventricle to the point where the left-ventricular ejection fraction is less than 35–40 percent, as opposed to the normal range of 50 percent or greater.

Orthopnea: Dyspnea experienced when in the supine or prone position.

Radionuclide Ventriculography: A test of ventricular structure and function in which images are produced through external detection of an intravascular ra-dioactive tracer.

Rales: Crackling or bubbling sounds heard during auscultation of the lungs. The presence of rales indicates that fluid has permeated the terminal bronchioles and alveoli, which can be due either to heart failure or to primary pulmonary disease, especially pneumonia.

Tachycardia: Disturbances in cardiac rhythm that result in an abnormally rapid heart rate.

Acronyms

ACE inhibitor	Angiotensin-converting enzyme inhibitor
AHCPR	Agency for Health Care Policy and Research
AV block	Atrioventricular block
BID	Twice a day
BUN	Blood urea nitrogen
CABG	Coronary artery bypass graft
CASS	Coronary Artery Surgery Study
CBC	Complete blood count
CONSENSUS	Cooperative New Scandinavian Enalapril Survival Study
COPD	Chronic obstructive pulmonary disease
ECG	Electrocardiogram
EF	(Left-ventricular) Ejection fraction
FDA	Food and Drug Administration
FFS	Fee for service
HMO	Health maintenance organization
HRQOL	Health-related quality of life
HYD/ISDN	Hydralazine and isosorbide dinitrate
MI	Myocardial infarction
NIH	National Institutes of Health
NHLBI	National Heart, Lung, and Blood Institute
NYHA	New York Heart Association
PET	Positron emission tomography
PTCA	Percutaneous transluminal coronary angioplasty
QD	Once a day
RCT	Randomized controlled trial

SAVE Trial	Survival and Ventricular Enlargement Trial
SOLVD	Studies of Left-Ventricular Dysfunction
TID	Three times a day
TSH	Thyroid-stimulating hormone
VHeFT	Veterans Affairs Vasodilator Heart Failure Trial

Index

Chest x-ray, 31
CHF STAT trial study, 67, 97
Chlorthalidone, 68–69
Chronic obstructive pulmonary disease
  (COPD), 23
CIBIS (Cardiac Insufficiency Bisoprilol
  Study), 93
Clinical trials. *See specific clinical trials*
Clonidine, 96
Cocaine use, 52
Cognitive function, assessment of, 118
Complete blood count (CBC), 32
Compliance, patient, 6
Congestive heart failure, 2. *See also* Heart
  failure
CONSENSUS trial, 4, 75, 86
CONSENSUS II trial, 21, 74
Coronary artery angiography, 46, 48, 110,
  111–112
Coronary artery bypass graft (CABG)
  benefits of, 3, 102–107
  risks of, 107–109
Coronary artery disease
  diastolic dysfunction and, 48
  with heart failure, evaluation/treatment
    of, 101
  heart failure and, 99–102
  left-ventricular systolic dysfunction
    and, 51
Costs, for heart failure monitoring, 7
Cough, ACE inhibitor-induced, 77–78
Counseling
  general, 53–58
  for revascularization decisionmaking,
    110–113
  topics for, 55
Creatinine, serum, 32, 73, 76
Creatinine clearances, 73, 79–80

D

Death. *See also* Mortality rates
  sudden, 62
  sudden cardiac, 34, 62, 63, 96
Decompensation, heart failure, 6
Decompensation, of heart failure, 6, 33,
  66

Diagnosis. *See also* Diagnostic tests; *specific diagnostic tests*
  errors in, 7–8
  psychological implications of, 55, 56
Diagnostic tests, 28–36. *See also specific
  diagnostic tests*
  for arrhythmias, 34–35
  for atrial fibrillation, 35–36
  laboratory
    errors in, 8
    for monitoring, 120–121
  selection of, 42
Diastolic dysfunction
  chronic, 47
  diagnosis of, 49
  differential diagnosis, 43
  incidence in symptomatic heart failure,
    48
  left-ventricular, 39–40
  mortality rates, 51
  prognosis, 51
  treatment of, 49–50
Diet
  compliance, 64
  low-fat, low-cholesterol, 61
  recommendations for, 60–62
  salt-restricted, 6, 60–61
Digitalis, 50
Digoxin
  for atrial fibrillation/flutter, 35
  clinical trials, 80–81
  discontinuation of, 83
  dosages of, 82–83
  ejection fraction and, 47
  for left-ventricular dysfunction, 82
  serum levels, 82–83
Digoxin Investigation Group, 80
Diltiazem Post-Infarction trial, 95
Diuresis, excessive, 50
Diuretics. *See also specific diuretics*
  with ACE inhibitor, 67, 73–74
  adverse reactions, 69
  for diastolic dysfunction, 49, 50
  dosages of, 66, 68–69, 91
  for elderly, 41

FFS (fee-for-service), 6
Flecainide, 35
Fluid intake, 60, 62, 88
Follow-up, patient, 117–121
Food and Drug Administration (FDA), 85, 93
Framingham Heart Study, 41
Furosemide, 66, 67, 68–69, 88

G

GESICA trial, 97
GISSI-3 trial, 74
Global hypokinesis, 45–46
Guanabenz, 96

H

Health maintenance organization (HMO), 6
Health-related quality of life (HRQOL), 118–119
Heart failure. *See also specific aspects of*
  algorithm for, 10, 11
  with angina, 94–95
  definition of, 2
  diastolic. *See* Diastolic dysfunction
  evaluation/care, cost of, 2–3
  incidence of, 2
  signs/symptoms of, 1–2, 23–25, 32, 56
  systolic. *See* Systolic dysfunction
Heart transplantation, 106, 114–115, 120
Hemochromatosis, 52
Hemodynamic monitoring, with pulmonary artery catheter, 90
Hepatic engorgement, 66
Hibernating myocardium, 102
HMO (health maintenance organization), 6
Holter monitoring (ambulatory electrocardiography), 8, 34
Hospitalization
  admission criteria, 36–37
  discharge criteria, 37
  for inotropic therapy, 90–91
  readmission, 37–38, 64
HRQOL (health-related quality of life), 118–119

Hy-C trial, 84
HYD/ISDN. *See* Hydralazine/isosorbide dinitrate (HYD/ISDN)
Hydralazine
  dosing, 68–69, 96
  with isosorbide dinitrate. *See* Hydralazine/isosorbide dinitrate (HYD/ISDN)
  for persistent dyspnea, 92
  side effects of, 96
Hydralazine/isosorbide dinitrate (HYD/ISDN)
  coughing and, 77
  indications for, 79, 84–85
  mortality rates and, 5, 75
Hydrochlorothiazide
  dosage, 66, 67, 68–69
  for persistent heart failure, 88
  side effects, 69
Hypercholesterolemia, 61
Hyperkalemia, 89
Hypertension. *See also* Blood pressure reduction
  angiotensin-2 receptor antagonists for, 85
  diastolic dysfunction and, 48, 49
  left-ventricular systolic dysfunction and, 51
  persistent, 95–97
  poorly controlled, 25
  uncontrolled, 6
Hypocalcemia, 72
Hyponatremia, 91
Hypotension, ACE inhibitor usage and, 73, 78

I

Incidence/prevalence, in elderly, 41
Inotropic therapy, 90
Iron, serum, 52
Iron deficiency anemia, 33
Ischemia
  evaluation for MI history, 112
  with heart failure, 76, 100
  with left-ventricular hypokinesis, 46
  myocardial, 51

Myocardial perfusion scintigraphy, 114
Myocardial relaxation, 49
Myocarditis, 52

N

Nitrates. *See also* Isosorbide dinitrate
for diastolic dysfunction, 50
for heart failure with angina, 94
for persistent dyspnea, 92
Nitroglycerin, 92
Noncompliance, 63–64
Nonsustained ventricular tachycardia
(NSVT), 97
NSVT (nonsustained ventricular tachycardia), 97

O

Omnibus Budget Reconciliation Act
(Public Law 101-239), 1
Orthopnea, 23, 24
Orthostatic hypotension, 77
Outcome
assessment, 117–121
impact of poor quality care on, 6
Outpatient care, quality of, 6

P

Paroxysmal nocturnal dyspnea, 23, 24
PEACE trial, 22
Percutaneous transluminal coronary angioplasty (PTCA), 109
Peripheral edema, 8, 24, 27, 28, 91, 66
Persistent heart failure, treatment of,
88–93
PET (positron emission tomography),
113–114
Pharmacological management, 57, 87–88.
See also specific drugs
algorithm for, 70–71
anticoagulation for, 85–87
hydralazine/isosorbide dinitrate, 84–85
over-the-counter drugs and, 57
for persistent heart failure, 88–93
Physical examination, 27–28
Positron emission tomography (PET),
113–114

Potassium, serum
ACE inhibitors and, 76–77
depletion of, 67, 72
total potassium body stores and, 72
Potassium chloride, 61
Potassium-sparing diuretics, 68–69, 72,
76, 91
Potassium supplements, 77, 89, 91
PRAISE trial, 95
Prazosin, 96
Primum non nocere dictum, 86
Prognosis
for diastolic dysfunction, 51
discussion with patient, 62–63
left-ventricular ejection fraction and, 47
Prothrombin time ratio, 85, 86
Psychological aspects, of diagnosis, 55,
56
PTCA (percutaneous transluminal coronary angioplasty), 109
Public Law 101-239 (Omnibus Budget
Reconciliation Act), 1
Pulmonary capillary wedge pressure, 24,
25
Pulmonary edema, 48, 51, 65, 66
Pulmonary vascular congestion, 66

Q

Quinapril, 68–69, 78
Quinidine, 83

R

RADIANCE trial, 80, 81, 82
Radionuclide ventriculography
advantages/disadvantages, 44, 45
of left-ventricular function, 27, 40, 41
Rales, 27, 28, 65, 120
Randomized Aldactone Study (RALES),
72
Regional wall motion abnormalities, 45
Rehabilitation programs, 59
Renal artery stenosis, 76
Renin-angiotensin-aldosterone, 67
Research, future, recommendations for,
14–17
Revascularization

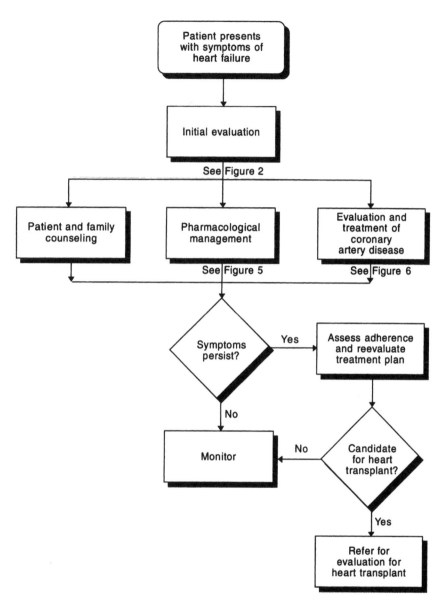

Overview of Evaluation and Care of Patients With Heart Failure

From Kasper, EK, *Heart Failure: Evaluation and Care of Patients with Left-Ventricular Systolic Dysfunction.* Copyright © 1997 by Chapman & Hall.

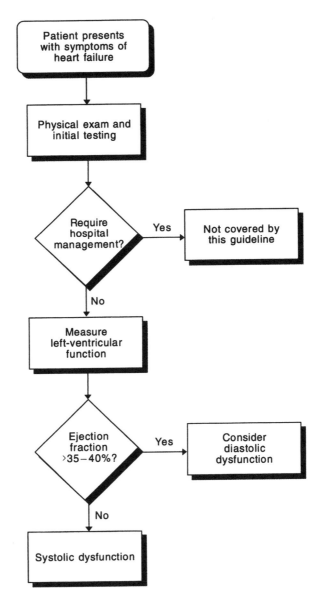

Initial Evaluation of Patients With Heart Failure
From Kasper, EK, *Heart Failure: Evaluation and Care of Patients with Left-Ventricular Systolic Dysfunction.* Copyright © 1997 by Chapman & Hall.

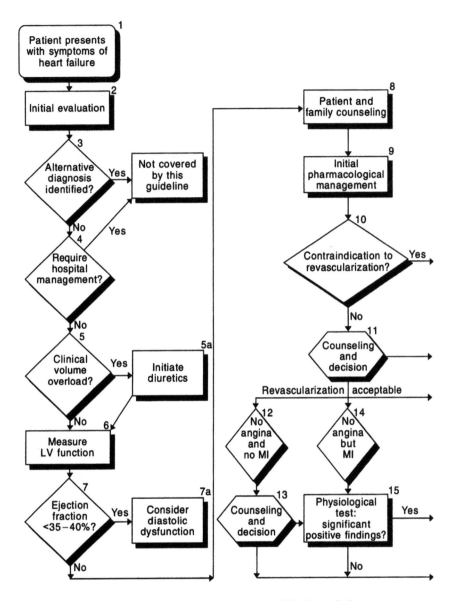

Clinical Algorithm for Evaluation and Care of Patients With Heart Failure
Note: See Executive Summary for annotation. LV = left-ventricular, MI = myocardial infarction.

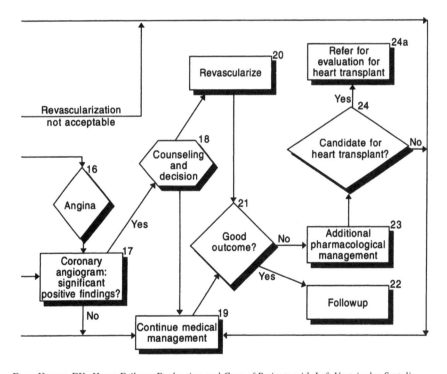

From Kasper, EK, *Heart Failure: Evaluation and Care of Patients with Left-Ventricular Systolic Dysfunction.* Copyright © 1997 by Chapman & Hall.

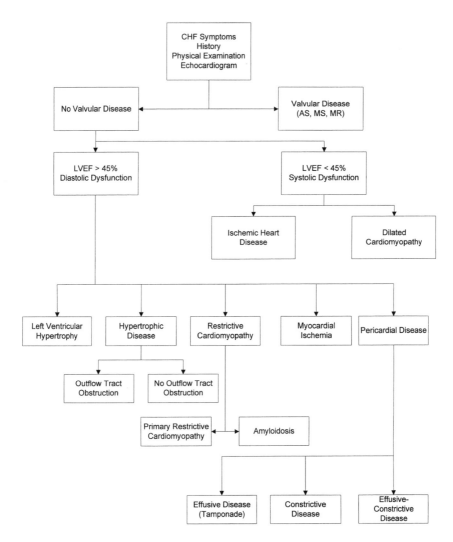

Diagnostic Algorithm for Differentiating Causes of Systolic and Diastolic Heart Failure by Two-Dimensional Echocardiography

Note: CM = Cardiomyopathy.

From Kasper, EK, *Heart Failure: Evaluation and Care of Patients with Left-Ventricular Systolic Dysfunction*. Copyright © 1997 by Chapman & Hall.

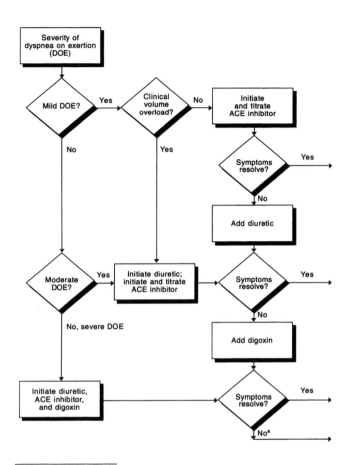

—————————

^a Obtain cardiology consult if not already done.
^b Beta blockers and calcium-channel blockers may also be effective but should be considered
investigational.

Pharmacological Management of Patients With Heart Failure

[a]Obtain cardiology consult if not already done.

[b]Beta blockers and calcium-channel blockers may also be effective but should be considered investigational.

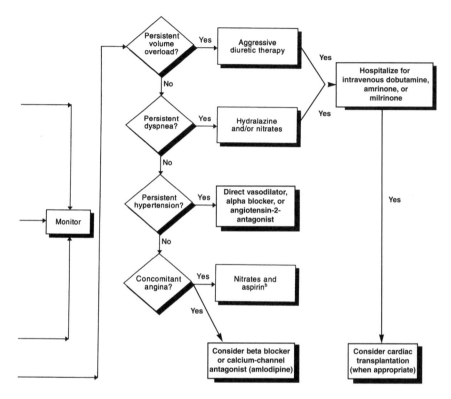

From Kasper, EK, *Heart Failure: Evaluation and Care of Patients with Left-Ventricular Systolic Dysfunction*. Copyright © 1997 by Chapman & Hall.

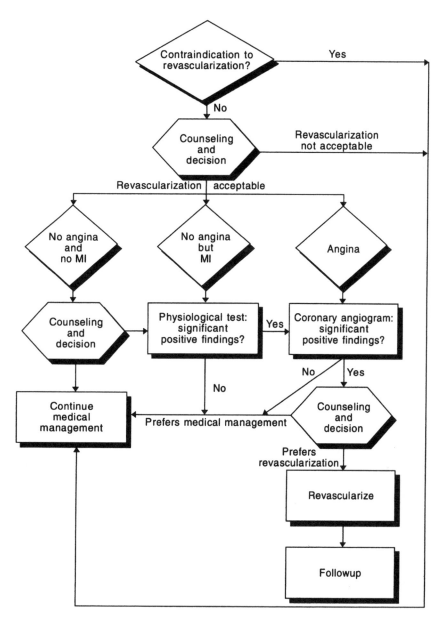

Evaluation and Treatment of Coronary Artery Disease in Patients With Heart Failure
From Kasper, EK, *Heart Failure: Evaluation and Care of Patients with Left-Ventricular Systolic Dysfunction.* Copyright © 1997 by Chapman & Hall.